Rural Racism

*To Mum and Dad who introduced me to 'England's green and pleasant land',
with much love.*

Neil

*To Mum and Dad who introduced me to the joys of 'The Singing Postman', with
much love.*

Jon

Rural Racism

edited by

Neil Chakraborti and Jon Garland

Routledge
Taylor & Francis Group

LONDON AND NEW YORK

First published by Willan Publishing 2004
This edition published by Routledge 2012
2 Park Square, Milton Park, Abingdon, Oxon OX14 4RN
711 Third Avenue, New York, NY 10017 (8th Floor)

Routledge is an imprint of the Taylor & Francis Group, an informa business

First issued in paperback 2012

First published 2004

ISBN 978-1-84392-056-4 (hbk)
ISBN 978-0-415-62800-6 (pbk)

British Library Cataloguing-in-Publication Data

A catalogue record for this book is available from the British Library

Typeset by GCS, Leighton Buzzard, Bedfordshire
Project managed by Deer Park Productions, Tavistock, Devon

Contents

Acknowledgements

A considerable debt of gratitude is owed to a great many people, without whose help and support the book would not have been completed. First and foremost, we would like to thank each of the contributors to this volume for providing us with such insightful material and for being a pleasure to work with. Thanks also to Brian Willan for his advice and thoughtful comments, and to Ben Bowling for interrupting his study leave in the sun by offering to help with the book.

Much of the thinking behind the book's conception was originally inspired by the editors' own research, and we are grateful to all those who helped us to develop our ideas. A special mention goes to Sam Johnson and his son for inadvertently paving the way for our initial research; to Mike Rowe for acting as an academic sounding-board to our various ramblings; to Parvinder Sandal and Katie Keetley whose assistance was greatly valued; to staff at Suffolk County Council's Community Safety Unit, as well as Ivan Balhatchet, Carolyn Went and Andy Johnson, for recognising the importance of this area of work; and to participants in our research studies, particularly minority ethnic households who were so open in sharing their harrowing experiences of victimisation with us.

Further inspiration for the book has come from our first-hand experiences of racism in the rural, and we are especially thankful for all the 'fan mail' that we have received from Mr 'Death Incarnate' [sic] and other critics. Thanks are also due to Derby County FC and Norwich City FC, the respective failures and successes of whom have provided the editors with rather contrasting emotions during the course of this book's completion.

Finally, our families and friends deserve enormous praise for their love and support during times of stress (of which there have been many) and for patiently listening to us when they would really have preferred not to.

And to Michele, Laura and Enrico: *Tante grazie ai nostri amici ... viva la gnocca!*

Foreword

by Ben Bowling

This is a valuable contribution to the literature on a set of complex issues that have long deserved far greater attention by academics and policy-makers. The research set out in this book will chime with the experiences of black and brown-skinned people who have, like me, grown up or live in the British countryside. It will inform and stimulate students, academics and policy-makers to think afresh about rural racism. Collectively, the authors challenge prevailing assumptions, raise new themes and issues for research and point out new directions for politics, policy and practical action.

The book confronts the fact the while the ethnic minority population of Britain is concentrated in the urban sphere, people of colour can be found living in almost all parts of England, Scotland and Wales. Encouragingly, our presence in rural environments is increasing. The book engages with the paradox that black and brown people are often highly visible within rural towns and villages and yet seem invisible to policy-makers. As has long been accepted in the urban environment, diversity of physical appearance and cultural practice are also part and parcel of the rural landscape. Acknowledging this reminds us of the diversity of the white population and takes us past the widely held, but erroneous, assumption that if your skin is dark you must *really* be from somewhere else. It is now a simple empirical fact that you can be 'visibly different' and yet still *from* Worcestershire, the Highlands of Scotland, the Welsh valleys or wherever.

The book challenges the curious belief that there cannot be racism in rural Britain because there are relatively few people of colour resident there. Many ethnic minority rural dwellers will know that the reverse is more to the point – rural racism is one of the reasons that more people of colour do not choose to live outside the cities. At the same time, the book avoids characterising minorities as inherently victims, simply objects of hate and exclusion rather than complex, active subjects with diverse experiences – both positive and negative – of country life. It shows that people of African, Caribbean and Asian descent enjoy living in the countryside for the same reasons as their white counterparts – the love of rural terrain, the availability of country pursuits and the emotional tranquillity that comes from living in a peaceful natural environment. It shows that many black and Asian people find themselves welcome in the rural environment and enjoy a contented life there. Nonetheless, the authors do not shy away from documenting the effect that racist violence and exclusion has on many people and how it can have deep psychological effects in itself and in the way that it echoes other aspects of racism in British society.

It is understandable that engagement with anti-racist politics has tended to focus on areas of extensive ethnic minority settlement; the cities are, after all, where the 'problem' was thought to be located. This raises the question of how a politics based on respect for diversity and anti-racism can be mobilised in areas where there are few black and brown faces. This book shows that there is a real need to think about how best to respond to rural racism and how policy can meet the needs of individuals and families with diverse backgrounds. It can perhaps build on the shared experience – articulated by both rural dwellers in general and individuals from minority ethnic communities – of economic marginalisation, social isolation, poor infrastructure, absence of decent public services and invisibility in mainstream urbanist public debate. Together, the chapters of this book point to the need for an alternative politics emphasising a 'countryside of difference' that will enable us to redraw the rural landscape in ways that reflect the experiences of all.

Ben Bowling
King's College London
and The University of the West Indies

Notes on Contributors

Neil Chakraborti is a Lecturer in Criminology at the Department of Criminology, University of Leicester. In addition to his research with Jon Garland on the subject of rural racism, he has published more broadly on issues of racism, ethnicity and victimisation, with a particular interest in multi-agency responses to racist crime; fear of crime among minority ethnic communities; racism and anti-racism in football; and policing diversity.

Jon Garland is a Research Fellow at the Department of Criminology, University of Leicester. He has researched and published widely on issues of racism, anti-racism, ethnicity and identity; policing diversity; community safety and football-related disorder. His books include *Racism and Anti-Racism in Football* (with Michael Rowe; Palgrave, 2001) and *The Future of Football* (edited with Michael Rowe and Dominic Malcolm; Frank Cass, 2000). In the last three years he has been conducting extensive research into issues of rural racism with Neil Chakraborti.

Paul Cloke is Professor of Human Geography in the School of Geographical Sciences at the University of Bristol. He is also Founder Editor of the *Journal of Rural Studies*. He has published extensively on issues of rural change and social marginalisation, and recent books include *Country Visions* (Pearson) and *Rural Homelessness* (Policy Press, with Paul Milbourne and Rebekah Widdowfield, 2002). His current research focuses on urban homelessness, ethical consumption, and the nature–society relations of adventurous and eco-tourisms.

Philomena J.F. de Lima is a Lecturer and Researcher in Sociology at Inverness College, where she is examining access to further and higher education among minority ethnic groups in the north of Scotland. She authored the influential *Needs Not Numbers* report in 2001, and completed a study, *Rural Racism: Mapping the Problem, and Defining Practical Policy Recommendations* for the CRE in 2002. She has an active involvement in policy issues, including participating in the Scottish Further Education Council and the Cooperative Diversity Working Group (UK), and is a member of the Steering Group for the National Resource Centre for Ethnic Minorities and the Scottish Advisory Group for the Equal Opportunities Commission.

Dominic Malcolm is Director of Masters Programmes at the Centre for the Sociology of Sport, University of Leicester. He has edited three books in this area, the most recent being *Sport: Critical Concepts in Sociology* (with Eric Dunning; Routledge, 2003) and *Sport Histories: Figurational Studies in the Development of Modern Sports* (with Eric Dunning and Ivan Waddington; Routledge, 2004). He has also written articles on race relations in cricket for the *Sociology of Sport Journal*, the *Journal of Historical Sociology* and the *Journal of Ethnic and Migration Studies*. He is currently writing a *Dictionary of Sport Studies* for Sage.

Vaughan Robinson is Professor of Human Geography and Director of the Migration Unit at University of Wales Swansea. His research interests are in human migration broadly, and in the social demography of minority populations, and geographies of asylum and refugee-seeking in particular. He has written or edited eight books on these themes, the two most recent being *Spreading the 'Burden'? European Policies to Disperse Asylum Seekers* (Policy Press, 2003) with Roger Andersson and Sako Musterd; *Understanding the Decision Making of Asylum Seekers* (Home Office, 2002) with Jeremy Segrott, and *Migration and Public Policy* (Edward Elgar, 1999).

Hannah Gardner is currently a Research Fellow at the University of Wales, Swansea where she is working on a project funded by the Crown Prosecution Service investigating the experiences of black and minority ethnic people with the criminal justice system. Before that, Hannah researched issues surrounding rurality and ethnicity for her doctoral thesis at the same institution. This was submitted in late 2004, and explored black and minority ethnic lived experiences in rural Wales. She has already published a joint research paper and book chapter on these themes with Vaughan Robinson.

Paul Iganski is a Lecturer in Sociology and Criminology at the University of Essex. He specialises in teaching, research and writing on bigotry, hate and violence. He is co-author of the book *Ethnicity, Equality of Opportunity and the British National Health Service* (with David Mason, Ashgate, 2002), editor of *The Hate Debate: Should Hate Be Punished as a Crime?* (Profile, 2002) and *A New Antisemitism? Debating Judeophobia in 21st Century Britain* (with Barry Kosmin, Profile, 2003). He is also co-author with colleagues from the Essex Sociology Department of the textbook: *Criminology. A Sociological Introduction* (with Eamonn Carrabine, Maggy Lee, Ken Plummer and Nigel South, Routledge, 2004).

Jack Levin, PhD is the Irving and Betty Brudnick Professor of Sociology and Criminology at Northeastern University in Boston, where he directs its Brudnick Center on Conflict and Violence. He has authored or co-authored 25 books including *Hate Crimes Revisited* (Westview Press, 2002), *The Functions of Prejudice* (Harper and Row, 1975), *Why We Hate* (Prometheus Books, 2004), and *The Violence of Hate: Confronting Racism, Anti-Semitism, and Other Forms of Bigotry* (Allyn and Bacon, 2002). Dr Levin has also published numerous articles in professional journals such as *Justice Quarterly, Criminology, Journal of Interpersonal Violence* and *Youth and Society*. He lectures widely on issues of prejudice and violence.

Shammi Jalota is the manager of the Racial Harassment Initiative (RHI) at Suffolk County Council, where he has worked since 1998. In 1999, the RHI was one of the top ten crime prevention projects across the UK and won the prestigious CGU British Crime Prevention and Community Safety Award. Between 1996 and 1998, Shammi was coordinator of Leicester City Challenge's Anti-Racism Project, and before this worked on a Crime Concern study which investigated business crime and its effect on the black and ethnic minority community.

Kate Broadhurst is currently the Head of Community Safety at Perpetuity Research and Consultancy International (PRCI). Her role includes managing a programme of research funded by the National Association of Schoolmasters Union of Women Teachers exploring violence and indiscipline in schools. Prior to joining PRCI, Kate worked for Crime Concern as senior consultant and before this, she was a research associate at the Department of Criminology, University of Leicester.

Andi Wright has extensive experience of undertaking research and consultancy in the fields of crime and disorder, community safety, hate crime, youth offending and education. He is currently employed by the Youth Justice Board for England and Wales as a performance monitor for Youth Offending Teams and secure estates including Secure Training Centres, Local Authority Secure Children's Homes and Her Majesty's Young Offender Institutions, working across both the East Midlands and Eastern Government Office regions. Previously, Andi was employed as a research consultant by Perpetuity Research and Consultancy International and worked in the areas of youth crime prevention and drug and alcohol mapping, and has investigated black markets for illicit goods.

Richard Pugh is Reader in Social Work at Keele University and has worked as a residential and field worker in the UK and the USA. He has published widely on minority language issues, child care, social work theory and rural social work, with most of this work being explicitly located within a broad anti-discriminatory perspective. He has extensive links with academics and practitioners in Australia, Canada and Europe, and is a visiting researcher at the University of South Australia. Currently, he is researching black and ethnic minority social work staff perceptions of racism and agency response.

Introduction

Justifying the study of racism in the rural

Neil Chakraborti and Jon Garland

Living here makes me proud to be British. Everything's so peaceful, and despite everything that's changed in this country over the years, we've managed to keep hold of our traditions, of our rural way of doing things. How could anyone not want to live here? (White male and lifelong resident of rural Suffolk)

We were getting dogs' mess thrown at the door, stones at the window, and then you [the husband] stood at the door one night and they threw an egg at you. I chased after them and they called me a 'Paki loving bitch' who needed shooting. (White wife of a Pakistani Muslim, rural Suffolk)

During the course of their studies of rural life in various towns and villages, the editors of this volume, and no doubt many of its contributors, have encountered a staggering degree of surprise, complacency and in some cases overt hostility from numerous stake-holders in rural affairs who have questioned the legitimacy of researching racism in a rural context. It would appear that a 'no racism here' mentality permeates much popular imagery surrounding the rural, a line of thought that takes its basis from the rosy veneer that has shaped public opinion over the years. The above quotations are illustrative of the variations in perception between those who adhere to the more traditional, somewhat romanticised conceptions of the rural, and those who have an altogether different lived experience of rural life. The first observation, from an elderly gentleman who had lived his entire life in one particular rural village, refers to his feelings of pride in his area of residence, and exemplifies the idyllic notions often used in references to the rural. The second observation, meanwhile, refers to the ongoing experiences, recounted during an interview conducted by the editors of this book, of a dual heritage family living in that same county, an ostensibly 'peaceful', to coin the previous interviewee's description, part of the English countryside. These experiences contrast markedly with the conception of country life referred to in the first quotation, and point to an alternative, and often overlooked, version of rural reality.

Dominant conceptions of the rural

Why though are particular conceptions of the rural overlooked, while others prevail? To a large degree this can be explained by the extent to which certain representations of rurality have been allowed to dominate popular discourse unchallenged by critical social scientific enquiry. Sustained attempts to adequately conceptualise rurality have been widely absent from contemporary criminological and sociological debates which have tended to neglect rural perspectives (Moody 1999; Dingwall 1999), and instead, the task of conceptualising the term has been left largely to rural geographers who have adopted a range of different perspectives and foci in helping to shape our understanding of how the rural has come to be defined (see, for example, Cherry 1976; Cloke 1977, 1980).

Among the most popular ways of viewing the rural has been to dichotomise 'the rural' and 'the urban', commonly by drawing upon historical references to the polarisation of the two forms of place. Robinson (1990: 37–8), for example, reflects on the one hand upon the work of authors such as Ferdinand Tonnies (1887), who perceived rurality in its ideal sense to be typified by features like 'kinship', 'familiarity' and 'understanding', while noting the quite different set of characteristics attributed to urbanism in the writings of Louis Wirth (1938) such as 'impersonality', 'superficiality' and 'transition'. Similar assertions have been made by sociologists working within the tradition of the Chicago school, for whom problems of crime and deviance have long been associated with the dehabilitating environmental conditions of the city.[1] Consequently, this suspicion of the 'urban' has remained a recurring theme in much popular and academic discourse. Murdoch and Marsden (1994: 9) emphasise this point by referring to Raban's (1974) influential description of the city as 'a place of great uncertainty and instability where individuals may find extreme difficulty in achieving any real sense of security', and subsequently arguing that such descriptions of urban life have shaped people's desires to seek alternative forms of space. By way of contrast, the rural has traditionally been presented as a sanctuary from the harsh realities of the urban world, a way of life that embraces a very different, and wholly preferable, set of values to the urban such as honesty, kinship, solidarity and paternalism (Little and Austin 1996: 102).

Conceptualising the rural through this dichotomisation of the rural and the urban has retained a strong influence, and this direct comparison between the landscapes of city and countryside has been central to the way in which rural areas have been 'romanticised' over the years as problem-free 'idyllic' environments (Little and Austin 1996; Scutt and Bonnett 1996; Cloke 1997). Positive associations are seen to surround different aspects of rural lifestyle and landscape, thereby reinforcing nostalgic representations that refer to the distinctive, timeless and ultimately desirable qualities of the rural which provide a welcome escape from the hassles of modern-day living. Such a conception is encapsulated in the oft-used term the 'rural idyll', which in the words of Cloke and Milbourne (1992: 359) 'presents happy, healthy and problem-free images of rural life safely nestling within both a close social community and a contiguous natural environment'.

The term 'community' has particular resonance here, with a number of authors having highlighted the appealing imagery of romanticised notions of the 'rural community'. As Francis and Henderson (1992: 19) suggest:

> There is no doubt that community, especially when prefixed by 'rural' is a powerful and emotive concept ... [it] includes notions of reciprocal human relationships, voluntary effort, interest in local affairs, neighbourliness: above all, the village is seen as a place where everybody knows and cares for each other.

A vivid illustration of the way in which such imagery has transcended popular opinion can be found in television and radio broadcasting, where the romanticisation of a singular, homogeneous rural community has long been a feature of programmes transmitted through the popular media in the UK. Bunce (1994: 50–5), for example, has pointed to the 'nostalgic veneer' surrounding long-running shows such as *The Archers* and *All Creatures Great and Small* that depict a seemingly happier way of life and a greater sense of harmony, while Fish (2000: 19) refers to the attraction of prime-time entertainment such as Yorkshire Television's adaptation of H.E. Bates's series of books *The Darling Buds of May* to show how such programmes play a major role in disseminating and perpetuating the idea of a rural idyll to all sections of the general public, often by positioning the rural experience as the antithesis of the urban experience and thereby reinforcing separate images of the two forms of space. As with simple rural–urban dichotomies, this notion of rural community has attracted criticism, most notably for perpetuating ambiguous, nostalgic and ultimately exclusive constructions of rurality (Philo 1992; Murdoch and Day 1998), although some (see, for example, Liepins 2000) have argued for reconceptualisation, rather than rejection, of the notion so that it embraces the heterogeneity of rural life. Certainly, if one is to acknowledge the existence of multiple experiences of the rural, a logical consequence would be to reject the idea of a particular rural culture or way of life, as encapsulated within the arguably outdated notion of a singular rural community, in favour of an approach which recognises the diversity of rural *communities*. This will be discussed at greater length during the course of this volume.

A further dominant feature within popular constructions of rurality, certainly within the English context, has been the extent to which the rural is seen to capture the very essence of national identity. When conceived in such a way, the rhetoric of rural living has the capacity to evoke powerful feelings of patriotism and nationalism characterised, for example, by enduring images of 'England's green and pleasant land' (Milbourne 1997: 95). By drawing parallels between rural and national identity, constructions of rurality have sought to highlight the 'timeless' and 'quintessential' national virtues that constitute a priceless part of the nation's heritage (Sibley 1997; Murdoch and Pratt 1997; Howkins 2001). Such constructions have prevailed despite the growing recognition afforded to multiple conceptions of identity which cast doubt upon the relevance, and indeed the validity, of singular notions of nationality.

The appeal of nationalised notions of the rural is evident in the sentiments expressed by William Whitelaw, the former UK Home Secretary and Deputy Prime Minister during the Thatcher administration. In his memoirs (1989: 249) Whitelaw speaks of his feelings of relief on returning to his country home following a tour of the inner-city areas of London affected by the disorders of 1981, asserting his belief that the countryside 'represents more accurately the character and mood of the vast majority of the British people'. Another illustration is provided by former UK Prime Minister John Major, who chose to interpret Orwell's (1941) portrayal of Englishness in a rather different manner from which it was originally intended to describe his own vision of present-day England: 'County grounds, warm beer, invincible green suburbs ... and old maids cycling to Holy Communion through the morning mist' (Major 1993, quoted in Garland and Rowe 2001: 121). Once again, notions of national identity are seen to correlate directly with monocultural, retrospective yet apparently comforting images of rurality, while less nostalgic multidimensional and multicultural images are ignored.

Political groups and institutions have certainly made use of popular nationalistic notions of rurality to support their own arguments. Such notions have potentially broad appeal to all sides of the political spectrum: Robinson (1992: 13), for example, notes that while those associated with the political right can draw comfort from the rural imagery of 'the country house, the church and traditional hierarchical rural society based on the squire, parson and a deferential labour force', those on the left can eulogise over visions of 'rural folk society, the village community, rural crafts and the worthiness of farm labour'. However, it is the political right, and most commonly the Conservative party in the UK, that perhaps has drawn the strongest associations between the rural and national identity, as exemplified by the aforequoted comments of former leading Conservative politicians. Certainly it would seem that the peculiarly 'English' traits of the countryside enshrined within popular constructions of the rural fit broadly with a Conservative ideology that promotes the importance of maintaining the traditions of rural communities, and this has helped to perpetuate dominant typologies of rurality (Francis and Henderson 1992: 22).

Indeed, the potential of the rural to be utilised as a political pawn has not gone unnoticed by parties further to the right of the political spectrum. During the early 1990s prominent members of British far-right groups, such as John Cato, himself a leading white supremacist who had moved from London to a Lincolnshire village, advocated the establishment of an autonomous whites-only 'homeland' in rural parts of the country that would act as a stronghold for white supremacists throughout the land (Lowles 2001: 150). While the creation of a rural 'homeland' never took shape in the manner envisaged by Cato and his followers, the rural arena has nonetheless maintained its sense of popularity among supporters of the far-right, as illustrated in the following extract from the British National Party website (and as discussed more fully in Iganski and Levin's later chapter in this volume):

You can't help but notice the presence of new housing development all over the British countryside, destroying the character and in most cases the sense of community in the areas affected ... But has anyone stopped to consider where all these people who are moving into these developments come from, who they are and why they are there? ... [They are] people who see rural Britain as a refuge – a place to make a fresh start, away from the sordid, squalid towns and cities of Blair's new Babylon. (British National Party 2002)

Recognising a more plural rural

Despite the enduring influence of particular stereotypes, the important contributions made by a number of academics, most notably those from the field of rural geography, have helped to cast doubt upon the relevance of traditional representations by highlighting some of the social and spatial complexities of rural life. Rather than taking these representations at face value, attention has instead been focused on the extent to which such representations have been used as exclusionary devices to decide who does and does not belong in the English countryside (Cloke and Little 1997). This is usefully articulated in Philo's (1992) description of the 'othering' process, where he sees the unwarranted focus upon the interests of powerful rural groups as resulting in the active exclusion of many different social groups from what he refers to as the zone of 'Sameness', a zone in which mainstream values such as Englishness, whiteness, heterosexuality and middle-class occupancy are sustained. For Philo and other writers who have explored the possibility of a more diverse rurality (see, for example, Sibley 1997; Murdoch and Pratt 1997; Cloke and Little 1997), certain groups are ostracised from mainstream society on account of a variety of 'undesirable' social characteristics alien to conventional rural society. Consequently, the interests of rural 'others' run the grave risk of being marginalised within the apparent rural hegemonic condition (or the 'cultural reservoir', to coin the term used by Scutt and Bonnett (1996: 8)) that is central to romanticised constructions of the countryside.

Recent studies have sought to highlight the experiences of a range of 'other' rural voices. A large proportion have examined the concepts of poverty and class as definitive features in rural imagery that tends to mask difference and promote the overriding impression of problem-freedom (Cloke 1997: 267). These studies have shown how the portrayal of rural locations as typically affluent, middle-class environments is seen as attractive both by established rural dwellers who seek to maintain this dominant ideology, and by new residents, themselves overwhelmingly middle-class, who are seeking a particular form of communal life which they believe exists in the rural. Hence, the argument runs, once middle-class incomers have begun to establish themselves in their new environments, they are sufficiently privileged to utilise political and cultural resources as a way of actively moulding the shape of rural policy to perpetuate the dominant representations of rurality, thereby bolstering the exclusionary process (Murdoch and Day 1998; Scutt and Bonnett 1996). Consequently, while the role of the affluent and the mobile is assured within these dominant representations, others may find it necessary to subscribe to these representations in preference to further exposing their own marginalisation (Cloke 1997: 261).

While a number of studies of rural life have used class as the central focus of their enquiry, reference has been made to the influence of alternative characteristics on constructions of rurality (see, for example, Agg and Phillips 1998; Phillips *et al.* 2001). Gender relations, and in particular the exclusion of women from dominant rural discourse, is one area that is said to be indicative of the inequity of power relations in rural society. It has been argued that traditional notions of rurality are based upon particular interpretations of masculinity and femininity that trivialise the actual activities of women except where they are seen to relate to the provisioning and sustenance of the male-headed household (Little and Austin 1996: 103). Similarly, Francis and Henderson (1992: 25) draw attention to difficult realities of rural living for women, which they suggest see women 'in a subordinate position to men, with little room given for self-expression, exercise of power or even equality of decision-making within the household'. Such authors therefore find it difficult to escape the conclusion that idyllic representations of the rural are instrumental in shaping patriarchal gender relations which operate to the detriment of women in the rural arena. Similar suggestions have also been made with reference to the social positioning of gay identities in the rural, where the othering of gay communities has been seen as integral to the maintenance of 'traditional' rural values (Kirkey and Forsyth 2001).

Minority ethnic communities are unquestionably one such group who have been 'othered' by traditional rural discourse. Dominant representations of the rural have been used to portray such areas as a predominantly 'white landscape' that masks the presence of visible and non-visible minority ethnic groups (see, for example, Agyeman and Spooner 1997; Chakraborti and Garland 2003); indeed, where recognition is afforded to other ethnicities in the countryside, this is portrayed in an almost inevitably negative light, as exemplified in recent times by the widely reported outrage among rural community groups surrounding government plans to build asylum-seeker accommodation centres in rural areas (Dyer 2004; Bright 2004), the violence targeted against refugees in Wrexham in June 2003 which led to several nights of disturbances (Bright 2003) and the burning of a mock 'Gypsy' caravan in a Sussex village in November of the same year (Carter 2003).

Not surprisingly, concerns of minority ethnic communities rarely feature in discussions of the rural, just as is the case with those of other social classes, other genders and other sexualities, thereby allowing simplistic, singular and largely outdated constructions of rurality to prevail. Previous studies of minority ethnic groups and their experiences of racism have for the most part tended to be based around the more urbanised areas which typically contain larger visible and non-visible minority ethnic populations. Even though recent years have witnessed a number of small-scale studies focusing on specific rural locales which have helped to raise some awareness of racism in rural areas as a problem in its own right (see, for example, Jay 1992; Derbyshire 1994; Malcolm 2000; de Lima 2001), the fact remains that away from the major towns and cities, racism is seldom recognised as being a significant problem on account of the small, and at times seemingly 'invisible', populations of minority ethnic residents. Moreover, this apparent *invisibility* of ethnic minorities amongst rural stakeholders and service providers is in many ways exacerbated by their simultaneous *high visibility* among local rural residents as a result of being one of few individuals or households from a different ethnic background (Chakraborti and Garland 2004). This 'double-bind' situation makes it all the more important to develop an accurate portrayal of the experiences of rural minority ethnic households.

Consequently, a logical position to adopt when attempting to create a more complete understanding of the rural would be to acknowledge the pluralistic nature of rurality. Dominant discourses have served to conceal particular features of rurality, to the extent where it is hard to disagree with Philo's (1992: 200) description of the average rural dweller as 'white and probably English, straight and somehow without sexuality, able in body and sound in mind, and devoid of any other quirks of (say) religious or political affiliation'. By moving away from broad interpretations of the nature of rurality, which in themselves promote assumptions, singularity and conjecture, studies should instead be devoted to exploring specific features of the construction of rurality and giving expression to the diversity of rural space. In so doing, such studies will help to develop a broader appreciation of the plurality of rurality which captures the views of traditionally 'invisible' rural groups.

About the book

This book aims to address the lack of critical academic enquiry into rural racism by highlighting key issues, concerns and preventative strategies that are central to contemporary debates on the subject. Throughout the course of their rural studies, the editors have observed considerable ambiguity surrounding the experience of rural minority ethnic households, ambiguity that, it was felt, a new text could go some way towards resolving. By the same token, the editors have also been drawn to the pioneering work of academics and practitioners who have sought to challenge traditional assumptions about that rural experience, and the prospect of assembling some of those ideas within a single edited volume was extremely appealing.

The book is divided into three distinct sections. Part 1 begins by helping to conceptualise rurality and the way in which the experiences of 'others' have been framed within the broader rural context. Debates around the term 'rural' have been alluded to already in this introduction, and Paul Cloke takes this discussion a step further in the next chapter as he examines how imagined, idyllic constructions serve to exclude particular social groups, both culturally and practically, in the purification of rural space. By drawing out the complexities and conjecture associated with rurality, Cloke goes on to identify a range of covert and overt processes of racism through which minority ethnic people are made to feel 'othered' in rural environments. Philomena de Lima then uses this basis in the subsequent chapter to provide a broad overview of racism in a rural context. As de Lima asserts, research has been undertaken across the UK on the subject of rural racism, though this tends typically to be small-scale and localised in nature, and she draws together this research to illustrate key issues that need to be considered as we develop a more informed understanding of rural racism.

Part 2 seeks to assess the problem in more detail by highlighting the different forms that racism can take in a rural context. Dominic Malcolm's chapter uses material elicited from a study based in the east of England to illustrate the diversity of racist experience affecting rural minority ethnic households, and his analysis helps to capture the subjectively defined 'low-level', or less tangible, types of racism that tend to be particularly common features of areas with low minority ethnic populations. The diversity of experience is also a theme picked up on in the chapter by Vaughan Robinson and Hannah Gardner, who warn against unwittingly stereotyping minority ethnic groups in the rural by assuming a commonality in their experience, regardless of differences between various sets of people and within alternative forms of rural space. Their chapter refers to research conducted in rural Wales as a way of unpicking conventional generalisations about minority ethnic people as victims and as a seemingly homogenous group.

The importance of drawing attention to different forms of rural racism is underlined by Paul Iganski and Jack Levin's discussion of the locational dynamics of racist hate crime in rural parts of the US and the UK. These authors focus specifically on the impact of white supremacist and far-right organisations in the rural, and suggest that individual acts of racism may be symptomatic of local cultures of bigotry in rural communities that extremist groups seek to inflame. Such cultures of bigotry also come under discussion in Jon Garland and Neil Chakraborti's chapter which utilises research material from a number of separate studies to analyse notions of community in the rural. The chapter details the perceptions of both white and minority ethnic rural communities to explore their perceptions of living in the countryside. It outlines the differences in these perceptions and suggests that 'traditional' notions of community are of little use in developing an understanding of contemporary rural living.

However, mapping the contours and dynamics of racism and rurality is not the sole concern of this volume. Developing responses to address the problem of rural racism must be a central component of the academic and political agenda, and Part 3 contains contributions from authors who have highlighted various ways in which prejudice can be challenged. Shammi Jalota outlines how a Racial Harassment Initiative based in the east of England works to tackle racism in rural and isolated areas, and suggests ways that this work can be applied to rural environments elsewhere. Issues of racism can often be marginalised by rural agencies in deference to other problems that show up more readily in official crime figures, and Jalota discusses ways in which the Initiative has coordinated a more prioritised response to rural-based victims of racist crime through its own range of services and through the multi-agency approach adopted in that area.

Introducing elements of diversity, multiculturalism and anti-racism into the classroom is a further challenge to those working in the field, particularly in the rural context where schools may have very few minority ethnic pupils and familiarity with 'other' cultures may be extremely low. Kate Broadhurst and Andi Wright refer in their chapter to steps that have been taken to develop a clearer understanding of the problem of racism within schools, drawing attention to the potentially enormous role that education can play in challenging racial intolerance. The importance of tackling intolerance and embracing difference are also key messages conveyed through the final chapter of this volume by Richard Pugh, who warns against the marginalisation and 'ghettoisation' of anti-racist initiatives in the context of local service delivery in rural areas. As Pugh asserts, responding to racism is now a statutory duty and professional obligation for service providers, and not merely a matter of discretion; as such, effective challenges to rural racism must be based upon widespread commitment to understanding different racisms, their context and their consequences.

As will be become apparent through the course of this book, rural racism is not a simple phenomenon: changing cultural norms, attitudes, geographical landscapes and political agendas will all impact upon the way in which different forms of racism manifest themselves in different forms of rural space, and indeed upon the way in which such behaviour is interpreted and challenged. With this in mind, a single volume as presented here cannot do justice to the full breadth of the subject, particularly in the current political climate where issues of 'race' and 'rurality' continue to be the source of considerable debate and conjecture. Nevertheless, it is the sincere hope of the editors that this collection of pieces helps to raise awareness of issues that, at least in the eyes of ourselves and our co-contributors, deserve far greater attention than they have hitherto received.

Note

1   The oft-referred to work of Clifford Shaw and Henry Mckay, for example, has argued that juvenile offending is a product of the societal transformations that result from rapid urbanisation, and as such that young people born and brought up in disorganised urban neighbourhoods are especially vulnerable to deviant behaviour (Shaw and Mckay 1972, cited in Hopkins Burke 2001: 104).

References

Agg, J. and Phillips, M. (1998) 'Neglected Gender Dimensions of Rural Social Restructuring', in P. Boyle and K. Halfacree (eds), *Migration Into Rural Areas: Theories and Issues*. Chichester: John Wiley and Sons.

Agyeman, J. and Spooner, R. (1997) 'Ethnicity and the Rural Environment', in P. Cloke and J. Little (eds), *Contested Countryside Cultures: Otherness, Marginalisation and Rurality*. London: Routledge.

Bright, M. (2003) 'Refugees Find No Welcome in City of Hate', *Observer*, 29 June, p. 14.

Bright, M. (2004) 'Asylum Seekers? Not Here, Not Even For a Few Minutes', *Observer*, 25 April, p. 5.

British National Party (2002) *Britain's Destiny: The New Atlantis?*, at http://www.land-and-people.org/atlantis_extinction.htm.

Bunce, M. (1994) *The Countryside Ideal: Anglo-American Images of Landscape*. London: Routledge.

Carter, H. (2003) 'Arrests for Burning of "Gypsy Caravan", *Guardian*, 12 November.

Chakraborti, N. and Garland, J. (2003) 'An "Invisible" Problem? Uncovering the Nature of Racist Victimisation in Rural Suffolk', *International Review of Victimology*, 10: 1, pp. 1–17.

Chakraborti, N. and Garland, J. (2004) 'England's Green and Pleasant Land? Examining Racist Prejudice in a Rural Context', *Patterns of Prejudice*, 38: 4, forthcoming.

Cherry, G.E. (ed.) (1976) *Rural Planning Problems*. London: Hill.

Cloke, P. (1977) 'An Index of Rurality for England and Wales', *Regional Studies*, 20, pp. 31–46.

Cloke, P. (1980) 'New Emphases for Applied Rural Geography', *Progress in Human Geography*, 4, pp. 181–217.

Cloke, P. (1997) 'Poor Country: Marginalisation, Poverty and Rurality' in P. Cloke and J. Little (eds) *Contested Countryside Cultures: Otherness, Marginalisation and Rurality*. London: Routledge.

Cloke, P. and Little, J. (eds) (1997) *Contested Countryside Cultures: Otherness, Marginalisation and Rurality*. London: Routledge.

Cloke, P. and Milbourne, P. (1992) 'Deprivation and Lifestyles in Rural Wales', *Journal of Rural Studies*, 8: 4, pp. 359–71.

de Lima, P. (2001) *Needs not Numbers: An Exploration of Minority Ethnic Communities in Scotland*. London: Commission for Racial Equality and Community Development Foundation.

Derbyshire, H. (1994) *Not In Norfolk: Tackling The Invisibility of Racism*. Norwich: Norwich and Norfolk Racial Equality Council.

Dingwall, G. (1999) 'Justice by Geography: Realizing Criminal Justice in the Countryside', in G. Dingwall and S.R. Moody (eds), *Crime and Conflict in the Countryside*. Cardiff: University of Wales Press.

Dyer, C. (2004) 'Judge Backs Asylum Centre', *Guardian*, 7 April.

Fish, R.D. (2000) *Putting Together Rurality: Media Producers and the Social Construction of the Countryside*. Unpublished PhD thesis, Leicester: University of Leicester.

Francis, D. and Henderson, P. (1992) *Working With Rural Communities*. Basingstoke: Macmillan.

Garland, J. and Rowe, M. (2001) *Racism and Anti-Racism in Football*. Basingstoke: Palgrave.

Hopkins Burke, R. (2001) *An Introduction to Criminological Theory*. Cullompton: Willan.

Howkins, A. (2001) 'Rurality and English Identity', in D. Morley and K. Robins (eds), *British Cultural Studies: Geography, Nationality and Identity*. Oxford: Oxford University Press.

Jay, E. (1992) *'Keep Them in Birmingham': Challenging Racism in South West England*. London: Commission for Racial Equality.

Kirkey, K. and Forsyth, A. (2001) 'Men in the Valley: Gay Male Life on the Suburban–Rural Fringe', *Journal of Rural Studies*, 17: 4, pp. 421–41.

Liepins, R. (2000) 'New Energies for an Old Idea: Reworking Approaches to "Community" in Contemporary Rural Studies', *Journal of Rural Studies*, 16: 1, pp. 23–35.

Little, J. and Austin, P. (1996) 'Women and the Rural Idyll', *Journal of Rural Studies*, 12: 2, pp. 101–11.

Lowles, N. (2001) *White Riot: The Violent Story of Combat 18*. Bury: Milo Books.

Malcolm, D. (2000) *West Norfolk Ethnic Minorities Research Report*. Leicester: Department of Sociology, University of Leicester.

Milbourne, P. (1997) 'Hidden From View: Poverty and Marginalisation in Rural Britain', in P. Milbourne (ed.), *Revealing Rural 'Others': Representation, Power and Identity in the British Countryside*. London: Pinter.

Moody, S.R. (1999) 'Rural Neglect: The Case Against Criminology', in G. Dingwall and S.R. Moody (eds), *Crime and Conflict in the Countryside*. Cardiff: University of Wales Press.

Murdoch, J. and Day, G. (1998) 'Middle-Class Mobility, Rural Communities and the Politics of Exclusion', in P. Boyle and K. Halfacree (eds), *Migration into Rural Areas: Theories and Issues*. Chichester: John Wiley and Sons.

Murdoch, J. and Marsden, T. (1994) *Reconstructing Rurality: Class, Community and Power in the Development Process*. London: UCL Press.

Murdoch, J. and Pratt, A.C. (1997) 'From the Power of Topography to the Topography of Power: A Discourse on Strange Ruralities', in P. Cloke and J. Little (eds), *Contested Countryside Cultures: Otherness, Marginalisation and Rurality*. London: Routledge.

Orwell, G. (1941) *The Lion and the Unicorn: Socialism and the English Genius*. London: Secker & Warburg.

Phillips, M., Fish, R. and Agg, J. (2001) 'Putting Together Ruralities: Towards a Symbolic Analysis of Rurality in the British Mass Media', *Journal of Rural Studies*, 17: 1, pp. 1–27.

Philo, C. (1992) 'Neglected Rural Geographies: A Review', *Journal of Rural Studies*, 8: 2, pp. 193–207.

Robinson, G.M. (1990) *Conflict and Change in the Countryside*. London: Belhaven.

Scutt, R. and Bonnett, A. (1996) *In Search of England: Popular Representations of Englishness and the English Countryside*, Centre for Rural Economy Working Paper No. 22. Newcastle Upon Tyne: Centre for Rural Economy, University of Newcastle Upon Tyne.

Sibley, D. (1997) 'Endangering the Sacred: Nomads, Youth Cultures and the English Countryside', in P. Cloke and J. Little (eds), *Contested Countryside Cultures: Otherness, Marginalisation and Rurality*. London: Routledge.

Tonnies, F. (1887) *Gemeinschaft und Gesellschaft*, 8: Auflage, Leipzig, 1935.

Whitelaw, W. (1989) *The Whitelaw Memoirs*. London: Aurum Press.

Wirth, L. (138) 'Urbanism as a Way of Life', *American Journal of Sociology*, 44, pp. 1–24.

Part I

Contextualising Rural Racism

Chapter 1

Rurality and racialised others: out of place in the countryside?

Paul Cloke

Ethnicity and the 'unusual' countryside

A recent report by Raekha Prasad (2004) in the *Guardian* newspaper deployed an orthodox shock tactic to highlight the complex inter-connections between ethnicity and rurality in the British countryside. Three people are pictured in the piece, posing against the background of a lake by a forest, and the banner asks 'What's unusual about this scene?'. The answer to the conundrum lies neither in the unspoilt solitude of the place, which might be expected to display the crowded nature of the rural honeypot, nor in the absence of the high-technology boots, anoraks and rucksacks which typically denote the paraphernalia of 'serious' walkers enjoying a highly embodied and entirely acceptable cultural experience of the countryside. No, the representation of 'unusual' in this context is signified by the clear non-white ethnicity of the subjects of the photograph – their 'Asian-ness' is stereotypically suggested in clothing, headgear, the men's beards and so on – and the intended shock counterposes the expectation that the countryside is typically a white domain.

To acknowledge that the presence of ethnic minorities in rural scenes is 'unusual' is one thing, but Prasad's report proceeds to identify more sinister links between rurality and ethnicity via vox-pop testimonies from black and Asian Britons who have variously found themselves 'disowned by rural England' (ibid.: S2). Andrea Levy, a black novelist, tells us that 'In the countryside I am so acutely aware of what I look like, not because people are hostile or unfriendly, but just because you are different. I always get the feeling when I walk into a country pub that everyone is looking at me, whether they are or not. You are glowing with colour' (ibid.: S3). Benjamin Zephaniah, a black poet, talks of the time when he was staying on a friend's farm and went out for a jog within the boundaries of the farm. 'When I got back to his house, the place was surrounded by police, a helicopter circling above. "We have had reports of a suspicious jogger" the police said' (ibid.: S2). Lemm Sissay, a black poet who was fostered and brought up in the country, tells of his experience in a countryside which he finds 'beautiful but incredibly damaged': 'Growing up, I used to ask myself why everyone had such a big issue with the colour of my skin. Men would shield their women from me, bars would go quiet. The incendiary racism that is in the country is never challenged' (ibid.: S3).

These autobiographical notes reflect on a range of identity clashes between minority ethnicity and rurality – difference, suspicion, marginalisation and racism all lurk behind the seemingly unusual presence of people of colour in countryside settings. While such identity clashes are highly visible in city sites, it is almost as if ethnic 'others' are typically rendered invisible by rurality, such that any moments of becoming visible represent unusual intrusions into the conventional cultural norms of rural life. In this chapter I want briefly to explore what it is about rurality and rural culture that sponsors this 'othering' of ethnic minority people, and to discuss the mechanisms of social and cultural regulation which position people of colour as 'out of place' in the countryside. Identities and subjectivities centred around ethnicity are by no means the sole axes of rural othering, but as this book portrays, both extreme and banal racisms represent very significant socio-cultural problematics in rural areas, and as with other axes of marginalisation, rendering them highly visible is the first step to a more socially inclusive future.

Rurality and otherness

Rurality is a complex concept. At one level, we are often content to fall back on key characteristics which historically have been associated with rurality and rural life and which translate into objects of desire in contemporary society. In these terms, the countryside is viewed as an area which fulfils three principal criteria (Cloke and Park 1985):

1   It is dominated (either currently or recently) by extensive land uses, such as agriculture and forestry, or large spaces of undeveloped land.
2   It contains small, low-order settlements which demonstrate a strong relationship between buildings and surrounding extensive landscape, and which are thought of as rural by most of their residents.
3   It engenders a way of life characterised by a cohesive identity based on respect for the environmental and behavioural qualities of living as part of an extensive landscape.

At another level, however, we draw from these material characteristics a series of ideas and understandings about the meaningfulness of rurality. Somewhere deep down in our cultural psyche there appear to be longstanding handed-down precepts about what rurality represents, emphasising the enabling power of nature to offer opportunities for lifestyle enhancement through the production and consumption of socially cohesive, happy and healthy living at a pace and quality which differs markedly from that of the city. Rurality has thus become cross-referenced with tranquillity, goodness, wholeness and problem-freedom, and at a more obviously political level it maps onto cartographies of identity, encapsulating for some a treasury of norms and values which both illustrate and shape what is valuable in a nation, a region or a locality.

Much has been written about the so-called 'rural idyll' in recent years (see, for example, Bell 1997; Bunce 1994, 2003; Cloke and Milbourne 1992; Halfacree 1995; Little and Austin 1996; Mingay 1989; Short 1991) both to confirm and to challenge these ideas of aesthetic pastoral landscapes acting as sites for humans working together in harmony and achieving both contentment and plenty. However, despite the over-arching and sometimes stereotyping characteristics of the concept of 'idyll', the idea endures both in the direct representation of a range of contemporary cultural paraphernalia, and in reflexive and instinctive knowledges about the rural which are lived out in perception, attitude and practice. As Bunce (2003: 15) explains:

> The values that sustain the rural idyll speak of a profound and universal human need for connection with land, nature and community, a psychology which, as people have become in-creasingly separated from these experiences, reflects the literal meaning of nostalgia; the sense of loss of home, of homesickness.

Rurality, then, not only represents spaces and values which satisfy basic psychological and spiritual needs, but also sponsors a cultural idyll which represents a natural and inevitable counterpoint to the rise of urban modernism.

This seemingly straightforward understanding of rurality needs to be tempered by a series of complicating acknowledgements about how rural metanarratives play out in real life, of which three will be summarised here. First, it is clear that rurality is not homogenous and that rural areas are *different*. In the English context, there are significant differences between the metropolitan ruralities of areas close to cities and the more peripheral ruralities of remoter areas. Equally, within the UK account has to be taken both of regional distinction and of the significance of nationhood in fashioning, for example, the ruralities of Wales and Scotland. Moving beyond the UK, the extensive ruralities of larger land continents exaggerate both materially and relatively the differences between rural areas. Outback Australia, the Canadian northern territories and the American mid-west, for example, can only loosely be treated spatially or conceptually as 'the same' as each other, and comparisons with, say, rural Berkshire are even more tenuous.

Secondly, rural areas are essentially dynamic. Far from being timeless, unchanging sites of nostalgia, they are being reconstructed economically and recomposed socially by the globalised food industry, by the increasing mobility of production and people, and by the niched fragmentation of consumption and the commodification of place. Wilson (1992) argues that the end-product of rural dynamism is a blurring of the boundaries between the urban and the rural. Rural areas are becoming culturally urbanised through the all-pervading spread of urban-based mass media and other cultural output. Social trends of counter-urbanisation have brought 'urban' people into rural areas, and out-of-town movements of factories and shopping malls have had similar impacts. In these and other ways, then, the city has moved out into the countryside. By contrast, the countryside has also, to an extent, been moving into the city, for example with the development of urban 'villages' and the now pervasive trend of heightening the visibility and performance of urban nature. As I have written elsewhere, all this renders the rural–urban distinction indistinct:

New regions focus on the hybrid relations between cities and surrounding areas; new information technologies permit the traversing of time–space obstacles; new forms of counter-

urbanisation result in spatial cross-dressing both by the arriving in
and leaving of places. (Cloke 2003: 2)

Thirdly, rural areas will often display dystopic characteristics in visible
illustrations of the seamier side of rural life. Bell's (1997) account of
cinematic depictions of small-town America demonstrates how the
'horror' of rural life counterposes any narrative of idyll. The foot and
mouth epidemic which consumed much of rural Britain during 2001
provided clear evidence of a non-idyllic countryside, as news media
portrayed vivid images of the funeral pyres of culled livestock, and the
curiously empty fields of farms deprived of their essential animality.
Whether in the imaginative texts of film, or in the seemingly more
mimetic (but equally imaginative) representation of news coverage,
there is now evidence galore of rurality without idyll. Previous
assumptions about rural areas as problem-free are challenged by a
determined flow of suggestions that rural life is little different from that
of the city in terms of crime, drug-addiction, poverty and other
apparently urban problems. The material realities of 'living-in-the-idyll'
are being seriously challenged by these depictions.

These characteristics of difference, dynamism and dystopia suggest
that the rural–urban dualism has been largely overtaken by events.
Rurality can no longer be regarded as a single space but is rather a
multiplicity of social spaces which overlap the same geographical area
(Mormont 1990). However, while the marked opposition between the
geographical spaces of urban and rural is being broken down, the
imagined opposition between the *social* significances of urban and rural
are being maintained and in some ways enhanced. Indeed it is the social
space of rurality – often fuelled by idyllistic concepts – which is the
magnetic force which pulls together the category 'rural' or 'countryside'
in the contemporary discourses of everyday life. And, as Halfacree (1993)
has explained, the multiple meanings which constitute the social space
of rurality are increasingly diverging from the geographical spaces of the
rural. The symbols of rurality are becoming detached from their
referential moorings, as socially constructed rural space is becoming
increasingly detached from geographically functional rural space. Thus,
despite our ever more nuanced understanding of the different
happenings in rural places, there is considerable scope for socially
constructed significations of rurality to dominate both the territory of
ideas and meanings about the rural, and the attitudes and practices
which are played out in and from that territory.

One of the most important outcomes of debates about socially constructed rurality has been a deep concern about the cultural and political domination afforded by hegemonic ideas about rurality and rural people. Philo's (1992) intervention to highlight the neglected rural geographies hidden away in and by such hegemonic social constructions was seminal in the search for ways to give voice to rural 'others'. He emphasised that social constructions of life are dominated by white, male, middle-class narratives (ibid.: 200):

> There remains a danger of portraying British rural people … as all being 'Mr Averages', as being men in employment, earning enough to live, white and probably English, straight and somehow without sexuality, able in body and sound in mind, and devoid of any other quirks (say) religious belief or political application.

Philo points to the discursive power through which the all-embracing commonalities suggested by social constructions of rural idyll serve in practice to exclude individuals and groups of people from a sense of belonging to, and in, the rural on the grounds of their 'race', ethnicity, gender, age, class and so on. Subsequent studies of rural 'others' (see Cloke and Little 1997; Milbourne 1997) have sought to identify the practices and devices which exclude particular individuals and groups in this way. For example, examinations of poverty in rural areas (see, for example, Cloke 1997; Cloke *et al.* 1995, 1997) have connected the idyllised, imagined geographies of rural lifestyles with the suggestion that poverty is being hidden or rejected *culturally*, both by decision-makers who refuse to accept that poverty can exist in idyllic rural areas, and by rural dwellers themselves who legitimise poverty as a disadvantage of rural life which is often compensated 'naturally' by the benefits of a rural setting. In this way, rurality can signify itself as a poverty-free zone, and socially constructed rural idylls both exacerbate and hide poverty in rural geographic space. Similarly, studies of rural homelessness (see Cloke *et al.* 2002) recognise that implicitly idyllised and romantic notions of rural living sponsor the idea that homelessness cannot occur in caring rural communities:

> The idea of a 'helpful' community, then, discursively constructs rural society, and problems such as homelessness within that society, in such a way that rurality and homelessness are further disconnected. (ibid.: 68)

A concern for 'other' people and practices of 'othering', then, have become of paramount importance in tracing the consequences of how cultural significations of rurality have impacts on and in rural life itself.

Racialised others in the countryside

> The countryside is popularly perceived as a 'white landscape' ... predominantly inhabited by white people, hiding both the growing living presence and the increasing recreational participation of people of colour. Thus in the language of 'white' England, ethnicity is rarely an issue associated with the countryside. Its whiteness is blinding to its presence in any other form than the 'non-white'. (Agyeman and Spooner 1997: 197).

The terms 'race' and 'ethnicity' are often substituted for each other without care for more precise definition. In this chapter, 'race' (following Jackson 2000) is taken to reflect a social construction which marks out human difference usually on the basis of distinct skin colour. By contrast, ethnicity is taken to be a more self-referential term by which particular groups linked by birth express the differences in their culture and lifestyle (Jackson 1992). The reference made by Agyeman and Spooner to how the 'whiteness' of the countryside reflects on its other as 'non-white' exemplifies an assertion that 'race' rather than ethnicity lies at the heart of processes and practices by which people of colour are 'othered' in and by the rural.

There is now a strong body of work which has demonstrated how rural landscapes have served as key symbols of English national identity (Kinsman 1993, 1995; Daniels 1992, 1993). The countryside, it is argued, is more than the sum of its parts; it reflects core qualities of Englishness and is inhabited by those who are intent on upholding the rural and social fabric of the nation. The absence of 'non-white' people in countryside landscapes, then, has reinforced a collaboration between whiteness and national identity in the symbolism of rurality – a collaboration which for the most part remains unspoken, but which has been detailed by extreme right-wing political parties such as the National Front (Coates 1993) and the British National Party (Roberts 1992) for whom a green and pleasant land free from invading (non-white) aliens represents ideologically potent fascist imagery.

Given these strong connections between rurality and the symbolisation of national identity, morality and social fabric, it is inevitable that social constructions of rurality will become embroiled, often unknowingly, in ideas of Englishness from which people of colour are excluded. Brace (2003) has argued that the mapping out of the nature of Englishness involves both 'the search for and valorisation of untouched, unsullied places that epitomised the things about Englishness which were so valued', and 'constructing a moral geography of places which were signally un-English' (ibid., 69). The vilification of problematic people and places is only made possible by its corollary – the celebration of unproblematic people and places – and rurality offers many opportunities for such celebration. However, the unsullied nature of rurality is predicated on a heritage which is assumed to be white and Anglo-Saxon, with other social and cultural groups being excluded because they potentially threaten the political narrative of 'acceptable' history and heritage. The glorious Englishness of the rural is founded on the relations and values of colonial history – a history told by white English historians who, as Agyeman (1995: 5) points out, have written out the stories of people of colour from their hegemonic narratives:

> Soldiers from North Africa used the Roman environment of the Borders. They were garrisoned on Hadrian's Wall. People from Asia were brought, often as whole villages, to Britain to work in the Yorkshire and Lancashire cotton mills. Many of our stately homes were financed, built and exotically landscaped through African-Caribbean slavery ... Has the presence of these and other people been routinely celebrated in visitor attraction and interpretation facilities, or has it been quietly and unceremoniously swept under the carpet?

If rurality has been linked with 'racial purity', and the countryside has been viewed as the core of national identity in which country people somehow become an essence of England, then such symbolisms are founded on skewed histories and deliberate exclusions which are bound to fuel unthinking partialities among the included, and fear and disenfranchisement among those excluded.

Explorations of racialised otherness in the countryside have been relatively few and far between. Most rural and social texts and commentaries acknowledge the othering of people of colour by turning to a particular contribution by the black photographer, Ingrid Pollard (see Kinsman 1995), whose series *Pastoral Interlude* comprises self-portraits and portraits of friends (also black) against rural backgrounds – a stone wall in front of an extensive landscape, a country churchyard, a stream. In these images, the picture of a black person in a rural setting is intended to be unusual, disconcerting, an interlude to pastoral norms. The mood of the images is enriched by their captions:

It's as if the Black experience is only ever lived within an urban environment. I thought I liked the Lake District, where I wandered lonely as a Black face in a sea of white. A visit to the countryside is always accompanied by a feeling of unease, dread …

… feeling I don't belong. Walks through leafy glades with a baseball bat by my side …

A lot of WHAT MADE ENGLAND GREAT is founded on the blood of slavery, the sweat of working people … an industrial REVOLUTION without the Atlantic Triangle …

Death is the bottom line. The owners of these fields; these trees and sheep want me off their GREEN AND PLEASANT LAND. No Trespass, they want me DEAD. A slow death through eyes that slide away from me.

(Pollard undated: emphasis in original)

According to Kinsman (1993) the lone black figures in Pollard's images are wistful and resigned, while the angrily ironic captions protest the white ownership of land which seeks to evict, repatriate or even destroy black 'intruders', even though their labour was a crucial factor in the economic development which underpins histories of land ownership. Pollard thus connects the historic death of black slaves with what she regards as the slower 'death' of black people in contemporary Britain, suffering – through racialised surveillance from country folk – from unease, dread, fear. Pollard's work has become an iconic source, turned to by academics wishing to illustrate racialised otherness in the countryside, although as the Women in Geography Study Group (1997) argues, her work also reflects gendered otherness. While Pollard's excellent work is certainly worthy of respectful re-examination, there is a whiff here of white academics (myself included) often being content just to have one (token?) example to reflect the non-white other. More recently, other academic studies have sought to widen the base of evidence (see, for example, Spooner-Williams 1997, reflecting on Dabydeen 1992 and Agyeman 1989, 1991, 1995) but the rural racialised other has certainly been given less attention than alternative othered groups.

The other major explorations of racialised otherness have come in a series of reports, for example: *Keep Them In Birmingham* (Jay 1992) a challenge to racism in south-west England published by the Commission for Racial Equality; *Staring At Invisible Women* (Esuantsiwa Goldsmith and Makris 1994) a report on the experiences of black and minority ethnic women in rural areas published by the National Alliance of Women's Organisations; and *Not In Norfolk* (Derbyshire 1994), a report on the experiences of ethnic minority people living in Norfolk, published by the Norwich and Norfolk Racial Equality Council. A feature of each of these outstanding reports is an emphasis on the invisibility of 'race' and racism in rural settings. To some extent, the mediated impression that 'race' issues are associated with urban areas means that their invisibility in rural areas is unsurprising. However, as the reports make clear, the popular myth that such invisibility is due to an absence of people of colour in the countryside is just a myth. There is a small, but significant, presence of people of colour living in and visiting the countryside, and the belief that no 'race' issues exist there is due only to cultural invisibility. Many of Jay's respondents from local authorities, health authorities and other voluntary organisations felt that questions of racial equality were 'not applicable' in their areas of jurisdiction, both because they seriously underestimated the scale of ethnic minority presence and because of a broad cultural denial of any 'problems with race'. He concluded that 'the commonest response to the project was one of indifference or even hostility; racial equality is evidently not part of the agenda' (Jay 1992: 43). Esuantsiwa Goldsmith and Makris (1994) experienced similar attitudes from statutory and non-statutory organisations which denied that race-related problems occurred in rural areas. However, their evidence from women of colour confirmed the presence of racism in the countryside:

> Racism was experienced by the women we consulted as a lack of acceptance into white society, and discrimination against minority culture, religion, colour and way of life through fear and ignorance of other people. (ibid.: 23)

Moreover, they concluded that women of colour suffered from a double dose of othering practices because rural communities tend to be dominated by patriarchal structures which prevent consultation with women and therefore render invisible their needs, views and aspirations. These women are additionally disadvantaged because of the invisibility of issues connected with 'race'. Derbyshire's findings add a further dimension to the invisibilty of rural racism. She records the almost universal reaction from white respondents that 'there is no problem here' and suggests that the reasoning behind this response is because:

> Those [people of colour] who are here are encountered individually and so constitute no real threat, or they are working within the context of restaurants and takeaways and in this sense 'know their place'. (Derbyshire 1994: 21)

This reference to 'knowing their place' seems crucial to the understanding of racialised others in the countryside, because ethnic minorities not only find themselves positioned culturally as 'out of place' in the countryside, but also experience practices and attitudes which seek to purify that place should it be transgressed.

In place/out of place in the countryside

The othering of ethnic minorities in rural areas needs to be understood against a broad-brush background of how idyllistic cultures of rurality serve to signify key facets of what rural life should be like (Cloke *et al*. 2000). Cresswell's (1996) discussion of how uses of space come to be constructed as 'appropriate' or 'inappropriate' is instructive here, in that it suggests not only that an established social order is reproduced by a naturalisation of common sense, but also that boundaries will be erected between common-sense notions of what is appropriate or inappropriate in particular places. He argues that there is therefore a 'taken-for-granted' doxa of what goes on in places, and that different places display different such doxa or senses of the obvious. When such common-sense doxa are transgressed, things will seem out-of-place because of a lack of doxa conformity. Cresswell concludes that particular places are implicated in the construction and reproduction of particular ideologies, and that socially constructed meanings of place can become naturalised as they are taken for granted.

Cresswell's ideas fit well with Sibley's (1995: 78) arguments about the geographies of social exclusion, in which spatial purification is seen as a key factor in the organisation of social space:

> The anatomy of a purified environment is an expression of the values associated with strong feelings of objection, a heightened consciousness of difference and, thus, a fear of mixing at the disintegration of boundaries.

So not only do we need to acknowledge a taken-for-grantedness about what is 'in place' or 'out of place', but we need to grasp how places assume a symbolic importance which constructs and reproduces a desire for order in which local environments require ordering and purification. It is by these means that spaces become implicated in the construction of deviancy. The purity of spaces reinforces their difference from other places and sponsors a policing of social and spatial boundaries. Speaking of New Age Travellers, Sibley (ibid.: 107–8) argues:

> A rigid stereotype of place, the English countryside, throws up discrepant others ... These groups are other, they are folk-devils, and they transgress only because the countryside is defined as a stereotypical pure space which cannot accommodate difference.

Although it is important to reiterate that rurality should not be viewed as any kind of self-defining or naturalistic category, we can use Cresswell's and Sibley's arguments to suggest a thesis about the othering of ethnic minorities in rural areas. First, the lived presence of ethnic minorities in Britain tends to be spatialised as 'in place' in urban environments. Secondly, rural areas are typically understood as signifying essentially white characteristics of Englishness. Taken together, the presence of non-white ethnic minorities in rural areas is not just 'unusual' (as discussed in the introduction to this chapter) but may be deemed as out of place, representing a transgression of the orthodoxies assured by socio-spatial expectations. We might therefore expect to find the countryside policed as a purified space in this respect, because a rejection of difference is deeply embedded in its social system.

Such expectations find echoes in studies of 'race' and ethnicity in rural areas. Agyeman (1989) for example reflects that for white people, 'ethnicity' is viewed as being out of place in the countryside, and Spooner-Williams (1997) interprets white women's narratives of 'race' in the village in terms of attempts by middle-class residents to purify their local space. Evidence on these issues needs to be treated with care, as personal statements of individual attitudes towards 'race' and ethnicity in the countryside may well contrast with attitudes attributed to 'the village' collectively. In this way, white people can deny their own complicity in racist purification yet can sometimes acknowledge the existence of racism by displacing it onto other individuals or onto 'the village' more generally.

Rachel Spooner-Williams assesses these contrasting discourses of rural 'race' in terms of the 'public' and 'private' faces of racism. She found that many white women claimed not to recognise 'race' as an issue in rural settings: a denial which often assumes away the difference in others of colour so as to maintain the dominance of the presumed sameness of whiteness. The public discourse of 'we are all the same' is sometimes accompanied by displacement of racist attitudes to other (often older and longer-standing) village residents, but is mostly twinned with discourses of 'we all have every opportunity' and thereby with a blindness to racial difference and to the presence of prejudice and discrimination. She also found that many women of colour in rural settings become co-opted into these discourses through a desire to 'fit in'. The private face of rural 'race', however, strongly reflects a purification of village spaces in which white residents demand conformity to their perceived orthodoxies and exclude those who transgress these boundaries of what is in place in the village setting. Sometimes being 'out of place' seems to be a matter of constructions of cultural incompetence (Cloke 1994; Cloke *et al.* 1997) reflected in cultural distinctions relating to how to keep house, tend a garden or join in with village society. However, such constructions often represent the superstructure of a far deeper vessel of anxiety, discrimination and racism in rural settings, which collectively serve to bleach the cultural identity of people of colour, and to police the cultural boundaries of rural whiteness.

Rural racisms

While it would be erroneous to assume all white rural residents to be racist, the evidence from available research nevertheless clearly points to the presence of rural racism which polices the 'purity' of rurality in a number of different ways, ranging from the subtle to the downright criminal. The purification of rural space varies in visibility – a village up in arms over proposals to establish a centre for asylum seekers in their vicinity seems to be 'acceptable' as a very public expression of outrage, while the miseries suffered by a black child in a village school will be more private yet equally reflect processes and practices of rural purification. Despite the risk of over generalisation, a useful starting point for the identification of rural racism is therefore to identify a range of covert and overt practices and experiences by which people of colour are made to feel excluded, marginalised and othered in rural environments.

Covert racism comes in many forms, but at its heart lie mechanisms, assumptions, inflections and orthodoxies which serve to deny people of colour any distinct cultural identity in rural settings, presenting them with lifestyle choices involving a denial of ethnic identity so as to 'fit in', or a celebration of ethnic identity often leading to cultural isolation. Derbyshire's (1994) study in Norfolk demonstrates how the onus is always on ethnic minority people to fit into rural society, and her interviews with people of colour illustrate how coping with life in white rural society requires compromise and self denial:

> I have to make changes to fit in, for my own mental health. I'm not sure it's the way I should go. There is no platform for me ... I'm allowed to entertain but they are toning me down!

> If you don't fit in you pay the price. It's hard to have the confidence to fight back – if you are the one who suffers. You must try and fit in and suppress any feelings against this.

> Here I keep a large part of myself hidden. It's like I have two lives. (ibid.: 33)

Even where people of colour are content to strive for community acceptance, they face an inevitability that acceptance will usually only be partial. Esuantsiwa Goldsmith and Makris (1994: 22) quote an Asian woman interviewee as suggesting that:

> The attitude of white society in rural areas appears contradictory. They imply that if minority people conform and adopt white culture they will be accepted. But even if we do we are still regarded as different.

This cultural isolation is often compromised by difficulties in receiving community support and a lack of information networks or links for ethnic minority residents in rural areas. These covert racisms are often cloaked in a façade of polite condescension, as rural residents will assume a public face of tolerance of the 'strangers' in their midst. Jay (1992: 21) illustrates this point through the life-experiences of a black interviewee living in the rural south-west of England:

> For one man, the experience of being a black person in an almost totally white environment was that he encountered great ignorance and was regarded as a piece of 'exotica'. 'They treated me as someone who needed to be patronised; it was as though I had just stepped off the boat.'

While people of colour may experience such ignorance in all kinds of spatial settings, the white heat of the localised cauldron of rural society, where everybody knows everybody else, exacerbates the isolation and othering which results.

More overt forms of rural racism are also evident from these research studies. Narratives of straightforward discrimination in rural areas abound, and it is interesting to note in the following two examples drawn from Jay (1992: 17) that discrimination often seems to result from transgression of the *imagined* spaces of rurality – what is and what is not 'in place' – which can be as much to do with the expectations of wider society as it is constructed by rural people themselves:

> A young black student working for a degree in institutional management arrived at a hotel in Cornwall to begin an industrial placement … The hotel management was surprised to find that the trainee was black, and the following day he was asked to leave, since his colour 'might affect the trade' … at a different Cornish hotel, a black woman who had just started work as a chambermaid was dismissed because members of a coach party staying there 'expressed virulent dislike' at the idea of a black chambermaid attending their rooms.

Such obviously discriminating racisms were dealt with under race relations and employment legislation, but other practices of racialised purification in rural areas take the form of sustained harassment which is more difficult to counteract both in legal terms and because of the costs of resultant exclusion in a small community. People from ethnic minorities who operate restaurants and shops in rural areas, for example, will often have to tread a precarious line amongst the abusive harassment attracted by their non-white identities. Derbyshire (1994: 32) reports the story of one such takeaway owner in rural Norfolk:

> Children are the worst. They say so many rude words to you. 'You

fucking foreigner' ... You go and talk to their parents. They don't take it seriously. They laugh at you or say the same thing ... People leave without paying. Do they do that to the English? ... Children threw a condom through [the] window. We sent the mother a solicitor's letter. It means she never comes anymore and she has told all in the neighbourhood not to come here for food ... Windows have been broken and the insurance won't pay anymore ... I'm stressed, I can't sleep. We are selling up and going after 15 years.

Such violent harassment is not confined to a few isolated cases. Jay's (1992) research in Dorset and Somerset uncovered a series of incidents in which Asian families had been forced to leave their homes and businesses because of the hostility of other villagers, and from Devon and Cornwall he gathered reports of racial abuse and threatening and violent behaviour experienced by restaurant workers and owners.

These covert and overt examples of rural racism clearly illustrate some of the practices used to 'purify' the whiteness of rural space, when transgressions occur through what are constructed as the 'out of place' presence, activities or cultural differences of non-white others. At a time when the cultural politics of rurality appear to have focussed sharply on developing a 'rural voice' to speak for the countryside against a range of perceived threats from the urban, there is an urgent need to evaluate that rural voice in terms of its potentially exclusive vision of rural affairs. Hegemonic speaking out on behalf of rural people inherently reinforces the processes and practices of exclusion which accompany hegemonic rurality. An alternative cultural politics emphasising a countryside of difference seems long overdue but is essential if we are to break down the interior boundaries of rurality which both concrete difference and 'purify' otherness.

References

Agyeman, J. (1989) 'Black People, White Landscape', *Town and Country Planning*, 58 (12): 336–8.
Agyeman, J. (1991) 'The Multicultural City Ecosystem', *Streetwise*, 7: 21–4.
Agyeman, J. (1995) 'Environment, Heritage and Multiculturalism', *Interpretation*, 1: 5–6.
Agyeman, J. and Spooner, R. (1997) 'Ethnicity and the Rural Environment', in P. Cloke and J. Little (eds), *Contested Countryside Cultures: Otherness, Marginalisation and Rurality*. London: Routledge.

Bell, D. (1997) 'Anti-idyll: Rural Horror', in P. Cloke and J. Little (eds), *Contested Countryside Cultures: Otherness, Marginalisation and Rurality*. London: Routledge.

Brace, C. (2003) 'Rural Mappings', in P. Cloke (ed.) *Country Visions*. Harlow: Pearson.

Bunce, M. (1994) *The Countryside Ideal*. London: Routledge.

Bunce, M. (2003) 'Reproducing Rural Idylls', in P. Cloke (ed.), *Country Visions*. Harlow: Pearson.

Cloke, P. (1994) '(En)culturing Political Economy: A Life in the Day of a Rural Geographer', in P. Cloke, M. Doel, D. Matless, M. Phillips and N. Thrift, *Writing The Rural: Five Cultural Geographies*. London: Paul Chapman Publishing.

Cloke, P. (1997) 'Poor Country: Marginalisation, Poverty and Rurality', in P. Cloke and J. Little (eds), *Contested Countryside Cultures: Otherness, Marginalisation and Rurality*. London: Routledge.

Cloke, P. (2003) 'Knowing Ruralities?', in P. Cloke (ed.), *Country Visions*. Harlow: Pearson.

Cloke, P. and Little, J. (eds) (1997) *Contested Countryside Cultures: Otherness, Marginalisation, and Rurality*. Routledge: London.

Cloke, P. and Milbourne, P. (1992) 'Deprivation and Lifestyles in Rural Wales', *Journal of Rural Studies*, 8 (4): 359–71.

Cloke, P. and Park, C. (1985) *Rural Resource Management*. London: Croom Helm.

Cloke, P., Goodwin, M. and Milbourne, P. (1997) 'Inside Looking Out, Outside Looking In: Different Experiences of Cultural Competence in Rural Lifestyles', in P. Boyle and K. Halfacree (eds), *Migration Into Rural Areas: Theories and Issues*. Chichester: Wiley and Sons.

Cloke, P., Milbourne, P. and Thomas, C. (1997) 'Living Lives in Different Ways? Deprivation, Marginalisation and Changing Lifestyles in Rural England', *Transactions Institutes of British Geographers*, NS 22: 210–30.

Cloke, P., Milbourne, P. and Widdowfield, R. (2000) 'Homelessness and Rurality: "Out-of-place" in Purified Space', *Environment and Planning D: Society and Space*, 18: 715–35.

Cloke, P., Milbourne, P. and Widdowfield, R. (2002) *Rural Homelessness*. Bristol: Policy Press.

Cloke, P., Goodwin, M., Milbourne, P. and Thomas, C. (1995) 'Deprivation, Poverty and Marginalisation in Rural Lifestyles in England and Wales', *Journal of Rural Studies*, 11 (4): 351–66.

Cloke, P. and Park, C. (1985) *Rural Resource Management*, London: Croom Helm.

Coates, I. (1993) 'A Cuckoo in the Nest: The National Front and Green Ideology', in J. Holder, P. Lane, S. Eden, R. Reeve, U. Collier and K. Anderson (eds), *Perspectives on the Environment: Interdisciplinary Research Network on the Environment and Society*. Aldershot: Avebury.

Cresswell, T. (1996) *In Place, Out of Place: Geography, Ideology and Transgression*. Minneapolis, MN: University of Minnesota Press.

Dabydeen, D. (1992) *Disappearance*. London: Secker and Warburg.

Daniels, S. (1992) 'Place and Geographical Imagination', *Geography*, 77: 310–22.

Daniels, S. (1993) *Fields of Vision*. Cambridge: Polity Press.

Derbyshire, H. (1994) *Not In Norfolk: Tackling the Invisibility of Racism*. Norwich: Norwich and Norfolk Racial Equality Council.

Esuantsiwa Goldsmith, J. and Makris, M. (1994) *Staring at Invisible Women: Black and Minority Ethnic Women in Rural Areas*. London: National Alliance of Women's Organisations.

Halfacree, K. (1993) 'Locality and Social Representation: Space, Discourse and Alternative Definitions of the Rural', *Journal of Rural Studies*, 9 (1): 23–37.

Halfacree, K. (1995) 'Talking About Rurality: Social Representations of the Rural as Expressed by Residents of Six English Parishes', *Journal of Rural Studies*, 11 (1): 1–20.

Jackson, P. (2000) 'Race', in R. Johnston, D. Gregory, G. Pratt and M. Watts (eds), *Dictionary of Human Geography*. Oxford: Blackwell.

Jackson, P. (1992) *Maps of Meaning: An Introduction to Cultural Geography*. London: Routledge.

Jay, E. (1992) *'Keep Them In Birmingham': Challenging Racism in South West England*. London: Commission for Racial Equality.

Kinsman, P. (1993) *Landscapes of National Non-Identity: The Landscape Photography of Ingrid Pollard*, Working Paper 17. University of Nottingham, Department of Geography.

Kinsman, P. (1995) 'Landscape, Race and National Identity: the Photography of Ingrid Pollard', *Area*, 27 (4): 300–10.

Little, J. and Austin, P. (1996) 'Women and the Rural Idyll', *Journal of Rural Studies*, 12 (2): 101–12.

Milbourne, P. (ed.) (1997) *Revealing Rural 'Others': Representation, Power and Identity in the British Countryside*. London: Pinter.

Mingay, G. (ed.) (1989) *The Rural Idyll*. London: Routledge.

Mormont, M. (1990) 'Who is Rural? Or How to Be Rural: Towards a Sociology of the Rural', in T. Marsden, P. Lowe and S. Whatmore (eds), *Rural Restructuring*. London: David Fulton.

Philo, C. (1992) 'Neglected Rural Geographies: A Review', *Journal of Rural Studies*, 8 (2): 193–207.

Pollard, I. (undated) *Monograph*. London: Autograph.

Prasad, R. (2004) 'Countryside Retreat', *Guardian*, 28 January, pp. S1–S3.

Roberts, L. (1992) 'A Rough Guide to Rurality: Social Issues and Rural Community Development', in *Talking Point*, No. 137. Newcastle upon Tyne: Association of Community Workers.

Short, J. (1991) *Imagined Country*. London: Routledge.

Sibley, D. (1995) *Geographies of Exclusion: Society and Difference in the West*. London: Routledge.

Spooner-Williams, R. (1997) 'Interpreting Cultural Difference: Articulations of "Race", Gender and Rurality in Britain and New Zealand/Aotearoa'. Unpublished PhD thesis, University of Bristol, School of Geographical Sciences.

Wilson, A. (1992) *The Culture of Nature*. London: Routledge.

Women in Geography Study Group (1997) *Feminist Geographies: Exploration in Diversity and Difference*. Harlow: Longman.

Chapter 2

John O'Groats to Land's End: racial equality in rural Britain?[1]

Philomena J.F. de Lima

Introduction: is there a problem?

Following the publication of two ground-breaking examinations of rural racism in the early 1990s (the Fife Regional Council Report (1991) in Scotland and the Jay Report (1992) in England) there has been an increase in the number of reports that have highlighted the problem in various localised contexts (see, for example, Derbyshire 1994; Nizhar 1995; Suzin 1996; Kenny 1997; Dhalech 1999; de Lima 2001a; and Garland and Chakraborti, 2002). These reports have consistently highlighted racism as an issue that requires acknowledgement for a number of reasons. For example, 1991 and 2001 census data have recorded a presence of minority ethnic groups or households across all local authority areas (Scottish Executive 2004; de Lima, ongoing;[2] Office for National Statistics 2003), including rural ones. Moreover, more recently a number of studies have reaffirmed the persistence of negative stereotypes and attitudes towards minority ethnic groups across Scotland, including rural areas (see, for example, Bromley and Curtice 2003; Scottish Civic Forum 2002), while the chances of being a victim of a racist assault may be higher pro rata in rural than in urban areas (Lemos 2000; Rayner 2001). Furthermore, the need for anti-racist action in predominantly white areas may in fact be more important because of a greater likelihood that racist practices and attitudes go unchallenged in the absence of routine contact with minority ethnic people (Gaine 2000).

Drawing on a wide range of research (often small-scale and conducted at a local level) as well as national research funded by the Commission for Racial Equality (CRE),[3] this chapter focuses on experiences of minority ethnic households and communities mainly in rural Scotland and England. The chapter will start off by providing a brief overview of definitions highlighting the problematic nature of current discourses, and will then provide an overview of the rural policy context, assessing some of the themes that emerge from research on the experiences of rural minority ethnic households. Such households, however, are not passive victims and the chapter will briefly highlight practical action that has been designed to address issues such as social isolation. The chapter will conclude by identifying some overarching themes and issues which need to be addressed on any future agenda on 'race' in rural areas.

Definitions: problematising the 'rural', ethnicity and 'whiteness'

This chapter does not address in any detail the many well-rehearsed and highly debated controversies surrounding terms such as 'race', 'ethnicity' and 'rural', but provides a brief overview to set the context and to acknowledge the diversity, as well as the various power dimensions, that may be exercised within seemingly homogenous categories such as 'rural' and 'ethnicity'.

An important aspect of making sense of the experience of minority ethnic households in rural areas is arriving at an understanding of how 'rural' is defined. The tendency of discourses on the 'rural' until recently has been to ignore the diverse nature of rural communities. In addition, a review undertaken by Copus *et al.* (1998) in Scotland demonstrated that the dominant emphasis with regard to definitions of 'rurality' has been on population-based measures. However, over the years it would seem that a number of different definitions of 'rural' have evolved and population measures are supplemented from time to time by the use of other indicators, such as economic activity, car ownership or age structure, to develop typologies of rural areas (Cloke 1977; Cloke and Edwards 1988, cited in Department of Environment, Food and Rural Affairs (DEFRA) 2000: 60).

In 2001 the Scottish Executive, while acknowledging that a single definition of rural was unlikely to be achieved, nevertheless advocated the need to adopt a more consistent approach. Subsequently, a six-fold categorisation of rural/urban, using settlement sizes and drive times, has been adopted as follows: 'large urban areas' (settlements of over 125,000 people); 'other urban areas' (settlements of 10,000 to 125,000 people); 'accessible small towns' (settlements of between 3,000 and 10,000 people and within 30 minutes' drive of a settlement of 10,000 or more); 'remote small towns' (settlements of between 3,000 and 10,000 people and with a drive time of over 30 minutes to a settlement of 10,000 or more); 'accessible rural' (settlements of less than 3,000 people and within 30 minutes' drive of a settlement of 10,000 or more); and 'remote rural' (settlements of less than 3,000 people and with a drive time of over 30 minutes to a settlement of 10,000 or more). Using this classification, the Scottish minority ethnic population is predominantly urban-based, though it is important to highlight that there is a presence of minority ethnic households across all 32 Council and 15 Health Board areas in Scotland (Scottish Executive 2004: 24–6). In England and Wales, DEFRA (2000) has also argued for a revised approach to rural typologies particularly drawing on the 2001 Census.

The debate on rural definitions has yet to take into account the views and needs of rural minority ethnic dwellers, and studies that focus on these groups rarely make explicit their definitions of rurality. The need to arrive at a working definition of 'rurality' is critical to developing an accurate profile of minority ethnic populations in rural areas, which in turn can be used as a basis for appropriate policy development and interventions. This is particularly pertinent in light of the analysis of reports and information uncovered by a CRE mapping study undertaken in 2001, which suggests that the term 'rural' tends to be used to refer to a wide range of contexts, many of them purely subjective.

There is a need to move beyond fixed and rigid notions of racialised identities, taking into account the multidimensional aspects of individual and group identities that have been emphasised by a number of authors (for example, Brah 1998; Hall 1997; Rattansi and Westwood 1994). For instance, in a study undertaken in the Scottish Highlands, young people did not find questions on ethnicity helpful in portraying their experience, as reflected in this statement made by a secondary school pupil with reference to questionnaire 'tick-boxes' on ethnicity (de Lima 2001c: 14):

> They should have many boxes you know, not just a couple but many boxes. Because you're forced to choose between such closed-minded boxes. (Indian female, Scottish Highlands)

The study found that where a choice of labels is provided, young people prefer to use hyphenated identities, such as Scottish-Indian or Scottish-Muslim, a finding also supported by other research in Scotland (Saeed *et al.* 1999).

The problems of drawing boundaries around concepts such as 'race', ethnicity and racism is widely acknowledged and is reflected in the ongoing controversies surrounding the ethnic categorisation adopted in the 1991 and 2001 census data (for example, Ballard 1996; Fenton 1999). The most controversial element of the census categorisation in Britain has been an inconsistent approach: some groups are categorised by 'colour' (for example, by 'black/white' distinctions) and others by ethnicity or geographical regions which are quite specific (for example, Pakistani, Indian, *etc*.); this is in contrast to categories such as 'South Asian' and 'African' which mask the considerable diversity evident within each. Increasingly, categorisation based on 'colour' has come to be considered not only more closely related to the concept of 'race' in terms of phenotype, but also to imply a homogeneity of experience which is challenged by some as being untenable (see, for example, Modood *et al*. 1997; Scottish Executive 2001).

While acknowledging the continuing controversies on the issue of categorisation of groups, the term 'minority ethnic' is used in this chapter to refer to people sometimes described as the 'visible' minorities. The latter include those of African, Asian, Caribbean and South American descent, as well as Black British and people of mixed cultural or ethnic heritage. It is widely recognised that Gypsy Travellers face problems of racism based on cultural factors (see, for example, Morran *et al*. 1999; Morris 2001). However, this chapter cannot do full justice to this issue and therefore will limit its scope to 'visible minorities'. The term 'minority ethnic' is used in recognition of the fact that Britain is a society comprising many different ethnic groups, including Scots, Welsh and English, some of which are in the majority and others in the minority. In other words:

> Everyone has an ethnicity. To use ethnicity to discuss the location of black people is inaccurate. (Bhavani 1994: 5)

What is important to recognise and articulate clearly is the extent to which specific groups are in the majority or the minority, as this is often what determines their experiences in society and their access to power and resources. There has, however, been a tendency in discourses on 'ethnicity' to conflate the term with 'non-white', resulting in little or no understanding of the 'racialised identities of the ethnic majority' (Nayak 1999: 177). Dyer (1997) explores how through imagery and language white people will refer to or speak about the blackness or 'Indianness' of people they know or see in the street in everyday interactions, and yet make no reference to the whiteness of white people they interact with. He demonstrates how images and cultural narratives privilege 'whiteness' and the ways in which 'non-white' is racialised and accorded less status. 'Whiteness' is not something that has to be explained: it is perceived as the norm. 'White' is equated with being human, while 'non-white' is defined as 'the other':

> White people have power and believe they think, feel and act like and for all people; white people, unable to see their particularity, cannot take into account other people's [particularity]; ... white people set standards of humanity by which they are bound to succeed and others bound to fail. (Dyer 1997: 9)

Rural discourses and ethnicity

The assumption that racialised identities apply to mainly 'non-white' people is even more evident in rural areas. Research in the Highlands of Scotland demonstrates how 'colour' continues to play an important role in defining notions of 'belonging' and 'identity' (de Lima 2001c: 13–14):

> I get a lot of people that ask 'Where are you from?' and I say 'From Inverness'. And they say 'Well, how come you are a different colour?' and I say 'Well, my mum and dad were from India' ... I am from Scotland and have lived here all my life and my parents happened to have come from India. People should step back and think about what they are doing rather than stereotype people all the time. (Indian female, Scottish Highlands)

Studies have illustrated that despite considerable effort on the part of minority ethnic households to adapt to their local communities, such households continue to feel that they do not belong to the local communities in which they live (de Lima 2001b; Garland and Chakraborti 2002). The myth of a 'common rural culture' serves as an exclusionary device, resulting in the marginalisation of some groups and individuals from a sense of belonging to rural places, on the basis of a variety of factors including their ethnicity.

The image of the 'rural' as homogenous and a 'good place to live in' continues to be deeply embedded in popular culture and exerts a powerful influence on the way in which rural life is perceived and at times experienced, despite attempts to challenge these perceptions and to recast and reinterpret the meanings of 'rurality', consequently moving beyond the notion of 'the rural as physical space' to the *symbolic significance* of rurality within which social and cultural characteristics are bound up (see, for example, Cloke and Little 1997; Philo 1992). The 'purity' of the rural is contrasted with the 'pollution' of the city, often closely associated with the presence of visible minority ethnic communities (Lowe 1983, cited in Agyeman and Spooner 1997: 199). There is a great deal of anecdotal evidence, for example in the Scottish Highlands, to suggest that one of the underlying considerations for whites moving from English cities to areas like the Highlands is precisely because of the perception that such areas are unlikely to contain the large numbers of visible minorities associated with cities.[4]

Ethnicity and 'race' have rarely been issues associated with the countryside. Agyeman and Spooner (1997: 199), like Dyer (1997), argue that one of the main reasons why ethnicity is not problematised within concepts of rurality is due to the 'invisibility of whiteness as an ethnic signifier':

> For white people 'ethnicity' is seen as being 'out of place' in the countryside, reflecting the Otherness of people of colour. In the white imagination people of colour are confined to towns and cities, representing an urban, 'alien' environment, and the white landscape of rurality is aligned with 'nativeness' and the absence of evil and danger. The ethnic associations of the countryside are naturalised as an absence intruded upon by people of colour.

Against the background of such associations and the lack of recognition afforded to the diversity of heritages which exist in rural Britain, life can be problematic for minority households living in rural areas, as well as being off-putting for those wishing to access the countryside as a source of recreation and leisure (for example, Wong 1999a, 1999b, 2000; and Cloke in this volume).

While discourses on the neglect of 'others' in the rural have provided a mechanism for focusing on ethnicity, there has been relatively little research that has sought to include the voices and experiences of minority ethnic groups within rural discourses. The neglect of minority ethnic perspectives in rural studies research is paralleled by the exclusion of ideas which may seem to constitute a challenge to established categories of knowledge and power structures in academia. This point is illustrated by Sibley (1995: 137), who with reference to the discipline of human geography argues that:

> The postmodern enthusiasm for difference seems rather unconvincing when the presence of authors other than white ones in the literature is such a meagre one, but it is clearly difficult to shake Eurocentric and imperialistic impulses in a subject whose history is so bound up with colonialism.

The invisibility of minority ethnic groups – the rural policy context

The government focus on 'rural' has intensified in the face of the various crises that have affected rural areas of Britain. However, an examination of government policy documents (for example, Countryside Agency 2000; DEFRA 2000) reveals that the neglect of 'ethnicity' in rural research and theoretical discourses is also paralleled by neglect in the rural policy arena. Although new policies and strategies relating to areas such as social inclusion, community cohesion and rural partnerships present an opportunity to develop a synergy between the issue of rural development and equality issues such as ethnicity, the evidence suggests that the presence and contribution of rural minority ethnic dwellers has largely been ignored.

The CRE mapping exercise mentioned earlier found that many individuals working in a rural context felt that the lack of an overall strategy has resulted in rural racism not being taken seriously, thus leading to an ad hoc and unsustainable approach which is heavily dependent on a few committed individuals or concerned agencies in communities. Consequently, the overwhelming feeling is that resources have gone into urban areas. In the words of one respondent interviewed as part of the CRE mapping exercise in 2001:

> Ethnic minorities are living in the year 2001 in urban areas. We cannot say this of rural areas, they are still seemingly stuck in 1961. If the Government wants to create a socially just society which is inclusive, this cannot happen so long as rural race issues are not tackled. (Director of two rural Race Equality Councils in England)

Often workers involved in tackling rural racism are made to feel that they are 'working against the grain', as illustrated by cynical comments such as the following:

> We had to overcome a great deal of scepticism. One response that sticks in mind is 'You are surely not suggesting that we are going to have race riots in Ystrad?' (Powys Victim Support 2000: 11)

It is important to acknowledge that the CRE mapping exercise did find a small increase in race equality policy activity in contrast to the pre-Macpherson Report (1999) era, albeit within a limited context. Discussions with respondents revealed that much of this activity could indeed be attributed to the recommendations emerging from the Macpherson Report. Other factors which respondents believed had facilitated the process of getting 'race' on the policy agenda included community safety strategies, the Human Rights Act, 'Best Value',[5] as well as the Crime and Disorder Act 1998. Since the mapping exercise, the Race Relations (Amendment) Act 2000 has also been vital in getting racial equality issues on the agenda, although its impact has yet to be evaluated (CRE 2003).

The following section details the key themes that emerge from research on rural minority ethnic groups and households.

Demographic issues

Lack of reliable demographic statistics

Evidence, often based on inadequate data sources, suggests that the key features of rural minority ethnic populations are that they are small in number, diverse and scattered. This raises some interesting questions about the extent to which one can refer to minority ethnic people in rural areas as 'communities' where there is little or no contact between households or awareness of the presence of other fellow minority ethnic families (for further discussion of this issue, see Chapter 6 in this volume, by Garland and Chakraborti).

The CRE mapping exercise found that a recurrent issue highlighted by all those working in rural areas is the lack of reliable local demographic data. The most common motivation for gathering such data is often to counter the assumption that exists among local agencies that 'there isn't a problem here'. The 1991 Census has until recently been the main data source, despite the unreliability of the statistics which have tended to understate the minority ethnic population size (Dhalech 1999). At a local level, agencies often supplement census data by using other data sources, such as information on ethnicity and first language spoken by bilingual pupils gathered by local education authorities to provide English as an additional language support if it is required. Consequently statistics gathered at a local level in rural areas seem to be at best guestimates. The difficulties of attempting to update demographic data are highlighted by Magne's (2001: 1–2)[6] research in Devon:

> Statistical and demographic information just wasn't there to be had … The intention had been to track down ethno-demographic information, compile it and correlate it with a projection of the 1991 Census. Straight away it was a struggle to get hold of the 1991 Census data in a detailed enough form to be useful as baseline data.

Undoubtedly the nature of the rural minority ethnic population does pose challenges. For example, agencies are often uncomfortable about implementing monitoring systems when there are very small numbers or single minority ethnic families in an area for reasons of confidentiality. It is also the case that minority ethnic families may not wish to identify themselves due to a fear of making themselves even more 'visible'. In addition, recent studies have demonstrated that there are also differences between generations, with young minority ethnic people, for example, commonly not perceiving themselves as actually being from an 'ethnic minority' (de Lima 2001c). One possible way out of this that could be explored further would be to deconstruct 'whiteness' so that the gathering of ethnicity data is seen as relevant not only to 'visible minorities' but to all. This would also go some way towards addressing the issues raised in this chapter regarding defining ethnicity and 'whiteness' as the norm.

The spatial distribution of rural minority ethnic populations

There have been some isolated attempts to identify the spatial distribution of rural minority ethnic populations. In England, for example, Esuantsiwa Goldsmith and Makris (1994: 7–9) reported that over 27 per cent of black and minority ethnic people lived outside the metropolitan counties of the North West, Yorkshire and Humberside, with some shire counties (especially Leicestershire and Bedfordshire) showing substantial representations. Similarly, in Scotland an analysis of the 1991 Census revealed that 60 per cent of the minority ethnic population were living in Scotland's four main cities,[7] with the remaining 40 per cent dispersed throughout out the mainland and islands (de Lima 2001a: 15). As previously discussed, a similar trend is confirmed by the 2001 Census, with some minority ethnic presence being recorded for all local authority and health board areas across Scotland (Scottish Executive 2004).

Racism in rural areas

The extent of racial harassment

In England, the report *Keep Them in Birmingham* (Jay 1992) was an important milestone in putting rural racism on the policy agenda and, as has been highlighted, led to a number of local reports on the experiences of minority ethnic groups in rural England, though there has been less evidence of such research activity in Scotland (Netto *et al.* 2001). Additional information sources on racist incidents for many rural areas in Britain have become more readily available since 1998. Such sources at a local level tend to be predominantly race equality initiatives, where they exist, or police forces. Without exception, the majority of reports highlight the prevalence of racism and discrimination in the day-to-day lives of rural minority ethnic households, and where monitoring information is available the data also points to an increase in reported incidents. Rayner (2001) reported that in England and Wales ethnic minorities living in low-density minority ethnic areas were at greater risk (ten times more likely) of being attacked on racial grounds. On the issue of racial incidence, the Rayner report suggested that Northumbria topped the list and was closely followed by Devon and Cornwall, and South Wales, while other areas defined as 'hot spots' were Norfolk, Avon and Somerset, Durham and Cumbria. The vulnerability of minority ethnic households is an issue that has also been highlighted by Lemos (2000: 8) who suggested that:

> … racist attacks can also occur in areas where few black people live or are seen about. Those that are present are therefore more isolated, and in that sense more vulnerable.

The CRE mapping exercise, drawing upon information from areas in which the relevant data was made available,[8] confirmed the upward trend in reported racist incidents highlighted by Rayner (2001). This exercise also highlighted a small but growing number of rural multi-agency racial equality initiatives (notably in places such as Suffolk, Norwich and Norfolk, and central Scotland) established to address racist incidents. However, the robustness and comparability of racial incident data across areas is problematic, due to variable data gathering mechanisms and the lack of consistent classification and disaggregation systems for recording data.

Despite the increase in reported racist incidents, it is widely acknowledged that they are under-reported and under-recorded. There continues to be a lack of confidence and trust in the system and minority ethnic households are often reluctant to take action against perpetrators for fear of reprisals, as expressed by one rural local worker interviewed as part of the CRE mapping exercise:

> People are 'spat at' on a daily basis … they put up with it because they have got to live here. In the past when they have contacted the

police they [the police] did nothing, so people feel 'Why bother?'
(Rural race equality worker, northern England)

Nature, location and impact of racial harassment

Although evidence suggests that the majority of racial harassment cases
involve verbal abuse, incidents involving damage to property and
personal attacks are also highly prevalent. At a UK level, research
suggests that the location of racial harassment is more likely to be close to
or at aimed at people's homes (Chahal *et al.* 1999; Lemos 2000). Although
such data is not readily available for rural areas, studies have noted that
racism occurs in a wide range of public settings, such as schools, on the
streets and at the workplace (Garland and Chakraborti 2002; Kenny
1997). It would appear that ethnic businesses are particularly vulnerable
to racial harassment. For example, a study undertaken in Leicestershire
interviewed 17 businesses, all of which had experienced racism
manifesting itself through verbal abuse, racist chanting, customers
leaving without paying or criminal damage (Scoon 1998: 23–4).[9]
Similarly, PROSPER (2000) reported that one in five businesses in the
south-west of England had reported incidents of racial harassment
mainly by customers and occasionally within the workforce. In Wales,
Powys Victim Support have observed that minority ethnic-owned
restaurants and shops are frequently the victims of abuse and criminal
damage (Spackman 2000), while research in Scotland has highlighted
that as many as 63 per cent (106) of the 169 racist incidents recorded in
that area occurred within business premises (RAHMAS 2001: 3).

On the issue of the impact of racism on people's lives, a report by
Suzin (1996) in the south-west of England explored the subjective
feelings of those who had experienced racism, highlighting the different
coping mechanisms adopted by individuals in the face of racist
experiences, ranging from withdrawal to 'fighting back'. Other authors
have noted similar responses to victimisation. Kenny (1997) in Somerset
developed a picture of the 'emotional and psychological' impact of
racism, which included despondency, despair, resignation, defeat and
loss of self-esteem. RAHMAS (2001: 3) found that racist crimes on
minority ethnic businesses affected the confidence, self-esteem and
ultimately the physical and mental health of victims, contributing
to social exclusion and leading to constraints on business growth
and development. Garland and Chakraborti (2002) noted depression
and restricted access to public spaces as consequences of racial
harassment.

Far-right group activities

Research undertaken by the National Council for Voluntary Organisations (NCVO) in the mid to late 1990s uncovered activity by far-right groups such as the British National Party (BNP) and Combat 18 in parts of Norfolk, Leicestershire, Derbyshire, Hertfordshire and the Midlands (Acton *et al.* 1998; Dhillon 1994; NCVO 1997). Written submissions received from organisations and a number of local reports (for example, The Valleys Race Equality Council in Wales;[10] Craig *et al.* 1999) identified by the CRE mapping exercise have reported the presence of far-right groups in areas such as South Wales, Lincolnshire and recently in parts of rural Scotland. It is difficult to assess how extensive these extremist activities are in rural areas across Britain or indeed the extent to which racial harassment is linked to them. The CRE mapping exercise, however, did find some documented evidence for England which suggests that there is a potential link between the presence of far-right groups and racial harassment. For example, in a part of East Northamptonshire, Combat 18 stickers were placed on cars outside a shop that had also been receiving threats of damage to property, while a local organiser distributed Holocaust denial leaflets at a Holocaust memorial ceremony in Wellingborough (MAGRAH – Eastern Area 2001: 16–17).[11] More recently, Norwich and Norfolk Racial Equality Council (NNREC) reported an increase in 'fascist group' activities and expressed concerns about their possible impact on the reporting of racial incidents (NNREC 2002: 40).

Although there is a dearth of research on the activities of groups such as the BNP in Scotland, it would appear that increasingly their targets are migrant workers in a number of rural areas (see Lawrence 2003). The BNP have established a number of branches across Scotland, including the Highlands and Islands, and much of the information on the BNP website for the Highlands focuses on Kurdish and Iraqi migrant workers and their perceived negative impact on the local communities.[12] At present it is difficult to assess the impact of increased BNP activity on racist incidents; however, it is notable from the local press letters pages in the Highlands that it is a subject of lively debate (*Inverness Courier* 2003a, 2003b). Undoubtedly there are serious issues to be addressed in relation to the recruitment, deployment and settlement of migrant workers, particularly against a background of little or no consultation with local communities. However, the question of whether the presence of the BNP results in the politicisation of 'race' in Scotland has yet to be explored.

Access to services

The numbers-led approach to service provision

While the experiences of rural minority ethnic households may not be too dissimilar in some respects from those identified in urban contexts, two underlying issues which underpin discrimination in rural areas are the continuing lack of commitment to racial equality at a strategic level and the ways in which the demographic and spatial features of rural minority ethnic populations serve to amplify the discrimination they experience. A recurrent theme that emerges from much of the research is the appeal of a 'numbers led' rather than 'needs or rights led' approach, with key public, private and voluntary sector agencies often reluctant to recognise that they have a responsibility to address the needs of minority ethnic communities, as noted by the Lincolnshire Forum for Racial Justice (1999: 4):

> It is clear, despite some interesting and significant advances, that statutory and mainstream voluntary service providers within the county are overwhelmingly white and ethnocentric … On the whole there is still a tradition of organisations offering what they see as 'colour-blind' services, i.e. service provision is open (in theory) to everyone regardless of race colour or creed, and a resistance to 'special provision' for particular groups.

Although there is very little information specifically focusing on service provision in this context, research has confirmed that rural minority ethnic populations tend to lack access to appropriate and relevant services, and their situation is compounded by issues of size, dispersion and heterogeneity. Experiences of discrimination at the points of access and delivery of services are well documented (see, for example, Craig and Manthorpe 2000; Garland and Chakraborti 2002; NNREC 2002), and consistently reports have identified a range of barriers to a whole host of services such as health, education, housing and business advice. These barriers include poor access to information and advice; inappropriate and culturally insensitive services; a lack of capacity building support to develop their ability to influence service provision; an absence of an infrastructure to address issues of discrimination; communication and language barriers; a lack of interpretation and translation facilities; stereotyping; a lack of strategic commitment and leadership; and a dearth of representation on decision-making bodies (Craig and Manthorpe 2000; Garland and Chakraborti 2002; NNREC 2002).

Moreover, there appears to be little or no minority ethnic presence in local authority councils, management or governing boards of schools, and other relevant local and regional decision-making bodies, making the nature of racial equality work precarious:

> During the period when a governor was appointed with special responsibility for them, bilingual pupils began to be integrated into the school, but with the departure of this individual, the management and governors moved closer to ignoring them again … Compliance with legislation (for example, the Race Relations Act 1976; the Children Act 1989) depended in large measure upon an agent (in this case the governor/researcher) who was prepared, and able, to confront the passive attitudes that prevailed. (Kerry 2000: 62)

The CRE mapping exercise found that workers employed to address race equality issues in rural areas tend to find themselves working in isolation and are often overwhelmed by the scale and nature of the issues to be addressed. As a result, the challenge of addressing racial equality and discrimination issues tends to depend on committed individuals with little or no democratic or wider infrastructure to underpin such work.

Multiple discrimination and the needs of specific groups

The interrelationship between ethnicity and other factors such as gender, age, religion, class, or disability, can be complex, making some groups particularly vulnerable to social isolation and experiences of racial discrimination and harassment. In the rural context, with a few notable exceptions (Esuantsiwa Goldsmith and Makris 1994; Marsh 1996), there is a distinct shortage of research focusing on the interaction between ethnicity and other variables.

The evidence, limited though it is, suggests that the interaction of gender, for example, with ethnicity can reinforce the vulnerability of some women to discrimination. Minority ethnic women in rural areas would appear to face a number of specific problems. For example, isolation is more likely to be a problem for these women due to their restricted or lack of access to transport and their roles as carers; moreover, this latter role means that they are all the more likely to require support for health issues, but, as argued previously, services such as health tend not to take into account the cultural needs of minority ethnic groups. In addition, the common absence of culturally sensitive support structures in a small community can act as a deterrent with regard to the reporting of crimes such as rape and domestic violence, while the lack of locally based refuges and affordable housing, together with the experience of racism, can exacerbate the vulnerability of minority ethnic women both inside and outside the home. Communication can also be a problem, particularly in rural areas where there may be little or no accessible translation, interpretation or language facilities (Esuantsiwa Goldsmith and Makris 1994; Marsh 1996).

There is little specific information on the young and the elderly in rural areas. What little evidence there is suggests that young minority ethnic people face similar problems to other young people in rural communities generally, typically with regard to issues such as a lack of transport and leisure facilities (Esuantsiwa Goldsmith and Makris 1994; Marsh 1996). However, a key finding from research conducted in the Scottish Highlands relates to the issue of maintaining cultural identity in the context of a monocultural environment. Evidence suggests that the cultures of minority ethnic young people are rarely valued or recognised in schools, youth groups and in the community in general, and their situation can be made worse by the lack of contact with other fellow minority ethnic youths (see Arshad and Syed 1998;[13] Nizhar 1995).

Social isolation and maintaining cultural identities

Social isolation

A recurrent theme emerging from the literature is the vulnerability and social isolation experienced by rural minority ethnic groups that is attributed to their small populations and diversity, as well as to their being subjected repeatedly to racism. The demographic features and the spatial distribution of rural minority ethnic households raises questions about the appropriateness of terminology such as 'community', highlighting a need to assess the implications for developing specific intervention strategies which do not privilege notions of 'community'.

Contact with fellow minority ethnic households is considered important in helping people to cope with feelings of social exclusion and isolation. Mike Prescott, a participant at an NCVO Conference (Dhillon 1994: 16), described his experience of 'being black in the countryside':

England's so-called green and pleasant land is not like the inner cities. It is a mythical picture of the countryside that racists will go to any lengths to preserve. Living in a rural area is very different for black people compared to living in towns and cities. It is even more stressful.

The cause of this stress was attributed to the lack of access to a 'multicultural community', as well as to the entrenched attitudes of local rural residents and stereotypes portraying black people as 'the natives, uncivilised, ignorant, having no refinement ...' (Dhillon 1994: 15).

Maintaining cultural identities

The emphasis in rural areas continues to be on integration and assimilation. Derbyshire (1994: 33) found that those who succeed in fitting in on terms set by the majority community found a high level of acceptance but at the cost of keeping their own cultural identity hidden, and participants in a focus group undertaken for the CRE rural mapping exercise also supported this view, highlighting some social class differences:

> The society takes away your identity and gives it back when it wants to. You are an 'honorary white' when it suits them ... If you are wealthy and middle-class and if you do the right things, you have the right accent, then you experience less racism. (Asian Muslim female, south-west England)

Maintaining self-esteem and a sense of identity in the absence of others from a similar background can be felt acutely by minority ethnic groups living in rural areas and, as discussed previously, the issue is brought into sharp focus in relation to young people growing up in a white monocultural rural environment. As discovered in the CRE mapping exercise, for some, faith-based activities are perceived as one way of positively reinforcing one's sense of identity as well as helping to overcome personal, social and cultural isolation:

> There are no opportunities for positive identity, there is negative reinforcement of our identity on a daily basis, undermining our sense of identity ... Faith based activities are not based on colour, they are based on the need to associate with something positive. (Asian Muslim female, south-west England)

Overcoming social isolation

Evidence across many rural areas suggests that there is very little social interaction between minority ethnic families and the majority communities, despite efforts on the part of minority ethnic households to fit in. Much of the evidence suggests that minority ethnic activities tend to be based in cities and towns, necessitating travel over long distances. In addition, given the small numbers of very diverse (in terms of culture, faith, etc.) individuals in rural areas, there rarely is the critical mass to get together (de Lima 2001a; Garland and Chakraborti 2002).

It would seem that much of the community-based activity, where it exists in the rural context, is dependent on the initiative and commitment of a few individuals with a limited capacity for community development activity to enable minority ethnic groups to network and organise on a sustainable basis (Henderson and Kaur 1999). When agencies have provided a funded resource to engage with rural minority ethnic groups,[14] communities seemed generally more empowered and better networked, enabling them to overcome social isolation and access services more effectively.

However, it would be misleading to portray rural minority ethnic households as 'passive victims'. Households use a variety of methods to overcome social isolation and maintain links with their cultures, which can include travelling great distances to access relevant facilities. A study in Leicestershire (Scoon 1998),[15] for example, found that no such facilities existed for minority ethnic residents of the rural villages which were the focus of the study, and instead members of minority ethnic groups travelled to nearby cities in the East Midlands for leisure, cultural and religious purposes. Similar practices have been documented in areas such as Lincolnshire (1998, LFRJ) and North Wales Moreover, the CRE mapping exercise did find examples of well-established faith and non-faith groups. For example in the south-west of England there is an active Islamic society, in the north-east of Scotland in Moray there is a thriving Chinese Christian community group as well as an Islamic society, and more recently an Indian Association has been established in the Highlands of Scotland. The main challenge for these groups is sustainability, given the small size and scattered nature of the populations.

Conclusions: a rural 'race equality' agenda for the future?

Although it could be argued that the challenges faced by rural minority ethnic households are not too dissimilar from those found in urban areas, their situation has undoubtedly been compounded by at least three factors: the persistent lack of acknowledgement that minority ethnic people are a part of rural communities; a 'numbers' rather than a 'needs' or 'rights' based approach to service provision; and the small size, and diverse nature, of black and minority ethnic rural populations. The demographic features of rural minority ethnic populations highlight the need for more exploration and experimentation of different service delivery models within the broader context of equalities to address the needs of small and diverse groups in a rural context.

Undertaking research on minority ethnic households in rural areas is a challenging task. In the absence of reliable data and given the sparseness and diversity of the populations, identification of households can be problematic and has to be treated with sensitivity, particularly in addressing issues of confidentiality and anonymity. Moreover, there is a tendency for some of these communities to be feeling 'over-researched' (Stevenson Ltd 2003), while traditional methods of sampling populations can be inappropriate given the demographic features of rural minority ethnic communities. Consequently, creative solutions must be found to resolve this aspect of the research process. Even when households have been identified, persuading them to become involved in research can often be a difficult and time-consuming as building trust is a crucial component of the research process. However, the experience of undertaking such studies in areas like the Scottish Highlands and Islands has also demonstrated that research can be part of a process of capacity building, helping isolated individuals and households to come together to address problematic issues (de Lima 1999).

Despite the growing number of reports since the 1990s which underline the ways in which rurality impacts on the lives of minority ethnic households, combating rural racism and promoting racial equality has yet to be fully integrated into the rural policy agenda, and rural race equality initiatives, where they exist, tend to operate in isolation from rural policy-making in general. Consequently, initiatives undertaken by rural agencies need to incorporate the perspectives of rural minority ethnic dwellers within their policy and strategic discussions. In the funding of research and initiatives, rural agencies should ensure that race equality perspectives are embedded, exploring innovative ways of including the views of diverse minority ethnic populations.

The current situation in rural areas underlines a need to 'think outside the box' in addressing the needs of minority ethnic households. It is important to explore creative solutions by involving minority ethnic individuals as active agents. Rather than focusing upon deficit models of addressing needs and portraying minority ethnic households as passive victims, the emphasis ought to be on the contributions, current and potential, that such groups and households make to the rural communities, thus focusing on minority ethnic households as 'assets' in a rural context.

The need to address race equality issues is even more compelling given the demographic trends highlighted by the 2001 Census which point to a declining and ageing 'white population' and a young and growing minority ethnic population (GROS 2002). While some rural areas are benefiting from 'counterstream' migration[16] (see, for example, Findlay *et al.* 1999), the question of whether this is enough to repopulate and regenerate rural areas such as the Scottish Highlands and Islands is very much on the minds of government agencies. Against this background, policy-makers in Scotland have been highlighting the need to attract migrants and people of diverse backgrounds into rural areas to help the economic regeneration of those areas.

However, given the hitherto poor track record of agencies in addressing the needs of rural minority ethnic groups, it would seem that there is still a long way to go. The assumption of a 'homogenous cultural majority' has arguably led to a lack of a voice and the power to shape the 'mainstream agenda' for rural minority ethnic groups. Counterstream migration can also lead to antagonism between the so called 'locals' and 'incomers', sometimes resulting in racist prejudice being directed towards the white communities, as exemplified by reports of racism towards English people in some parts of rural Scotland (Jedrej and Nuttall 1996). This highlights a need to challenge the view that addressing issues of 'ethnicity' and 'racism' is only relevant when referring to visible minority ethnic groups. Rather, there is a need to explore ways of deconstructing 'whiteness' and to understand the racialised identities of 'white people' within rural contexts, exploring different ways in which is power is exercised within and between groups.

In countries such as Scotland, devolution[17] has undoubtedly opened up opportunities for both rural and 'race' issues to be examined in a way that has not happened before. There are a growing number of opportunities to address the issues facing rural minority ethnic people in Scotland, and these opportunities need to be pursued proactively by agencies in order to develop a more strategic and sustainable response to rural racism. In addition, Scottish devolution is also creating opportunities for debate and discussion on issues of identity and belonging in a way that has not hitherto been possible, thus contributing to a developing conceptual framework for analysing identity issues for minority ethnic households in a rural context.

Notes

1 Thanks to Jon MacKenzie, South West Race Equality Project, National Association of Citizens' Advice Bureaux (NACAB) who suggested this title.

2 The ongoing project referred to in this chapter is focusing on minority ethnic participation in further and higher education in Moray and the Highlands and Islands. This has been funded by the North Forum on Widening Access and is due to be completed in 2004.

3 The Commission for Racial Equality (CRE) funded a project *Rural Racism: Mapping the Problem and Defining – Practical Policy Recommendations*, which took the form of a rural mapping exercise on 'race' issues. The research was commissioned in 2001 and undertaken between 2001 and 2002 by the author and was submitted to the CRE in 2002. Although, the research was primarily a review of secondary sources of information (published and unpublished), this was supplemented by focus groups and semi-structured interviews with key stakeholders working on rural race issues in different parts of Britain. The CRE are considering ways of publishing the report. Much of the material referred to in this chapter draws from the research undertaken for this project with the permission of the CRE.

4 This issue is also explored in the context of the city of Leicester by Tyler (1999) as part of an ongoing PhD thesis.

5 'Best Value' is a framework for local government and public bodies to measure, manage and improve their performance. Consulting users of services, including minority ethnic groups, is an important aspect of implementing the framework (http://www.idea.gov.uk/bestvalue/).

6 This refers to unpublished research conducted by S. Magne (2001) entitled 'DEREC Rural Outreach Project: Annual Report', March 2000–1.

7 Scotland's four main cities are Glasgow, Edinburgh, Dundee and Aberdeen as defined in the Scottish Executive (2004) *Analysis of Ethnicity in the 2001 Census – Summary Report*.

8 Data was drawn from the following sources: Suffolk's Multi-Agency Forum Against Racial Harassment, 2001; Norwich and Norfolk Racial Equality Council, 2000; The Valleys Race Equality Council (VALREC) 2001; Northern Constabulary (Highlands and Islands), 2001; Lothian and Borders Police, 2001.

9 F. Scoon (1998) *Nearly All White, So Why Bother?* A report produced for the Action for Racial Equality Across Leicestershire Multi-Agency Forum.

10 This refers to written evidence submitted by The Valleys Race Equality Council in 2001 as part of the CRE mapping exercise.

11 Multi Agency Group against Racist Attacks and Harassment (MAGRAH) is a multi-agency initiative covering the East Northamptonshire District Council and Wellingborough Borough Council areas. The information provided to the CRE rural mapping exercise was based on presentations made to statutory and voluntary agencies in 2002–3.

12 See the BNP's websites at
www.bnp.org.uk/freedom/regions/scotgroups.html,
www.bnp.org.uk/freedom/regions/handi.html, and
www.bnp.org.uk/freedom/regions/dingwall2.html.

13 This refers to unpublished research conducted by R. Arshad and R. Syed (1998) entitled 'Black and Minority Ethnic Pupils' Experiences in Primary School: A Parent Opinion Study'. Edinburgh: CERES.

14 For example, the CRE mapping exercise found that a Community Education Worker had been employed to work with the Bangladeshi community in Suffolk, and a Chinese Development Worker had been appointed to work with the Chinese community in North Ayrshire (Scotland).

15 See note 9.

16 'Counterstream' migration refers to the trend where rural areas have switched from experiencing substantial 'net out-migration' to being areas of 'net in-migration'.

17 In 1707, the Act of Union combined the English and Scottish Parliaments in a UK Parliament at Westminster. Following a referendum on 11 September 1997, the majority of people in Scotland voted in favour of a Scottish Parliament with tax varying powers. In 1998 the Scotland Act was passed at Westminster devolving a range of powers to the new Scottish Parliament. This was followed by the first Scottish general election on 6 May 1999, when 129 Members of the Scottish Parliament (MSPs) were elected (http://www.scotland.gov.uk/about/CS/CS-CISD/00016282/devolution.pdf).

References

Acton, T., Samblas, C. and Coke P. (1998) *Land, Freedom and People: Conference Report*. London: National Council for Voluntary Organisations.

Agyeman, J. and Spooner, R. (1997) 'Ethnicity and the Rural Environment', in P. Cloke and J. Little (eds), *Contested Countryside Cultures: Otherness, Marginalisation, and Rurality*. London: Routledge.

Ballard, R. (1996) 'Negotiating Race and Ethnicity: Exploring the Implications of the 1991 Census', *Patterns of Prejudice*, 30 (3): 3–33.

Bhavani, R. (1994) *Black Women in the Labour Market: A Research Review*. Manchester: Equal Opportunities Commission.

Brah, A. (1998) *Cartographies of Diaspora*. London: Routledge.

Bromley, C. and Curtice, J. (2003) *Attitudes to Discrimination in Scotland*. Edinburgh: Scottish Executive Social Research.

Chahal, K. and Julienne, L. (1999) *We Can't All Be White! Racist Victimisation in the UK*. York: Joseph Rowntree Foundation.

Cloke, P. (1997) 'An Index of Rurality for England and Wales', *Regional Studies*, 20: 31–46.

Cloke, P. and Little, J. (eds) (1997) *Contested Countryside Cultures: Otherness, Marginalisation, and Rurality*. London: Routledge.

Commission for Racial Equality (CRE) (2003) *Towards Racial Equality in Scotland*. London: Commission for Racial Equality.

Copus, A.K., Gourlay, D., Chapman, P. and Shucksmith, M. (1998) *Small Area Data Sources for Socio-Economic Typologies of Rural Scotland*. Edinburgh: Scottish Office Central Research Unit.

Countryside Agency (2000) *Towards Tomorrow's Countryside*. Gloucestershire: The Countryside Agency.

Craig, G. and Manthorpe, J. (2000) *Fresh Fields?* York: Joseph Rowntree Foundation.

Craig, G., Ahmed, B. and Amery, F. (1999) ' "We Shoot Them at Newark!" The Work of the Lincolnshire Forum for Racial Justice', in P. Henderson, and R. Kaur (eds), *Rural Racism in the UK: Examples of Community-Based Responses*. London: Community Development Foundation.

de Lima, P. (1999) 'Research and Action in the Scottish Highlands', in P. Henderson and R. Kaur (eds), *Rural Racism in the UK: Examples of Community-Based Responses*. London: Community Development Foundation.

de Lima, P. (2001a) *Needs Not Numbers: An Exploration of Minority Ethnic Communities in Scotland*. London: Commission for Racial Equality and Community Development Foundation.

de Lima, P (2001b) 'Racism in Rural Areas', *Multicultural Teaching Journal*, 20 (1): 39–43.

de Lima, P. (2001c) *The Experiences of Young People from Minority Ethnic Backgrounds Living in the Highlands*. Inverness: Highland Wellbeing Alliance.

Department for Environment, Food and Rural Affairs (DEFRA) (2000) *Our Countryside: The Future – A Fair Deal for Rural England*. At http://www.defra.gov.uk/rural/ruralwp/whitepaper/default.htm.

Derbyshire, H. (1994) *Not In Norfolk: Tackling The Invisibility of Racism*. Norwich: Norwich and Norfolk Racial Equality Council.

Dhalech, M. (1999) *Challenging Racism in the Rural Idyll*. London: National Association of Citizens' Advice Bureaux.

Dhillon, P. (1994) *Challenging Rural Racism: Conference Report*. London: NCVO.

Dyer, R. (1997) *White*. London: Routledge.

Esuantsiwa Goldsmith, J. and Makris, M. (1994) *Staring at Invisible Women: Black and Minority Ethnic Women in Rural Areas*. London: National Alliance of Women's Organisations.

Fenton, S. (1999) *Ethnicity*. London: Macmillan.

Fife Regional Council (1991) *Race Equality in Fife*. Fife: Fife Regional Council.

Findlay, A., Short, D., Stockdale, A., Li, L. and Philip, L. (1999) *Study of the Impact of Migration in Rural Scotland*. Edinburgh: Scottish Office Central Research Unit.

Gaine, C. (2000) 'Anti-Racist Education in "White Areas": the Limits and Possibilities of Change', *Race Ethnicity and Education*, 3(1): 65–81.

Garland, J. and Chakraborti, N. (2002) *Tackling the Invisible Problem? An Examination of the Provision of Services to Victims of Racial Harassment in Rural Suffolk*. Leicester: Scarman Centre, University of Leicester.

General Register Office for Scotland (GROS) (2002) *Scotland's Census, 2001 Population Report Scotland*. Edinburgh: GROS.

Hall, S. (1997) 'Who Needs Identity?', in S. Hall and P. de Gay (eds), *Cultural Identity*. London: Sage.

Henderson, P. and Kaur, R. (eds) (1999) *Rural Racism in the UK: Examples of Community-Based Responses*. London: Community Development Foundation.

Inverness Courier (2003a) 'Stop the Surrender of Sovereignty', 10 August.

Inverness Courier (2003b) 'Democratic Process Will Decide', 11 December.

Jay, E. (1992) *'Keep Them in Birmingham': Challenging Racism in South West England*. London: Commission for Racial Equality.

Jedrej, C. and Nuttall, M. (1996) *White Settlers*. Luxembourg: Harwood Academic.

Kenny, N. (1997) *It Doesn't Happen Here?* Somerset: Somerset Equality Forum.

Kerry, C. (2000) 'Providing for Ethnic Minority Pupils in a Rural Primary School', *Education Today*, 48(4): 62.

Lawrence, F. (2003) 'The New Landless Labourers', *Guardian*, 17 May, pp. 24–5.

Lemos, G. (2000) *Racial Harassment: Action on the Ground*. London: Lemos & Crane.

Lincolnshire Forum for Racial Justice (LFRJ) (1998) *Ethnic Minorities in Lincolnshire, Forum Report No. 2: Local Employment Policies for Black and Minority Ethnic Groups*. Lincoln: Lincolnshire Forum for Racial Justice.

Lincolnshire Forum for Racial Justice (LFRJ) (1999) *Employment and Services: Forum Report No. 2*. Lincoln: Lincolnshire Forum for Racial Justice.

Marsh, B. (1996) *Community Care Needs of People from Minority Ethnic Groups in North Warwickshire*. Warwickshire: North Warwickshire Council for Voluntary Service.

Milbourne, P. (ed.) (1997) *Revealing Rural 'Others': Representation, Power and Identity in the British Countryside*. London: Pinter.

Modood, T., Berthoud, R., Lakey, J., Nazroo, J., Smith, P., Virdee, S. and Beishon, S. (1997) *Ethnic Minorities in Britain: Diversity and Disadvantage – Fourth National Survey of Ethnic Minorities*. London: Policy Studies Institute.

Morran, R., Lloyd, M., Carrick, K. and Barker, C. (1999) *Moving Targets*. Edinburgh: University of Dundee/Save the Children.

Morris, R. (2001) 'Gypsies and Travellers: New Policy and Approaches', *Police Research and Management*, 5 (1): 41–9, at http://www.cf.ac.uk/claws/tlru/Policing.pdf.

Nayak, A. (1999) 'White English Ethnicities: Racism, Anti-Racism and Student Perspectives', *Race, Ethnicity and Education*, 2 (2): 177–202.

National Council for Voluntary Organisations (NCVO) (1997) *Germinating the Seeds of Equality*. London: National Council for Voluntary Organisations.

National Council for Voluntary Organisations (NCVO) (2000) *Rural Anti-racism Project Report*. London: National Council for Voluntary Organisations.

Netto, G., Arshad, R., de Lima, P., Almeida Diniz, F., MacEwen, M., Patel, V. and Syed, R. (2001) *Audit of Research on Minority Ethnic Issues in Scotland from a 'Race' Perspective*. Edinburgh: Scottish Executive Central Research Unit.

Nizhar, P. (1995) *No Problem?* Telford: Race Equality Forum for Telford and Shropshire.

Norwich and Norfolk Racial Equality Council (NNREC) (1998) *Now in Norfolk: A 21st Century Partnership Against Racism.* Norwich: Norwich and Norfolk Racial Equality Council.

Norwich and Norfolk Racial Equality Council (NNREC) (2000) *Annual Report 1999/2000.* Norwich: Norwich and Norfolk Racial Equality Council.

Norwich and Norfolk Racial Equality Council (NNREC) (2002) *Norfolk at Ease.* Norwich: Norwich and Norfolk Racial Equality Council.

Office for National Statistics (ONS) (2003) *Census 2001: Key Statistics for Local Authorities in England and Wales.* London: Stationery Office.

Philo, C. (1992) 'Neglected Rural Geographies: A Review', *Journal of Rural Studies*, 8 (2): 193–207.

Powys Victim Support (2000) *Valuing Diversity – Progress Report for June–December 1999 on the 'Racial Awareness Helpline'.* Powys: Powys Victim Support.

PROSPER (2000) *Ethnic Minority Owned Businesses in Devon and Cornwall.* Plymouth: PROSPER.

Racial Attacks and Harassment Multi-Agency Strategy Partners (RAHMAS) (2001) *Tackling Crime Against Minority Ethnic Businesses.* Bid submitted to the Scottish Executive under the Make our Communities Safer Challenge Competition – 2001/2002.

Rattansi, A. and Westwood, S. (eds) (1994) *Racism, Modernity and Identity.* Cambridge: Polity Press.

Rayner, J. (2001) 'The Hidden Truth Behind Race Crimes in Britain', *Observer*, 18 February.

Saeed, A., Blain, N. and Forbes, D. (1999) *New Ethnic and National Questions in Scotland: Post-British Identities among Glasgow Pakistani Teenagers.* Glasgow: Glasgow Caledonian University (based on unpublished paper).

Scottish Civic Forum (2002) *Scottish Civic Forum Discrimination Survey.* Glasgow: Civic Forum.

Scottish Executive (2001) *Race Equality Advisory Forum Report.* Edinburgh, Scottish Executive.

Scottish Executive (2004) *Analysis of Ethnicity in the 2001 Census – Summary Report.* Edinburgh: Office of the Chief Statistician, Scottish Executive.

Sibley, D. (1995) *Geographies of Exclusion: Society and Difference in the West.* London, Routledge.

Spackman, P. (2000) *Researching Racism in Rural Areas, Victim Support Magazine*, Spring, p. 12.

Stevenson, B. Ltd (2003) *Focus Groups with Minority Ethnic Communities.* Edinburgh: Scottish Executive Social Research.

Suffolk Multi-agency Forum Against Racial Harassment (2001) *Annual Report 2000–2001.* Ipswich: Suffolk Multi-agency Forum Against Racial Harassment.

Suzin, K. (1996) *Voices from the Margins: A Qualitative Study of the Experiences of Black People in Devon.* Exeter: University of Exeter.

Tyler, K. (1999) *Making Gramsci's Notion of Hegemony Anti-Essentialist*. PhD Student at University of Manchester, Paper ID No. 106. Presented at British Sociological Conference, 6–9 April 1999, University of Glasgow, Scotland.

Wong, J.L. (1999a) *Multi-cultural Interpretation and Access to Heritage.* Wales: Black Environmental Network (BEN).

Wong, J.L. (1999b) *Ethnic Environmental Participation, Volume 2.* Wales: Black Environmental Network (BEN).

Wong, J.L. (2000) *Visualising Heritage Participation by Ethnic Groups.* Wales: Black Environmental Network (BEN).

Part 2
Assessing the Problem

Chapter 3

Outsiders within: the reality of rural racism

Dominic Malcolm

Although a range of statistics describing the extent of racial violence in the United Kingdom is available, for a variety of reasons most statistical sources inaccurately portray the real-life situation. Police figures are deemed to be misleading because a large proportion of victims either do not report the crimes against them or do not – often because they do not have sufficient evidence – report them as racially motivated (CRE 1999; Clancy *et al.* 2001). While more comprehensive in nature, the British Crime Surveys have been criticised for failing to capture a number of forms of racist incidents, especially cases of 'low-level' harassment (Virdee 1997: 263). The most adequate statistics, derived from the Policy Studies Institute's (PSI) *Fourth National Survey of Ethnic Minorities* (Modood *et al.* 1997), do record such 'low-level' incidents, however. This research found that 13 per cent of respondents had been subjected to some form of racial harassment in the preceding year and that considerable diversity existed between minority ethnic groups, with Caribbeans most likely, and Chinese least likely to experience physical attacks (ibid.: 265). Furthermore, it was found that while one in seven of all ethnic groups (including whites) experienced damage to property during the same period, Bangladeshis were only half as likely as the other minority ethnic groups in the sample to report such damage. As Virdee notes (1997: 263): 'The more we learn about racial violence and harassment, the clearer it becomes that the publicly reported police statistics represent the visible tip of an iceberg.'

There remain, however, two fundamental problems with these kinds of data. First, and perhaps not surprisingly, most of the research into racially motivated violence and crime focuses on areas that have a relatively high concentration of minority ethnic populations. What Virdee describes as 'some anecdotal evidence' (1997: 271) had suggested that levels of harassment may even be worse in areas with very small minority ethnic populations (Jay 1992; Wrench *et al.* 1993), and although more recent research (Craig *et al.* 1999; de Lima 1999) has increased our understanding of rural racism, it remains the case that 'its existence is not recognised, it [racism] is associated in most people's minds with inner city areas and conurbations' (Henderson and Kaur 1999: 58). Secondly, the quantitative nature of these surveys means that they fail to capture the diversity of incidents we might wish to define as racial harassment, especially as there are distinct problems in defining incidents as either racially motivated or, indeed, as harassment. In essence, such large-scale quantitative surveys are 'not capable by themselves of giving a detailed and fully rounded picture of the nature of racial violence and harassment' (Virdee 1997: 272).

This chapter seeks to address these shortcomings by reporting the findings of an essentially qualitative study of racism, prejudice and discrimination in West Norfolk, a rural part of a county located in the east of England.[1] The research was funded by a number of local organisations[2] and encompassed the experiences of 60 households from a range of minority ethnic groups, including respondents from the black, Asian, Chinese, asylum seeker, Traveller and Irish communities.[3] The sample was assembled with the help of various local organisations, including Chinese and Asian societies, the borough and county council's social services and education departments, Norwich and Norfolk Racial Equality Council (NNREC), the local hospital's personnel department which the steering group identified as the largest local employer of minority ethnic workers (an assumption also made by Craig *et al.* about employment in Lincolnshire (1999: 23–4)), and through snowballing techniques.[4]

Initially, a core questionnaire was drawn up which reflected the concerns and priorities of the various parties involved in the project. This questionnaire was used in a number of ways. Some were distributed to individuals through the NNREC and returned to the researcher by post. Others were completed by the researcher during face-to-face interviews (which were also tape recorded and transcribed), and a number were distributed to individuals at the start of the four focus groups held (one with parents at a Chinese language Sunday school, two with Eastern European asylum seekers[5] and one at an English language adult education class). In the focus groups, individuals were first asked to complete sections of the questionnaire and the issues raised were then used as the basis of a more open-ended discussion which was tape-recorded and transcribed. Because of the relatively unstructured nature of some of this data gathering, not all questionnaires were fully completed and consequently 'response rates' for some questions were poor.

The chapter begins by providing some background context to the research, before outlining some of the experiences of racism detailed by respondents. The nature of the racist harassment suffered by different ethnic groups is explored and it is suggested that this victimisation can vary significantly depending upon the ethnicity of the victim. The chapter suggests that some of those who took part in the research had difficulty with identifying the nature of the harassment suffered and were reluctant to identify too explicitly a racist element to the victimisation experienced. It is also posited that 'low-level' forms of harassment are more common in rural than in urban areas but that, due to the nature of this harassment, incidents are not commonly reported to the police.

The context of the research

The borough in which the research was undertaken has a small but rapidly growing minority ethnic community. According to the 1991 Census, minority ethnic groups constituted just 0.8 per cent of the population. However, mid-Census data indicated that this figure had more than doubled to 1.8 per cent in 1996 and by 2001 the number of residents defining themselves as 'white-British' had fallen to 96.1 per cent (ONS 2003). In the space of ten years the total population had risen by 5,000, while the minority ethnic population of the area had risen from approximately 1,050 to 5,300. Particularly significant in this regard was the growth in the number of people identifying themselves as 'white-other' (i.e. not white-British or white-Irish), a large proportion of whom, the steering group felt and the research experience suggested, are asylum seekers from Eastern European nations. Moreover, as the research was being commissioned, 'race' issues rose in prominence on the local public agenda. This occurred partly due to an increase in the numbers of asylum seekers being housed in the borough but also as a result of the national debate which followed farmer Tony Martin's shooting of two burglars at his home near Emneth in the south of the West Norfolk borough.[6] Not only were the two intruders from Traveller families, but the debate was characterised by the perception of some that rural areas were becoming increasingly lawless and that the police were no longer able to protect the property of rural citizens. Martin's case was subsequently championed by the Countryside Alliance, an organisation centrally focused on, and funded by, those seeking to resist the anti-hunting movement. The popular support for the Countryside Alliance, however, is largely a consequence of the movement's mission of improving awareness and understanding of rural issues (see Milbourne 1997). This, in turn, can best be understood as the response of rural interests which perceive themselves to be 'beleaguered' in the face of urban – and to some extent urban can be taken to constitute multi-ethnic – dominance (Cox and Winter 1997). The Tony Martin case not only heightened the local population's sense of being 'beleaguered' but firmly placed the spotlight of blame on minority ethnic groups considered to be 'other' to the established, white, rural community (see also Agyeman and Spooner 1997: 199).

An unusual characteristic of the minority ethnic population in the area, however, was its relative affluence. Census data from 1991 indicated that a high proportion of research subjects would be drawn from higher socio-economic groups and while a large proportion of the sample assembled were unemployed (23 per cent, or 14), those from higher socio-economic groups were disproportionately represented among those in employment (see Table). Similarly, nearly 50 per cent (30) of the minority ethnic population on whom the research has data lived in owner-occupied accommodation. Therefore relatively few individuals from minority ethnic groups suffered from the 'compounded disadvantage' of poverty, low class status and ethnic marginalisation. It should be noted, however, that there were some individuals in the sample who were particularly impoverished, especially the Travellers and asylum seekers.

Having outlined some of the problems in using such data, it is still useful to look at official statistics for racially motivated incidents (RMIs) in the county, as these provide some indication of the changing status of this 'social problem'. Within Norfolk as a whole, reported incidents of racial harassment and discrimination have increased by 30 per cent or more every year since NNREC records began in 1995/96 (NNREC 1999). Whilst King's Lynn and West Norfolk accounted for just 5.4 per cent of the county-wide total of RMIs in 1998/99, local police figures indicated a similarly sharp rise in RMIs in recent years. The police division recorded only one RMI for the twelve-month period from April 1997 to March 1998, and during 1999 this figure rose to 17 recorded incidents. Impressionistic evidence relayed during the research suggested that this figure would dramatically increase again in 2000 and indeed, between 1999 and 2002 county-wide reporting of RMIs increased by 68 per cent.[7] Despite such increases, it remains the case that the low rate of recorded incidents meant that the establishment of a specialist department or

Table 1 Occupations and social class of respondents (according to the Registrar General's classification of occupations)

	Number	Per cent
Unemployed	14	23.3
Full-time education	4	6.7
Retired	3	5.0
Housewife/husband	4	6.7
Self-employed	7	11.7
Employed	24	40.0
Of those employed:		
Professional	7	25.0
Managerial and technical	10	39.3
Unskilled non-manual	2	14.3
Skilled manual	1	7.1
Partly skilled manual	4	14.3
Unskilled manual	0	0.0

section dealing with racism was felt to be unfeasible. As in Suffolk (Chakraborti and Garland 2003a: 12) comparisons were drawn between the relative 'rarity' of RMIs and the regularity of domestic violence incidents, with the latter used to justify the low level of financial and human resources devoted to the former.

However, in sharp contrast to police figures, 29 per cent of research subjects who expressed an opinion (9 out of 31) stated that things were 'improving' in terms of racial prejudice and discrimination, with 68 per cent (21 out of 31) stating that things were 'staying the same'. The increases evident in official statistics, therefore, are as likely to be a reflection of changes in the method of recording as they are indicative of the number of actual incidents. The disparity in these figures provides a good indication of the way in which crime statistics fail to provide an accurate measure of racial harassment and how they should not be taken as an indication of actual trends.

While only half of the sample were able to compare the area with other parts of the country, 50 per cent (15) of these stated that in terms of racism West Norfolk was a 'relatively good' area in which to live. This view was most widely held by Chinese respondents. While one Chinese respondent noted that racism was 'occasional but not common compared to Birmingham, London or a bigger city', another more recently arrived Chinese woman, a translator relayed, was '... very worried about where she is now compared to Guildford where she was [previously].' One Asian respondent argued that the racism experienced in this rural area was simply 'different' to other parts of the country, suggesting: 'It's better in that there is less racism but there is also more ignorance.' All the Traveller respondents argued that the area was 'neither better nor worse' than anywhere else. These findings seem to contrast sharply with the research undertaken in neighbouring Suffolk where, '... the impression given by minority ethnic interviewees was that their experiences of living in rural Suffolk had been largely negative' (Chakraborti and Garland 2003a: 5).

Overall, most respondents considered racism, prejudice and discrimination in West Norfolk as relatively rare, with only 26 per cent (13) describing it as 'very' or 'quite common'. This figure, however, hides some considerable variance between members of different ethnic groups. For instance, around half the 'black' and Asian respondents described racism and prejudice as very or quite common whereas only one out of five Travellers, one out of 13 Chinese respondents and no asylum seekers did. While to some extent mirroring the trends identified in the PSI survey (cited in Virdee 1997), as we shall see, these data are a poor reflection of the actual differences in the racism experienced by members of these different groups. We might concede, perhaps, that the relative 'invisibility' (that is to say, whiteness) of Travellers and (Eastern European) asylum seekers insulated them from some of the more random forms of RMIs, but this would not account for the difference, for example, between the Chinese and Asian groups and would seem to contrast with the heightened emotion which has surrounded the issue of asylum in recent years. More likely, these figures reflect one or a combination of two things: that for the lay public, the definition of racism and 'racially motivated' is highly subjective and so varies greatly, and that the definition of 'common' is similarly subjective.

In the following section the multifaceted nature of racism in the rural community of West Norfolk is outlined, focusing on the extent of racism and on how membership of different minority ethnic groups acts as a significant influence on the types of racism experienced. Subsequently, the disparity between recorded and actual rates of racially motivated incidents is assessed, with three factors highlighted: the exclusion or withdrawal of minority ethnic groups from social life in rural areas,[8] the reluctance of many to define incidents as racially motivated and, finally, the widespread reticence to report such incidents through official channels.

Experiences of racism

In a similar fashion to the findings of de Lima (1999: 33) in Fife and of Chakraborti and Garland (2003b) in Suffolk, racist incidents were a regular feature of life for minority ethnic communities in West Norfolk. Twenty-eight per cent (14 out of 50) of respondents on whom there were data stated that they often or sometimes experienced verbal abuse, 20 per cent (10) that they often or sometimes experienced damage to property and 4 per cent (2) that they often or sometimes experienced physical abuse. In addition to these 'tangible' forms of racism, 36 per cent (18) said that they were often or sometimes the subject of unnecessary/ obtrusive staring and 22 per cent (11) said that they were often or sometimes avoided by people, something which led to, or compounded, the feeling of being an outsider within the rural community. In addition to this, a number of respondents volunteered examples where they had encountered other forms of prejudice, racial stereotyping or simply a lack of understanding of non-white cultures. Two points emerge from these data. First, within the broad 'brush stroke' of these quantitative findings it was apparent that, as official statistics had indicated, ethnic group membership was a significant mediator of the way in which racism and racial prejudice were experienced. Second, the more qualitative data discussed below highlight both the subjectivity of definitions of racism, and also that its regularity is underestimated by official statistics which seek to identify, with a relatively high degree of generality, the frequency of such incidents. Paradoxically, it may be the case that racist incidents are so common that the individual comes to view such incidents as unremarkable and does not, therefore, define them as racially motivated, or at least 're-categorises' them as 'not serious' enough to warrant this descriptor which legally, and popularly, has the potential to entail rather more severe consequences (a similar point has been made in relation to racist incidents in local cricket matches – see Malcolm 2002: 313).

Chinese, black and Asian respondents most regularly recalled experiences of verbal abuse. Name-calling was most commonly reported by young people, with two of the younger adult interviewees (i.e. aged in their late teens/early twenties) speaking of instances of name-calling from other pupils while at school. Other interviewees described how their children had experienced some racially motivated verbal abuse while at school. This is not, of course, to say that verbal abuse disappeared as people grew older, as Asian interviewees spoke of having suffered such abuse in the workplace. One locally born young black man noted that when he played football, and especially when playing in some of the area's smaller villages, he had experienced racist abuse from both players and spectators. This he dismissed, however, as being 'all part of the game'. One person stated that she no longer went to the local village social club with her (white) husband since encountering racism from bar staff, other patrons and, in particular, tourists.[9] Others spoke of problems which the local town's football club had encountered with racism shouted from the terraces (something which had also featured in police records of RMIs), chasing a group of teenage boys who had shouted racist abuse, or of correcting friends who had not seemed to realise that their language was racially offensive.

These data give some impression of the variety of forms and contexts in which racist verbal abuse is experienced. Yet in contrast to this, only two Traveller families spoke of being victims of such harassment, with one being abused by his neighbours and another Traveller couple detailing problems that their children had encountered with name-calling at school. Similarly, an Eastern European respondent described some children shouting insults in the street, and another woman cited 'one or two problems' that her children had at school with 'kids who were a little bit difficult and a bit rude sometimes'. Overall, however, it was clear that verbal abuse was more regularly experienced by those minority ethnic group members whose 'difference' was the most visible.

Again Chinese and Asian respondents most frequently reported damage to property. Occasionally interviewees mentioned vandalism to their domestic properties but more commonly vandalism was directed at business premises, as one Chinese person described:

> This would happen quite often ... it's frequent these days, probably to most restaurants ... especially during summer holidays ... [They] throw some rubbish into the door and run away and things like that.

Similarly an Asian owner of a town centre shop recalled how, on what he described as 'almost a weekly basis', he had to clean up or repair damage to his premises. He felt that, because no neighbouring shops experienced the same level of vandalism, many of these incidents were racially motivated. As with verbal abuse, we might link the frequency of such incidents to the visibility of such properties (for example, through the type of the business or its name), but, more pertinently, this issue raises the question of why the British Crime Survey does not record damage to commercial premises in its figures (CRE 1999).

While these findings indicate that verbal abuse and damage to property are by no means rare, more commonly respondents identified less tangible forms of racial prejudice such as 'staring' or being alienated by others in the community through the avoidance of social contact. Staring was commonly experienced by Asian, Chinese and black respondents but rarely cited by Traveller, Eastern European and Irish respondents. A Thai woman referred to the strange looks she had received from people in the street, while a Vietnamese woman echoed these sentiments, describing how she rarely left the house and avoided many social situations because she was 'scared'. Two other Asian interviewees noted that they had experienced a lot of 'staring' when they first arrived in the area and that, while it was less common now, it remained a problem 'in more rural parts of the region'. One black male respondent simply stated that 'the staring goes on all the time'. Conversely, however, many of the Eastern European interviewees argued that being white meant that they only occasionally experienced staring. As one (male) respondent noted:

When they hear us speaking our own language they look for a bit or when we are trying to talk English, but we never feel there is a problem. It's not for long and it's nothing like in our home country … here nobody seems to mind you speaking broken English.[10]

The feeling of being avoided was something identified largely by Asian and black respondents. Two Asian female respondents noted how they were regularly ignored by staff in fast-food restaurants and that often it was not until they explicitly asked for service (for example, by saying 'Excuse me', or 'I think that I am next') that they would be served. Male interviewees recalled similar experiences when trying to get served by bar staff in pubs. Two women (one black, one Asian) married to white husbands, spoke of experiences where people would freely talk to them when they (the minority ethnic women) were accompanied by their husbands but not when they were alone. Others recalled how they sometimes found themselves ignored by neighbours or the parents of their children's schoolmates. Two other interviewees spoke of their suspicion that the (white) parents of their children's friends had intervened more directly to limit contact between their respective children. Typically, the interviewees noted, a white child would accept a number of invitations to come to the interviewees' house but that their parents (usually the mother) would subsequently explain that, for various reasons, the child would not be able to visit. The regularity and/ or contrived nature of the 'reasons' given led to the growth of such suspicions. As outlined in other research (Derbyshire 1994; Chakraborti and Garland 2003a), experiences such as these can lead to, or exacerbate, feelings of isolation and loneliness. It is also likely that this form of racial prejudice is far less common in areas with significant minority ethnic communities. These urban locations have so far dominated official and academic research on 'race' and ethnicity and this has led to the peculiarity of rural manifestations of racism to be ignored or underplayed.

The relative frequency with which these 'tangible' and 'intangible' forms of racism occur indicates that police and other official statistics are unable to capture the extent of racist harassment experienced by members of minority ethnic groups. The types and range of other forms of racism identified by respondents further illustrates this point, grouped here in terms of problems related to a lack of understanding, a lack of acceptance into the community and the holding of negative racial stereotypes.

Chakraborti and Garland (2003a: 4) discovered that many members of the established white communities in rural Suffolk stressed 'narrow-mindedness' and a 'fondness for tradition' as common factors underpinning people's resistance to change in rural areas. In the present research this 'narrow-mindedness' was most clearly expressed through the widespread lack of understanding or awareness of different cultures. A number of hospital workers gave examples of this from their dealings with patients. Commonly interviewees spoke of 'friendly' but 'personal' questioning from patients which seemed to stem from the patients' lack of exposure to cultures other than their own. One Muslim woman in particular spoke of how patients would refer to other Asian staff as her 'brother' or 'sister' and another (dual heritage) woman who worked in the hospital said that patients often asked where she came from, only to be surprised to hear the answer that she had been born in the hospital itself some 20 years earlier.

This, perhaps 'well meaning', ignorance of cultures is undoubtedly more evident in areas with small minority ethnic populations such as West Norfolk than in larger urban areas, but this lack of understanding takes on greater significance because it can often merge with less tolerant, more resistant forms of behaviour. Interviewees spoke of the frustration of having to explain things twice, or what they perceived to be the unhelpful and obstructive behaviour they encountered (for example, in shops). A Thai woman recalled how a neighbour had questioned her (white) husband asking why he had married her, and then telling him that he should send his wife 'back home' because her English was not very good. One person mentioned a particular market stall which she avoided as she felt that the trader inflated prices because she was Asian. Some cited instances where they had made face-to-face enquiries and had left without receiving the information that they had requested. However, when they subsequently made telephone enquiries – that is to say, in a situation where visible characteristics are not important – they had felt that they had been given the information that they sought.

However, the prejudice experienced by Travellers in this respect was even more marked. Travellers regularly cited times when they had been turned away from local garages, for example, when they had asked for tap water. A woman who lived on a Traveller site explained how a portrait photographer, once he discovered where she lived, had insisted that the photographs were taken in his studio rather than in her home. The father of a housed Traveller family spoke of a sign outside a local pub banning 'van dwellers'. Stewart and Kilfeather (1999: 46) note that 'it is difficult to quantify the poverty and marginalisation suffered by the Travelling community' because the majority of available data are biased towards nomadic rather than housed Travellers. The present research, to some extent, replicated this bias but, if Stewart and Kilfeather are right, these examples only serve to underscore the greater regularity, and more overt character, of the prejudice that Travellers experience in comparison to other minority ethnic groups. If it is the case that prejudice is more likely to go unchallenged in regions where minority ethnic populations are relatively small and community groups are less well organised and less influential than their urban counterparts, then it would seem reasonable to suggest that a community as disparate as Travellers are even less able or less likely to challenge prejudicial attitudes.

Underlying many of these instances, however, was the acceptance of particular racial stereotypes. Indian men despaired at work colleagues' assumptions that they did not or could not undertake DIY tasks (a view famously made public by the Duke of Edinburgh[11]), or what they saw as teachers' lack of concern over their children's poor educational attainment. Both black and Asian men recalled incidents in which they felt persecuted by the police because of their colour. This might involve being stopped for what interviewees perceived to be 'no apparent reason'. An interviewee recalled a particular experience, following a road traffic accident, in which: 'The moment the police constable discovered I was Asian he sided with the other party who was white.' Finally, a questionnaire respondent reported an incident that occurred when he was paying money into a bank:

I went into a bank to deposit [a relatively large amount of] cash and was asked where it came from. The only explanation I can see for this question is that I am black.

Racial stereotyping is clearly apparent in these examples but they pale in comparison to the experiences recalled by Travellers. Travellers spoke of how they were often blamed for thefts, banned from shops (presumably on the basis of the same stereotype linking Travellers and crime) or perceived by others to be dirty or unclean. They also noted that police searched their homes looking for stolen property, that people often tried to sell them stolen goods or that their presence in a particular location encouraged others to steal because they felt that suspicion was likely to fall upon the Travellers. One interviewee stated that, with reference to a recent local theft, a policeman had made explicit his prejudice by saying, 'You're my number one suspect because of who you are.'

Recorded and actual rates of racially motivated incidents

The empirical examples revealed in the research have shown the multifaceted nature of racism in this rural community. The data also point towards a frequency of racially motivated incidents which is in excess of that recorded in official statistics, and the reasons behind this incongruity will be examined in this section. Three specific explanations became apparent from the empirical research: the exclusion/withdrawal of members of minority ethnic groups from some aspects of social life; the widespread reluctance to define incidents as racially motivated; and the tendency not to report even those incidents defined as racially motivated to the police or through other official channels.

How members of minority ethnic groups are excluded or withdraw from social life

Fifteen respondents (25 per cent) identified specific ways in which they had modified their lives in response to experiences of racial prejudice, but many others gave examples which suggested that the behaviour was so deeply ingrained in rural life that they did not consider it significant enough to mention. One person, when asked how racism affected their life stated, 'Of course it affects my life but you learn to live with racism daily.' As Dhalech (1999: 13–14) and Chakraborti and Garland (2003a: 8) have noted, racism is experienced in all areas of social life, such that some may come to perceive that there are no public places which are 'safe' from potential or actual racist victimisation. Consequently this may lead to 'self'-exclusion and, commonly, this was manifest in the avoidance of community groups, some shops (especially cheaper grocery stores), particular 'run-down' areas and the smaller towns or more rural areas where, perhaps, ethnic minorities or 'non-white' faces were less common. Though satisfaction with and use of local services by minority ethnic groups was not particularly different to the borough's population as a whole (as measured in the borough council's 'Citizens' Panel' survey), 3 out of 35 and 5 out of 35 respondents who provided an answer said that they did not use local services more widely because they felt 'unwelcome' or held the 'expectation of experiencing racism'. De Lima (1999: 34) notes, however, that one consequence of this withdrawal from participation within the community is that it can become interpreted by local service providers and the established white rural community as an indication that minority ethnic groups have little desire to be involved in these mainstream activities.

Yet the most striking finding in this connection was that it was the very groups that noted particularly low rates of racism, prejudice and discrimination that cited the most extreme forms of exclusion/ withdrawal. A number of Travellers, for instance, noted that they simply never went into public houses because it was so common for them to experience trouble. When the author asked one male Traveller who lived on the roadside whether he encountered problems in the towns he simply said, 'I don't go in them'. Speaking of his preference for seclusion, another Traveller explained: 'I don't like neighbours, I don't like visitors ... even with my own people' (i.e. other Travellers). He continued by noting that being able to move around and set up home on the roadside was essential to his quality of life: 'If I was getting aggro I wouldn't be [living] here'. The male head of another family living on the roadside was just as explicit, stating: 'Being on the road gives me security' (see Stewart and Kilfeather (1999: 46), who note that Travellers who live on un-serviced roadside sites tend to move location more frequently than other Travellers).

In contrast to this 'optional' withdrawal or 'self-exclusion',[12] asylum seekers are institutionally excluded because of their economic and legal status. Consequently, many asylum seekers simply do not encounter the everyday situations which others take for granted. Most could not, for instance, afford to visit public houses or cinemas. All were ineligible for work, the everyday situation which the sample as a whole identified as the most likely in which they would experience racial prejudice. The major problems they encountered related to their use of shopping vouchers and shop assistants' lack of familiarity with them, but then this, essentially, was their primary contact with mainstream culture.

A further, and major, limiting factor to their social experiences was language. An inability to communicate led many to limit their social contact to people from a similar background. Avoidance was not an option in healthcare and educational situations, however, and many spoke of problems negotiating with teachers and doctors. It should, however, be noted that the participants in the Chinese focus group made similar points to those made by the asylum seekers. In areas where the minority ethnic population is relatively small, the costs of translation and printing documents and information in a number of languages are particularly prohibitive. Craig *et al.* noted that the development of language skills was a central feature of Lincolnshire's programme for tackling racial injustice in the county (1999: 27), and the data presented here suggest that this policy priority is well-founded. Indeed, it is clear that one consequence of not addressing a language skills shortage is that minority ethnic groups become even less visible within the community and the multicultural reality is obscured.

The reluctance of many to define incidents as racially motivated

To some extent the non-defining of incidents as racially motivated related to a lack of evidence. One example was provided with the help of a more fluent English speaker in the Chinese focus group, who stated:

> The lady was saying that a lot of people ... don't know how to define racism and not everything needs to be called racism. She's saying that [they have] come into my shop and thrown eggs ... but she said that they're not saying silly names and things like that. But they're not doing next door or the other doors ... only to hers. Would that count as racism? Well, yes it's a question mark, isn't it?

The woman explained that this was an important dilemma for her. She recognised that the police took reports of racially motivated incidents more seriously but, subsequently, this increased the onus on her to make an accurate assessment of the motivation behind the incident. Asylum seekers relayed a similar lack of certainty about the motivation behind the problems they experienced. During one of the asylum seekers' focus groups, the translator relayed that there had been some experiences of verbal abuse in the street:

> They can have trouble in the street with kids, with teenagers, but not because they're foreigners they don't think. These sorts of kids are like that with anybody. It doesn't matter [who you are].

These examples were typical of respondents in general, but especially of the asylum seekers' attitudes to experiences which might, potentially, be defined as discriminatory, yet on the whole were not described as racially motivated. As one Chinese man argued: 'If there's a problem, it's a problem, it's not racism'. Though the quantity of empirical evidence for this point is not extensive, it may be the case that one unintended consequence of the political and social prioritisation of anti-racism, is an increased reluctance on the part of some individuals from minority ethnic groups to define incidents within this category.

At times, however, the ambiguity over the racially motivated nature of acts was alleviated either by the repetition of such incidents, or through comparison with the experiences of others. As one Chinese man explained:

> I think they still pick on the ethnic ones [restaurants or takeaways] … and not only me but some other places as well … in the balance, if there's a Chinese or Indian takeaway there, or a supermarket, they [target the Chinese or Indian business] … maybe ten times more.

While three out of the four interviews with Traveller families with children highlighted incidents at school of a racially motivated nature, the inter-view with one particular couple was revealing of the considerable tolerance with which members of this ethnic group viewed racism and prejudice. One couple told me that they did not have any problems at school but, with prompting from the Traveller Education Service officer present at this interview, they agreed that there had recently been some name-calling which had been quickly acted upon and resolved by the teacher. The mother said 'Bullying again'; the father added: 'Well, it wasn't bad'. The couple continued by recalling incidents such as the unexplained confiscation of a child benefit book at a post office, a doctor's refusal to provide a repeat prescription for medication prescribed by a previous doctor, and further incidents of fights at school involving their children. Despite this list of incidents, their overall judgement of the regularity of racial prejudice and discrimination was that it was 'rare'.

A similar instance, where the itemising of incidents seemed to contradict the more general impression given of the occurrence of racially motivated incidents, was provided by a retired Asian doctor. He argued that racism was 'very rare', that he 'never' experienced staring, physical abuse or racially motivated vandalism, that he could recall only one instance of verbal abuse in 40 years, and 'rarely' felt that he was being avoided. He stressed to me that people often made 'too much of such things', that prejudice should not be dwelt on, and that instead people should 'just get on with their lives'. However, as the interview progressed, he mentioned times when people had refused treatment from him on account of his skin colour. He also stated that he had 'often' sat on interview panels where he felt, indeed sometimes he even 'knew', that minority ethnic applicants had been racially discriminated against. Finally, he noted that he had not received the professional recognition he felt he deserved and that, since retirement, a number of (white) colleagues had said to him that they too felt he had deserved more appreciation for the work he performed. To some extent, this initial reluctance to admit experiencing racism seems to contrast with Chakraborti and Garland's research which found that 'ethnic minority victims often perceive a racial dimension to, or motivation behind, many of the crimes and incivilities suffered' (2002: 12). Clearly many members of minority ethnic groups do perceive themselves to have experienced racially motivated incidents, but it is only in the context of qualitative investigation such as this that a more rounded picture of the scale and type of racism which individuals suffer can be drawn out, and that we can start to understand more about the conscious and subconscious choices which form the process of deciding whether or not particular events are racially motivated.

The reluctance to report incidents through official channels

Given this reluctance to define incidents as racially motivated, it is not surprising that there is an even greater reluctance to report them in such a light. Only 13 respondents (21 per cent) stated that they normally responded in any way to instances of racial prejudice for, as one noted, 'you can't change everyone'. Most noted that they simply tried to ignore racist incidents when they happened. Despite this, 25 per cent (15) of the sample said that they had reported a racist incident to the police and 7 per cent (4) had reported incidents to the local authority. The main reason for not reporting such incidents, noted by 17 per cent (10), was that the victim felt it 'was not serious enough', or that too little evidence was available. Ten per cent (6) had decided not to report an incident because they felt that it would 'not be taken seriously' and 5 per cent (3) said that reporting such incidents 'only makes things worse'. The time involved in reporting incidents, and the fear of retribution, dissuaded people from acting: 'You have to think about when they come out ... otherwise it may get worse', noted one Chinese woman. Another man in this focus group added:

I reported [some] damage to [my] property. Personally I think it is racism but I don't say it ... We don't want the trouble. We don't want the trouble.

Among the Chinese and the Travellers in particular there was a feeling that it was preferable to sort problems out oneself. Such attitudes are symptomatic of the feeling that the police and other official agencies are ineffectual in combating racist victimisation.

These findings are similar to those of Chakraborti and Garland (2003a: 8) who argue that '"letting it go" or "turning a blind eye" were commonly regarded as the easiest, and least inflammatory methods of dealing with victimisation'. De Lima, for instance, notes that in rural areas there are 'considerable pressures operating on minority ethnic groups not to challenge harassment and discrimination' (1999: 36) and Dhalech (1999: 18) argues that any challenge to racist banter or joking in the workplace is normally interpreted as the individual's own personal failing, the inability to 'have a laugh' or the consequence of having a 'chip on the shoulder'. Overall, we can see that these actions, or indeed inactions, result from the 'common expectation ... that "outsiders" should make every effort to fit in and adopt mainstream values' (Chakraborti and Garland 2003a: 5).

Conclusions

In conclusion some general points can be made about the accuracy of official statistics relating to racial harassment and also some more specific points about their relevance to rural racism. Bowling (1998, cited in Chakraborti and Garland 2003a: 2) argues that victim surveys and official statistics typically highlight isolated incidents rather than ongoing events and that, consequently, little of the complexity or multifaceted nature of racial harassment is revealed. To this we might add that a qualitative understanding of rural racism highlights the importance of lived experiences in determining the individual's interpretation of the categories of incident about which such surveys typically ask. In this chapter it has been argued that self-defined, 'low-level' racial harassment, and hence officially recorded rates, depend considerably on the subjective assessments of individuals. In some examples it was indeed the case that, paradoxically, so common were such incidents that they were merely accepted as part of the individual's 'way of life', and hence were not remarkable enough to merit defining as a racially motivated incident. This dependence on subjective assessments clearly has an impact on all official statistics and explains why more qualitative forms of research identify a greater frequency of racially motivated incidents.

Furthermore, it may be the case that the specific characteristics of the rural context exacerbate this trend. From the descriptive passages above, it becomes evident that 'low level' harassment, or less tangible forms of racism are particularly common characteristics of the lives of minority ethnic groups in areas with a low minority ethnic population density. The regularity and low level of seriousness of these incidents leads to a widespread reluctance to report racial incivilities to the police or other official bodies. However, it should be stressed that this reluctance is also formed in the context of particular pressures on minority ethnic groups in rural areas not to 'rock the boat' or to upset the romanticised ideal of the countryside as a harmonious and placid place (see Milbourne 1997) which lies at the core of a British national identity that prides itself on being a civilised and moral people (Agyeman and Spooner 1997: 200). Interestingly, Solomos and Back, in a discussion of 'new racism', identify as significant 'the defence of the mythic "British/English way of life" in the face of attack from enemies *outside* and *within*' (Solomos and Back 1996: 18). The minority ethnic communities in rural areas are defined by the established white communities as one cause of their more generally disrupted or 'beleaguered' lives (Cox and Winter 1997). It is they (the minority ethnic groups) who are thus defined as the problem rather than the attitudes of the established white communities towards those who they perceive to be the 'outsiders' (see Small 1994). However, it should be noted that throughout the fieldwork not one respondent mentioned the presence or activities of far right groups. This may be an indication that, despite the British National Party's efforts to 'claim' rural issues through its *Land and People* campaign (Agyeman and Spooner 1997: 201), the party is making little notable impression in England's countryside.

Most commonly, members of minority ethnic groups who lived in this rural area experienced feelings of isolation and encountered people with little knowledge of, yet some prejudice towards, cultures other than their own. This lack of familiarity with visible or cultural difference is a characteristic of some rural populations that is noted elsewhere in this volume. Similarly economies of scale mean that for those with poor English, little help exists. Moreover, the lack of relevant channels through which help might be sought, for example from community clubs and networks to more politically active groups, means that experiences are rarely discussed or compared and so no common identity or consciousness as a group which is discriminated against develops. While in West Norfolk the emerging Chinese and Asian networks have gone some way towards the more effective mobilisation of these respective groups, their existence also clearly demonstrates the weaknesses of less well organised groups such as Travellers and asylum seekers.

Ten years ago, Helen Derbyshire wrote that 'racism in Norwich and

Norfolk, though as cruel and as dangerous as racism in places with larger ethnic minorities, is expressed in different ways and different strategies are needed to fight it' (1994, foreword). These strategies may not be so different in kind, but they should be in terms of emphasis. At the end of my research I urged the various commissioning parties to undertake a number of different actions. Most significantly in this context, it is clear that the development of minority ethnic community groups will have very real and tangible consequences in enabling individuals to cope with the problems of isolation and loneliness, as well as acting as the stimulus for mobilising minority ethnic groups for more effective action to counter racial prejudice. It is also clear that barriers related to language are significant and, to this end, a dual strategy of the wider provision of translation services and English language adult education would be effective. Finally, however, it should be noted that these policies would only scratch the surface of the rural racism issue for, most significantly, the established white communities need to become more aware of the increasingly multicultural character of the area. In possession of this greater understanding, it may be easier for these communities to relax from the existing siege mentality and embrace the future in a more optimistic frame of mind.

Notes

1 In addition to the research subjects who agreed to talk to me, I would particularly like to thank the research project's steering group of Roger Bennett, Steve Earl and Simon Phelan of King's Lynn and West Norfolk Borough Council, Sue Craythorne of the Norfolk County Council, DCI Martin Wright of Norfolk Constabulary and Anne Matin of the Norwich and Norfolk Racial Equality Council. I am also very grateful to the 'gatekeepers' in the community who helped me network and establish focus groups but regret that I cannot name them in person in order to preserve research subjects' anonymity.

2 Funding partners included King's Lynn and West Norfolk Borough Council, Norfolk County Council and Norfolk Constabulary, and the research was conducted with the help and guidance of the Norwich and Norfolk Racial Equality Council (NNREC).

3 The breakdown of respondents was as follows: 10 black (African Caribbean, African, black British, dual heritage); 15 Asian (Indian, Pakistani, Vietnamese and Thai); 15 Chinese; 14 eastern European asylum seekers; 5 Travellers; 1 Irish person.

4 See Malcolm (2000) for a more detailed description of the methodology and findings of this research project.

5   I am grateful to the translator who sat in on, and facilitated, these focus groups.
6   Martin was convicted in 2000 of the manslaughter of a burglar who had broken into his home, and had served two-thirds of a five-year sentence when he was released in July 2003 to something of a media 'frenzy'.
7   I am grateful to Norfolk Constabulary for providing these updated figures.
8   It would be inaccurate to draw a distinction between exclusion and withdrawal, as essentially these are interdependent features of the broader process of racism. This conception, I think, fits in better with Bowling's critique of official statistics (1997, cited in Chakraborti and Garland, 2003a) for their focus on specific events rather than the experience of racism as an ongoing process.
9   Interestingly, Dhalech (1999: 20) argues that the tourist industry is 'rife with racism' and that this has yet to be fully examined. Further, Agyeman and Spooner (1997) stress that recreational use of rural areas is largely a 'white' phenomenon.
10 It should be noted that all the Eastern European respondents had recently sought asylum in the UK and considered their experiences of prejudice in the UK here as relatively minor compared to the problems experienced prior to seeking asylum.
11 When visiting an electronics factory based in Edinburgh in 1999 the Duke spotted a fuse box that he felt was less sophisticated than the other electronic components on show, and commented: 'It looks as though it was put in by an Indian' (*source*: BBC News website at http://news.bbc.co.uk/1/hi/uk/416297.stm).
12 The terms 'optional' and 'self-exclusion' have been placed in inverted commas in recognition that such decisions are not made in a social vacuum.

References

Agyeman, J. and Spooner, R. (1997) 'Ethnicity and the Rural Environment', in P. Cloke and J. Little (eds), *Contested Countryside Cultures: Otherness, Marginalisation and Rurality*. London: Routledge.

Bowling, B. (1998) *Violent Racism: Victimisation, Policing and Social Context*. Oxford: Oxford University Press.

Chakraborti, N. and Garland, J. (2002) 'A Sense of Perspective: Assessing Minority Ethnic Communities' Views Towards Crime and Criminal Justice', *Criminal Justice Matters*, 49: 12–13.

Chakraborti, N. and Garland, J. (2003a) 'An "Invisible" Problem? Uncovering the Nature of Racist Victimisation in Rural Suffolk', *International Review of Victimology*, 10 (1): 1–17.

Chakraborti, N. and Garland, J. (2003b) 'Under-researched and Overlooked: An Exploration of the Attitudes of Rural Minority Ethnic Communities Towards Crime, Community Safety and the Criminal Justice System', *Journal of Ethnic and Migration Studies*, 29 (3): 563–72.

Clancy, A., Hough, M., Aust, R. and Kershaw, C. (2001) *Crime, Policing and Justice: The Experience of Ethnic Minorities – Findings from the 2000 British Crime Survey*, Home Office Research Study No. 223. London: Home Office.

Commission for Racial Equality (1999) *Racial Attacks and Harassment: CRE Factsheet*. London: Commission for Racial Equality.

Cox, G. and Winter, M. (1997) 'The Beleaguered "Other": Hunt Followers in the Countryside', in P. Milbourne (ed.), *Revealing Rural Others: Representation, Power and Identity in the British Countryside*. London: Cassell.

Craig, G., Ahmend, B. and Amery, F. (1999) ' "We Shoot Them at Newark!" The Work of the Lincolnshire Forum for Racial Justice', in P. Henderson and R. Kaur (eds), *Rural Racism in the UK: Examples of Community-Based Responses*. London: Community Development Foundation.

de Lima, P.J.F. (1999) 'Research and Action in the Scottish Highlands', in P. Henderson and R. Kaur (eds), *Rural Racism in the UK: Examples of Community-Based Responses*. London: Community Development Foundation.

Derbyshire, H. (1994) *Not in Norfolk: Tackling the Invisibility of Racism*. Norwich: Norwich and Norfolk Racial Equality Council.

Dhalech, M. (1999) 'Race Equality Initiatives in South West England', in P. Henderson and R. Kaur (eds), *Rural Racism in the UK: Examples of Community-Based Responses*. London: Community Development Foundation.

Henderson, P. and Kaur, R. (1999) 'Conclusions and Recommendations', in P. Henderson and R. Kaur (eds), *Rural Racism in the UK: Examples of Community-Based Responses*. London: Community Development Foundation.

Jay, E. (1992) *Keep Them in Birmingham: Challenging Racism in South West England*. London: Commission for Racial Equality.

Malcolm, D. (2000) *West Norfolk Ethnic Minorities Research Report*. Leicester: Department of Sociology, University of Leicester.

Malcolm, D. (2002) ' "Clean Bowled"? Cricket, Racism and Equal Opportunities', *Journal of Ethnic and Migration Studies*, 28 (2): 307–25.

Milbourne, P. (ed.) (1997) *Revealing Rural 'Others': Representation, Power and Identity in the British Countryside*. London: Pinter.

Modood, T., Berthoud, R., Lakey, J., Nazroo, J., Smith, P., Virdee, S. and Beishon, S. (1997) *Ethnic Minorities in Britain: Diversity and Disadvantage - Fourth National Survey of Ethnic Minorities*. London: Policy Studies Institute.

Norwich and Norfolk Racial Equality Council (NNREC) (1999) *Norwich and Norfolk Racial Equality Council Annual Report 1998/99*. Norwich: NNREC.

Office for National Statistics (ONS) (2003) *Census 2001: Key Statistics for Local Authorities in England and Wales*. London: Stationery Office.

Small, S. (1994) *Racialised Barriers: The Black Experience in the United States and England in the 1980s*. London: Routledge.

Solomos, J. and Back, L. (1996) *Racism in Society*. London: Macmillan.

Stewart, R. and Kilfeather, J. (1999) 'Working with Travellers in Northern Ireland', in P. Henderson, and R. Kaur (eds), *Rural Racism in the UK: Examples of Community-Based Responses*. London: Community Development Foundation.

Virdee, S. (1997) 'Racial Harassment', in T. Modood, R. Berthoud, J. Lakey, J. Nazroo, P. Smith, S. Virdee and S. Beishon, *Ethnic Minorities in Britain: Diversity and Disadvantage – Fourth National Survey of Ethnic Minorities*. London: Policy Studies Institute.

Wrench, J., Brar, H. and Martin, P. (1993) *Invisible Minorities: Racism, in New Towns and New Contexts*. Warwick: Centre for Research into Ethnic Relations, University of Warwick.

Chapter 4

Unravelling a stereotype: the lived experience of black and minority ethnic people in rural Wales

Vaughan Robinson and Hannah Gardner

Introduction

This chapter puts forward a very simple argument. It is that, in focusing on proving that black and minority ethnic people who live in rural areas suffer racism on a daily basis, academic research is in danger of unwittingly stereotyping those people and their lives. It is reducing them to the status of victims, and assuming a commonality in their lived experience, regardless of their personalities, nationalities, economic circumstances and where they live in the UK or within the countryside. This chapter, therefore, argues that now that the main contours of rural racism have been adequately charted, research needs to move on to the next task: demonstrating how, and explaining why, rural racism is not a monolithic entity that is the same everywhere and for every person. This argument will be illustrated by reference to the lived experience of black and minority ethnic residents of Powys in Mid-Wales, a diverse group of people who have led diverse lives in a distinctive place.

The contours of racism and racial harassment in urban and rural areas

The initial focus of research into racism in Britain was to demonstrate that the problem actually existed and required policies to challenge it. For example, Daniel's (1966) study sought to demonstrate that the black and Asian people who had arrived in Britain in the 1950s and 1960s did not receive the same treatment as their white counterparts and were systematically disadvantaged in the housing and labour markets by direct and indirect discrimination (Robinson and Valeny 2004). Smith's (1974) and Brown's (1984) second and third national surveys then told us more about the nature and impact of racism and made a strong case, both for further legislation and for more accurate monitoring of ethnic disadvantage, through the inclusion of an 'ethnicity question' for the first time in the 1991 Census. Not unnaturally, though, these pioneering studies concentrated on the experience of the urban black and minority ethnic (BME) population since, to use one particular example, seven out of every ten people in England and Wales describing their ethnicity as Pakistani lived in the seven largest conurbations (Robinson 1993a). Smith (1974) narrowed the focus of concern even further when he chose not only to oversample those black and Asian people who lived in cities, but to heavily oversample those found in the inner cities.

A different strand of research, which began in the 1980s, sought to focus not upon the structural position of the BME population in British society, but upon the impact of racism on the individual, particularly through racial harassment and racial violence. The Home Office's (1981) report *Racial Attacks* was the first to recognise these phenomena and to try to quantify their extent. It found, for example, that South Asian people were fifty times more likely to become victims of racially motivated incidents than white people. Following on from this, attempts were made to monitor the volume of such incidents, both through published police data and the British Crime Survey (BCS). Recent BCS analysis, for example, has estimated that 39,000 racially motivated incidents directed at ethnic minorities were reported in 1999 and that the risk of victimisation for a racially motivated incident was considerably less (0.3 per cent) for whites than it was for black people (2.2 per cent), Indians (3.6 per cent) or Pakistanis and Bangladeshis (4.2 per cent) (Clancy *et al.* 2001). However, it is now recognised that both police data and the BCS only record the most extreme forms of racial victimisation, and that there is another level of taken-for-granted or 'low-level' racial harassment that rarely appears in official data. The *Fourth National Survey of Ethnic Minorities* (Modood *et al.* 1997) attempted to provide a fuller picture by asking respondents about *all* forms of racial harassment, and Virdee (1997) used these data to estimate that over a quarter of a million people were subjected to some form of racial harassment in a 12-month period between 1993 and 1994.

Later still, academics turned their attention to the impact of racist victimisation upon people and their everyday lives. Chahal and Julienne (1999) interviewed 74 people in urban areas of the UK and found that 'the impact of racist victimisation had a profound effect beyond the actual event' (ibid.: vii) and that 'racist victimisation ... turns normal, daily activities into assessments of personal safety and security' (ibid.: 5). They described how one respondent had to hang her washing out at night-time so as to avoid an aggressively abusive neighbour.

However, if British academics were slow to chart racial harassment and its impact, they were even slower to address the issue of rural racism. Ingrid Pollard (1989) was one of the first to describe how BME people felt even more 'out of place' in the British countryside than they did in the inner cities. She used her photographs and their captions to describe how she felt an unwelcome visitor in the rural idyll, examples of which included 'walks through leafy glades with a baseball bat by my side', and 'the owners of these fields ... want me off their green and pleasant land ... they want me dead' (Pollard 1989: 42, 46). But only after the publication of Jay's (1992) seminal *Keep Them in Birmingham* did academics really take the issue of rural racism seriously. Jay had been commissioned by the CRE to study the extent, nature and impact of racism in the south-west of England. He concluded that BME people there felt threatened, isolated and vulnerable. He described how they experienced everyday racism and how their reaction had either been to leave the area, reduce their visibility or retreat into a compensatory stronger ethnic identity. His survey of service providers produced equally negative results, with institutions claiming either that there was 'no problem here' or that race relations were an issue only for parts of the country with sizeable BME populations.

Jay's work was subsequently replicated and confirmed by a series of other CRE-sponsored research projects (Derbyshire (1994) on Norfolk, Nizhar (1995) on Shropshire and de Lima (2001) on rural Scotland). Nizhar, for example, found clear evidence both of racist victimisation and of the unresponsiveness of officialdom, with one local government officer arguing that special services and support should not be provided for ethnic minorities because 'they should give up their identity and image and take on board white culture' (Nizhar 1995: 35).

Research on rural racism has since developed in four main ways. Firstly, some have studied why BME people not only feel out of place when they live in rural areas, but also when they visit rural areas for recreation and leisure (Agyeman 1989; Malik 1992). Secondly, additional studies have broadened the geographical coverage of the literature. Craig *et al.* (1999) considered Lincolnshire, for example, and pro-vocatively titled their report *We Shoot Them in Newark*, while Magne (2003) described the experience of racism and isolation for BME people living in rural Devon. Thirdly, a growing number of action-orientated researchers have looked at the policy responses to rural racism in various locations, especially in the light of the recommendations of the 1999 Macpherson Report and the subsequent Race Relations (Amendment) Act 2000. Most of these researchers also went on to make further recommendations for change. Henderson and Kaur (1999) identified the generic needs of rural BME populations and how these might best be met. Scourfield *et al.* (2002) made recommendations for initiatives in the South Wales Valleys. Both Dhalech (1999) and Magne (2003) have suggested how service providers in Devon could respond better to the problems experienced by the BME population there. Magne, for instance, suggested the appointment of community development workers to reach out into isolated areas and provide support directly and through the stimulation of multi-ethnic support networks. And, finally, a small number of researchers have focused specifically on the availability and quality of support services available to victims of racial harassment. Garland and Chakraborti (2002) studied rural Suffolk and made 32 recommendations to the County Council while praising its unique Racial Harassment Initiative, and Chahal (2003) considered the efficacy of racial harassment support projects, one of which was located in a rural area.

While this first phase of research on rural racism has thus given us a much clearer picture of the extent, nature and impact of racism and even described what is and what should be done about it, the literature has three main weaknesses.

First, much of the research to date has cast BME people in rural areas as victims. Casual reading of the literature on rural racism would leave a strong impression that all BME people in rural areas are unhappy, regretful, isolated, rejected and vulnerable victims of racial harassment, whose experiences are unremittingly negative. Undoubtedly there are mentions in the literature that BME people enjoy the 'peace and quiet' of the countryside or the lack of crime there (de Lima 2001), or the seaside and countryside of Devon (Magne 2003), or even the welcome received from some in the Welsh Valleys (Scourfield *et al.* 2002), but these positive experiences are overwhelmed by the accounts of 'perpetual', 'taken-for-granted', 'low-level' harassment and the psychological and behavioural adjustments to this. While for some people, racist victimisation can make their lives unbearable, we should be careful not to stereotype rural life and unthinkingly foreground the experience of some at the expense of others. Magne (2003), for example, recounts how two-thirds of her Devon sample had suffered racism, which presumably means that one-third had not.

Second, in our haste to demonstrate the existence of rural racism and the need for urgent policy responses to it, we have assumed that all black and minority ethnic people living in rural areas have the same experience despite their varied ages, incomes, qualifications, gender, nationality, religion, and reasons for moving to the countryside. Literatures that aim specifically to explore (and not just recognise) these variations within the minority ethnic population and how they may subsequently influence experiences are rare, with one exception being Scourfield *et al.* (2002), who describe how forms of racism faced by BME children differ according to class and gender, with young boys being the most likely to suffer.

Third, although research has been undertaken in a variety of rural locations, little research has yet considered the explicit role of place. Instead, there is assumed to be a single universal rural racism that exists in places as disparate as the Cotswolds and Welsh-speaking Mid-Wales, and which is characterised by the same manifestations. This is deeply paradoxical given that celebrating diversity is at the heart of post-modernist thinking and the 'cultural turn' in academia, and that those researching racism should be doing their best to challenge, not create, stereotypes. Again, however, there are exceptions. Robinson (1999, 2003) has considered the distinctiveness of Welsh rural racism, and Neal (2002) has begun to argue that there are not only fundamental differences between urban and rural racism but that there may also be parallel differences between different rural racisms.

Methodology

To advance the argument that there is more than one rural racism and that not every BME person living in rural areas suffers equally from this, this chapter will draw on material from a four-year project that has been completed as a joint venture between the authors and Powys Victim Support. This research was prompted by the success of Victim Support's helpline for those experiencing racial harassment in rural Powys (see Robinson 2003), and facilitated by funding from Powys County Council. Even though the helpline was only funded for six months and was only staffed one afternoon per week, it offered assistance to 65 people during that course of time. Victim Support Powys had thus identified both that minority people in Powys did have distinctive problems and needs, and that many local people and service providers denied these because they refused to acknowledge the local presence of a BME population.

The programme of research contained two main elements: a quantitative survey of white people living in Powys concerning their attitudes to national (i.e. UK) and local dimensions of 'race' and immigration; and an ethnographic and qualitative study of the lived experience of black and ethnic minority residents of Powys. Lack of space prevents us discussing the former, although it is covered thoroughly in Gardner (2004), Robinson and Gardner (forthcoming and Robinson and Gardner (2004)).

In order to capture the lived experience of black and ethnic minority residents of Powys, in-depth semi-structured qualitative interviews were undertaken with a variety of people from different parts of Powys. The selected sampling strategy was designed to capture a wide variety of experiences. Contact was made with those who had been victims of racial harassment and had reported it, those who had been victims and had not reported it, as well as those who had made no claims of victimisation whatsoever. Connecting with respondents was a lengthy process which involved snowballing from initial contacts, introductions by Victim Support, visiting schools, colleges and English-language classes, and working through 'community leaders'. Forty interviews were undertaken between October 2001 and August 2003, and they usually took place in the respondent's home, although interviewees were met in other locations when that was preferred. Interviews varied in length because people had very different stories to tell, but most lasted two hours, with some having a duration of six hours. These interviews sought to explore the lived experience of BME people in Powys, and a range of issues was covered in each, including motivations for rural living; expectations of rural living and life in Powys and whether these had been fulfilled; differences in attitudes towards 'race' in Wales and the impact of racism on everyday lives; service provision for ethnic minorities in Powys; the reporting of racial harassment; opinions on seeking help against racism; and people's hopes and plans for the future. The profile of respondents was designed to be as varied as possible to facilitate the unravelling of the stereotype of rural racism. Twenty-four were female and 16 were male, while nine were European, seven Black-Caribbean, seven South East Asian, six African, five Bangladeshi, three Indian, two Latin American, and one from the Middle East. The youngest was aged 15 while the oldest was 54, and their occupations varied from student to sculptor, with a range in between that included restaurant and hotel owners, waiter/waitress, housewives, a nurse, a pharmacist, a lawyer, a teacher and a graphic designer, to name but a few.

Black and minority ethnic people in Powys: a diverse population living in diverse rural places

Although the literature might give an alternative impression, the BME population of rural areas is by no means homogenous, nor does it live in homogenised 'rural space'. Rather, different people move to different rural areas for different reasons and with differing outcomes. It is this diversity of context and experience that we wish to explore in the remainder of the chapter by way of a challenge to the previous literature that has generalised the BME rural experience under the banner of rural racism.

The first dimension of this diversity is the variety of ethnic groups represented in Powys. Census data from 2001 tell us that the county has a BME population of 1,086, but that there is considerable diversity in the ethnic groups to which people recorded an allegiance. Even the largest ethnic group ('Other Asians') numbered only 21 per cent of the total BME population, and another four ethnic groups each individually formed more than 10 per cent of the BME population. In descending order, the largest ethnic groups in Powys were 'Chinese', 'Mixed: white and Asian', 'Other mixed' and 'Mixed: white and Black-Caribbean'. Furthermore, their distributions within Powys are rather different with, for example, the Chinese population being found in different wards to the Asian population.

Secondly, and rather obviously, Wales is not England! Evans *et al.*'s (2003) edited collection charts the past and present distinctiveness of 'ethnic' issues in Wales, and central to this are two myths. One is that migration has largely bypassed Wales, leaving it without the multi-cultural and multiracial character of its larger neighbour, and with a predominantly 'locally born' population. Robinson (2003) has shown how this myth cannot be supported by history, pointing to the sizeable migration of English and Irish people to Wales during industrialisation, the outflow of Welsh emigrants during the same period who neverthe-less maintained cultural links with the homeland, and the long history of ethnic minority settlement by colonial subjects. Williams (1998) described how Wales's BME population are often indigenous and have resided in Wales for many generations. Giggs and Pattie (1992) recounted how immigrants have travelled to Wales since the Middle Ages, with periods of increased immigration in the late eleventh century, during the Industrial Revolution and in postwar years. And Evans (2003) showed how it was not just the urban areas of Wales that attracted immigrants, but how ' "tranquil" rural Wales' became home to minority ethnic populations and the site of local resistance and prejudice. The other myth is that Wales is an inherently more tolerant society than its neighbour. Both Evans (1991) and Williams (1998) have debunked this myth by pointing to the history of intolerance towards immigrants and the per capita rate of racially motivated crime. However, although neither of these myths is true, they do shape both how the Welsh imagine themselves and the openness of their society. Williams (1998: 120), for example, has explained how people and policy-makers make 'the erroneous and dangerous assumption that there are few or no black and ethnic minority people in Wales'.

Thirdly, Wales differs from England in another important respect, namely the way in which 'ethnic issues' are defined. For many in Wales, the key axis of ethnic conflict is between the desire of the Welsh to maintain their culture, language and a distinctive Welsh 'heartland', and the arrival of English 'incomers' who bring with them a strong (and often unwelcome) 'anglicising' influence.

Fourthly, living in rural Mid-Wales is different for BME people because they can choose to integrate into either the 'Welsh' or 'Anglicised' versions of Welshness that exist due to past immigration patterns. For instance, in our sample a number of black and minority ethnic respondents proudly described themselves not as Black-Caribbean or Indian, but as Welsh, and a significant number were learning the language so as to participate more actively in Welsh culture.

Fifthly, Powys itself offers a variety of opportunities and possibilities as it is a very diverse county. Although it is the seventh largest county in England and Wales, it has the smallest population and is the most sparsely populated (Powys County Council website 2002): in other words, potentially the most isolated rural county in Wales and England. Even so, Powys contains former and current industrial settlements in the form of medium-sized towns, for example those at the head of the Swansea Valley, as well as Newtown and Welshpool further north. Therefore even though they live in a rural county, Powys' minority ethnic population actually resides in places which have very different characters, histories and economies.

Sixthly, minority ethnic residents of Powys have a variety of motivations for rural living. Many were born here (to the bewilderment of some 'locals'!), but those who have chosen to migrate have done so for reasons as disparate as a desire for a country lifestyle, the availability of economic opportunities or their partner or spouse being Welsh.

Finally, rural minority ethnic residents in Powys have often lived in diverse settings and had different past experiences. Some have lived in minority ethnic communities in multicultural cities such as Birmingham (the nearest large city to much of Powys) and London, others were born in Powys and have no experience of city living or multiculturalism, and yet others have come straight to Powys from their homelands.

Thus we can see that the BME population of Powys is not homogenous, either in its characteristics or its previous experience, and neither is it living in a homogenised rural space. Rather it has moved to different parts of a rural county that is both internally diverse and is sited within a nation that has a distinctive 'ethnic' agenda and immigration history.

Diverse experiences

This section unpicks the diverse experiences of BME people living in rural Powys and describes how this diversity precludes simple generalisation.

Not all bad news

Much of the literature on BME people in rural areas tends to label them as victims and focuses upon negatives: the name-calling, the isolation, the graffiti, the bullying and the attacks on property and person. We have no wish to deny that many people do suffer racism regularly, as witnessed by the following quotation:

> My aunt told me she'd been to the swimming pool one day in Rhayader and there was a hush when she entered the pool. Everyone just got out of the pool and they wouldn't get back in the pool after she [was] in there – she was with her children too. (Jamaican female[1])[2]

However, the authors also found that people had positive experiences that have been much less well reported. Favourable impressions of a rural idyll were often cited and these were contrasted with urban 'problems'. One respondent pointed out a particular benefit:

> At home – I know big city, I don't think maybe everyone welcome. I think people who live in the countryside are more welcoming, even more welcoming. (Chinese male)

A number of respondents commented on the way that the Welsh landscape offered them a more attractive setting for their lives, or a setting that reminded them of their familial homes. For example, one interviewee explained that he chose to live in Mid-Wales because of its similarity to the family farm in Bangladesh. Others said:

> It was when we visited Wales, I just fell in love with it and realised I wasn't a big city boy ... I love the Welsh countryside as it's not

synthetic, not so sanitised. The Welsh landscape is more rugged and natural. The landscape and rurality reminds me of when I grew up in Rhodesia. (Greek male)

I am very glad to be in Wales because I used to live in France close to mountains, big mountains, and I don't like flat ground. I love the ground in Wales, and around Llandrindod. (French male)

A significant number of interviewees commented about how they made a therapeutic connection with the environment through walking and cycling, and how this provided them with a sense of release and emotional peace, as one woman explained:

I like mountains, it's so good for me … I like nature as well. I like mountains and riding bicycles and sport and things like this. And now everything I can do because it is beautiful. (Portuguese female)

Another theme that arose in interviews was the perceived benefit arising from having being born in, or having lived in Wales for a significant period of time and the consequent acquisition of a dual identity. As one person stated:

I'd say I'm sort of Afro Celtic. That's a brilliant way of describing what my roots are. I'm Welsh and I'm very proud of it, but I also have Caribbean blood which is brilliant. I have a great love of both those cultures. I really don't have a problem with any of it. (Female interviewee of dual heritage)

One woman actively promoted her dual identity in Wales:

I want to promote my ethnicity, you know, I'm black and Welsh, I have a Welsh identity and I have a Welsh accent. I want to learn the language. I love being different and having two cultures. My family started the Caribbean Club here. We are proud to share our culture. (Jamaican female (2))

Indeed, many interviewees were also proud of their Welsh accents and took particular enjoyment from the 'surprised' reactions of 'locals' when they conversed in shops, especially in areas where they were not personally known. Elaborating upon the individual benefits of having dual identities, one man explained how local inhabitants also recognised and respected their cultural diversity and difference:

People sort of perceive you as being more cultural I think: you have got some sort of background, you got a [different] history, whereas they [the Welsh] have got exactly the same history. (Turkish male)

For some minority ethnic residents, being 'different' was perceived as creating social benefits. Some interviewees enjoyed standing out, being 'exotic', and welcomed the increased attention that they could garner as a result, as illustrated by the following comments:

In south London I would be just another black geezer, here I am a celebrity. (Jamaican male)

To be black and to live in [rural] Wales means something, whereas in Birmingham, you know, to see a black person it doesn't mean anything, it doesn't mean anything at all. (Trinidadian male)

Another interviewee noticed how local inhabitants were attracted to her 'mysteriousness', suggesting that '[local men] were just amazed at me you know, a gorgeous black woman! They'd never seen one before'. Another interviewee had even made a successful career out of her 'exoticism' by becoming a professional belly dancer. She recounted how 'people often used to call me a wild woman ... I found immense pleasure in that! I've never experienced racism when I was actually going out on jobs.'

For some, living in a rural area had been consciously chosen because of its isolation, and for others living outside an ethnic area offered freedom from the restrictions of community rules and expectation. As one person commented:

Those were tough times I think because home-wise your parents were really strict [on] what you could do, what you couldn't do, whereas now it doesn't really matter. You couldn't go out after eight o'clock at night and seeing girls was impossible – especially if it was an Asian girl. We were so restricted. I have total freedom now. (Bangladeshi male (1))

The following string of conversation highlights the sense of frustration that has now been left behind:

Interviewer: Was that good for you, do you think, initially [living in Bangladeshi community in London]?
Respondent: No ... because those people who are from Bangladesh

95

in this country, most, a high per cent of people from our district, can't read and I wanted to progress.

I: Could you tell me more?

R: They're not people like me, most of them are illiterate, so there is a massive difference between them and me. My status, the social status of my family is good, but I had to talk to the people, those who can't speak English. My environment, my colleagues, my classmates, my room-mates, all are educated. So I did have lots of problems. Not now though, in rural areas I have to speak English to everybody – I prefer. (Bangladeshi male (2))

Indeed, for some, part of the motivation for the move to rural Wales was to interact with 'different people' and reduce the chance of meeting those from their ancestral homeland. As one student put it:

I want to learn English and I want to mix with British people. I am not interested to interact with anybody from home – that would be cheating. (Nepalese male)

Different rural racisms and the uniqueness of Wales

Some of our respondents commented on how they had received a welcome in Wales that was particularly warm, and sometimes unexpected, as two respondents stated:

Here everybody's smiling to you on the street. In the shop, they are smiling. I am going to town and they keep smiling at me. I don't know, at times I thought, 'Do I know these people? Do I smile or not?' Everybody's very kind. (Iraqi female)

I was worried about it [coming to rural Wales]. But it was a surprise. It was better than England, nice people here and they wanted to help me. So really I still feel very good, like at home really. (Spanish female)

For some, such welcoming sentiments were felt to be the product of the unique politics of migration in Wales, that saw English incomers cast as the 'unwelcome outsiders', a role which they were themselves more used to occupying. 'It is easier to be a foreigner here, than it is to be English', commented one respondent. Or as another said:

I feel I fit in the equation better than an English person does. I am better off. I am in a much better position to move to Wales than an

English person ... There is more hatred for the English person to come and live in Wales ... I can tell from my own experience as an Asian coloured person coming to move into Wales. (Bangladeshi male (1))

Others commented on how their treatment depended upon exactly who they were interacting with in rural Wales. A significant number of minority ethnic individuals were able to distinguish between English in-comers and Welsh inhabitants, with the former recognised as being less receptive towards a minority ethnic presence in the countryside. The following individual summarised this dynamic, and also differences in tolerance within the host population:

The English, they themselves are the outsiders. You get the middle-class people who have moved from the Midlands or London or somewhere like that. They have come out of there probably, there have been a lot of Asian people or they are fed up with the hustle and bustle of life, and they come to move to Wales for the location and fewer Asian people, so they [the English] do have a resentment, it has happened to me. The Welsh are more tolerant people. I think they are – I speak as I find. (Indian female)

Another person expanded on this theme, highlighting a frequently cited view that English in-migrants are not just intolerant, but form a significant proportion of the perpetrators of racism:

The racism I find now is coming from the people who moved in. The English. They look at me. They don't want [me]. They start abusing me. (Jamaican female (3))

The racism and prejudice of some in-migrants is not a new issue. Jay (1992: 22) described how some incomers in south-west England defined themselves as 'refugees from multiracialism'. Derounian (1993: 71) commented upon the 'hardcore (urban in-migrants to rural areas) who believe they have left blacks behind in the city', and Neal (2002) cited evidence of a 'white flight' attitude on the part of some urban/rural migrants. In the context of Wales, Parker (2001) describes how the English leader of the British National Party has moved into north Powys and made Montgomery the centre of the party's activities, and how many of the incomers from Birmingham have brought their racism with them. Clearly then, the socio-cultural characteristics of different rural places across Britain make the minority ethnic experience more complex and changeable, with rural racism being expressed in different places through different social processes and being suffered in different ways, and thus rural racism in Powys is but one of many variants.

Distance and isolation

Another factor which seemed to shape rural life for BME people was the extent of their geographical isolation. Those living some distance from major towns described a different experience from those who had access to facilities and services. Rural Mid-Wales is a particularly sparsely settled part of the UK and produced a particular reaction in our respondents. They commented that the distances they had to travel, the mountainous landscape of Powys and the often poor weather (especially around the Brecon Beacons) can create a foreboding and very solitary existence, as one interviewee commented:

> Usually I'm really easy going ... then with the weather outside, it was not easy to meet people or to go outside. I couldn't walk far because of the rain and I had no car at all. I was trapped in the house really. (Lithuanian female)

There are numerous examples from interviews conducted of how such geographically isolating landscapes can contribute toward social isolation, particularly where individuals either cannot drive or do not have access to a vehicle. One interviewee recounted how their nearest significant town is Swansea, and how visiting there involves a round trip of eight hours on a train. They explained how this has become a regular excursion for them, in order either to go to the cinema or take the children to McDonald's.

The particular geography of Wales, and the widespread acknowledgement of its influence on all aspects of rural life, can negatively impact upon experiences in other important ways. For some, isolation takes on an additional dimension. Parts of Powys are also a considerable distance from most English cities which are the centres of settlement for the UK's BME population. Those who have moved to the more remote parts of Powys therefore often face long and difficult journeys when they want to visit family or friends back in England. This social isolation further heightens geographical isolation, as one person recounted:

> If I was Welsh I would have my family around me. They have their family near them so they can see their family. I called my mum [in Birmingham] a few times and said that I just want to go home. I'm

not happy. I'm on my own. I have no car. I felt alone for about a year. (Thai female)

Remoteness and isolation therefore affects and even worsens experiences by fuelling depression, and this can be accentuated by distance from family help and contact.

Economic leverage

A further factor which leads to a diversity in experiences for BME people in rural areas is their relative access to power or position. Our research suggests that individuals who tended to have the more positive experiences also occupied key economic and community roles. Those who were central to the local economy or, by virtue of this, central to the local community felt more included and respected. They felt that they were accepted because they had shown a commitment to the locality and its people, and perhaps also because they were in a stronger position to control the situation and disadvantage those who expressed racism. Both of these points are illustrated in the following quotation:

> As a landlady, I know all the locals, all the locals know me, I have a lot of interaction with the community. People know me, they know my principles, they know my behaviour … we had started running the local pub so … it wasn't a case of [people] sitting back and thinking 'Oh yeah, there's a new family moved in down the road' or whatever – they had to come in the pub. (Trinidadian female)

The actions of an Asian shopkeeper exemplify the latter point. He simply banned anyone from the shop who abused him, and since his was the only store for miles, perpetrators soon changed their behaviour. In many cases, interviewees stated that 'standing out' has been of economic benefit, as one local businessman stated:

> From a business point of view, part of my success is because I am different – because you are in a minority, sometimes you have to try that much harder to fit in. I have fitted in well with Welsh society because I have not alienated or segregated myself – because of that I am accepted as a service provider. (Bangladeshi male (1))

These examples show how discourses of a hegemonic rural white middle class *are* being challenged by black and minority ethnic individuals

99

becoming key members of village communities and carving out strong footholds in local businesses and social networks.

Personality

Experiences and the degree to which they were (and were thought to be) positive or negative also seemed to depend upon the outlook and personality of the individual in question. Many interviewees explained that, although they may face racism 'daily' or 'quite regularly', this need only be a problem if they allowed it to be. For example, one woman highlighted her own perception:

> I genuinely don't think anybody looks at my colour ... if people stare or point I think they are looking at me because I am an attractive woman. (Trinidadian female)

For some interviewees, it was felt that their personality and confidence had contributed to their acceptance and had decreased the chances of suffering hostility, as one person explained:

> We were accepted because we are very much outgoing you know, we would mingle with people and we would go out of our way to make sure that we were OK with everybody. We took it on ourselves to make sure we were accepted. I don't take remarks personally – not everybody will like you in life, whatever your colour. (Mauritian male)

Another person stated that his confidence had increased even more because of the attention he receives:

> I'm an extrovert, I like attention, it's just me being me. But the fact that I get noticed for literally doing nothing I see only as a good thing! If somebody notices me because I am black then fair enough, yeah, I just play on it. I don't mind getting noticed. That's just me at the end of the day. (Trinidadian male)

In contrast, one interviewee felt more vulnerable or sensitive to racism and believed that she would have felt the same regardless of whether she lived in a rural or urban environment 'because of my personality as well as ... being quite inward and quite self aware'.

Other interviewees felt they had had to suppress their personalities to achieve acceptance in rural communities. They had chosen to project a less confident and assertive persona so as not to appear to be 'taking over' or a threat, as one interviewee tellingly explained:

> I am in a better position because I don't try to join any of the groups … if you try to push into any group, they close ranks. If you are invited to join the group, it's different. I am, as I say, a floater! (Jamaican female (3))

Thus there appear to be various ways of coping with the experiences of rural living. Different people have adopted different personal strategies, ranging from challenging racists through to adopting a low profile out of keeping with their natural personality.

Social demography

Initial research findings from rural Mid-Wales have found that some minority ethnic individuals undergo double marginalisation/isolation because of their socio-demographics. They are marginalised or excluded because of their ethnicity and also because of other characteristics such as age or gender.

Children and young people appeared particular targets of racism, contrary to idyllised notions of rural childhoods, as the following individuals described:

> I actually thought that the [rural] people would be really nice, people would be really friendly, but no it wasn't like that because they only saw the skin colour and not the feeling. My whole life I actually … was this victim, the victim of hatred … I felt so isolated, I experienced racism everyday – like going into the playground, boys would say 'Paki, Paki'. I didn't go on school trips because of it. It shattered my self-esteem, I thought about suicide, that was my depth of sadness, and to this day my self-esteem is affected. I go to the gym a lot and I use weights – perhaps deep down it is something saying you have to be stronger to confront people mentally and physically. (Indian female)

> My son [aged ten] had this boy threatening to kill him, you know, to stab him in the head with his knife. He gets stones thrown at him, name calls. In Birmingham all the kids in our area were black. To us that was normal, but to them here it was totally shockable. It just shows you how different people are down here. (Female interviewee with dual heritage children)

These voices show how prolonged racism can impact on the everyday lives and routine of some young minority ethnic people as well as taking its toll on their mental well-being. The quotations also highlight how racism and its effects are different in rural areas because BME children are so visible in otherwise white communities. For some, visibility can produce benefits, as one father explained:

> I feel my children are quite better off than most really. In school they are the only coloured children and they are well respected, they take part in all the school plays and seem to get better roles! They are taking part in all sorts of social activities and things like that and they have lots of friends. (Bangladeshi female)

However, for most, visibility forced modifications to behaviour. One child talked about learning to 'keep out of the way', while for another it had meant being sent to a private school rather than a state school. He felt that 'If I went to a comprehensive school, I think it would have been a very, very different story. I guess I was lucky to go to a private school.'

Experiences of rural living were also gendered as it appears that women often confront racism within the domestic sphere and arguably become marginalised because of this. For example, some minority ethnic mothers felt very isolated, describing feelings of being 'trapped in the house', being unable to speak sufficient English, not having relatives nearby who could help with childcare, being unable to drive, and having few opportunities to meet people and make friends. For some women, racism also has a particular personal impact because it related to their physical appearance:

> People always go back to the same thing, 'Oh you're black, you look like a monkey, you're an ape', that sort of expression is quite common ... I just want the earth to swallow me up. (Female interviewee of dual heritage)

This perception of how racism might affect women differently from men was also commented upon by one individual, who explained how being a visible minority ethnic person in a rural area 'made a difference to my sister now [as opposed to the experience of living in an urban area], but I think that's just her being a girl'. In contrast, men were often subjected to racism within the public and work environment:

> In the kitchen, the relationship between the kitchen and the waiters is tense and sometimes I heard 'bloody French' or 'moody French' unpleasantness sometimes. (Republic of Congo male)

However, for the following man, racism in the workplace was more than the odd racist comment:

I: Tell me about your situation in work.

R: They bully, you understand, some of them. Look for mistakes.

I: How did it make you feel?

R: Well I felt bad. They talk about you in their own language.

I: In Welsh?

R: In Welsh if they want to talk about you.

I: How long did this continue?

R: Three months.

I: How did it affect you?

R: You are emotionally distraught. It affects your routine. It affects you, all the things you are doing. They report that you've done this, you've done that. You're too slow. It certainly affected my work. It played on me psychologically.

(Nigerian male)

Thus, although the effects of racism (and the emotions associated with suffering it) are shared by both genders, it appears that the instances and contexts of racism may be different for men and women.

Religion and skin colour also appear to be important personal characteristics that shape experiences of rural racism. Initial findings indicate that visible ethnic and religious groups face greater overt racism, as one Polish woman explained: 'When they [new residents] are black or they have different colours of skin, it's much more difficult … people will be afraid of them.' This situation was also commented upon by another eastern European resident, as illustrated in the following observation:

I have been to the library many times and see people like me from abroad, some black people, some people from Asia, and I know this many times that people stare and act different. That doesn't happen to me and they know I am foreign too. (Hungarian female)

However, even among those minorities that were visibly different, experiences varied, with three groups in particular having very different stories. For the Bangladeshi community the majority of racism took the form of 'usual' comments and 'drunken ramblings' in restaurants on a Friday and Saturday night which they did not take seriously. However, during the week, local behaviour is very warm towards them, something that was commented upon by several respondents, for example: 'A lot of people know me and know I work in the restaurant and say hello when I go out shopping.' Another group who appear to live through a particular form of rural racism are those of dual heritage, as the following quotation reveals:

My sister has problems because she's half-caste. She's quite a lot whiter than I am but you can see black in her features and she gets picked on … people call her nigger when she is not even black. So she's really conscious of herself and her features. My sister was offered tickets to go back to the Caribbean from the family for a holiday and she turned it down because she feels too white. (Male interviewee with sister of dual heritage)

A third group are those thought by local people to be asylum seekers dispersed to Powys under the arrangements introduced in the Asylum and Immigration Act of 1999 (see Robinson *et al.* 2003), as one person explained: 'The problem I am having now is like I am outside sweeping on the steps and a car pulls up, and this man starts abusing me because I'm an asylum seeker.' Because of this, some minority ethnic people have, themselves, become resentful toward asylum seekers:

I blame my racism on asylum seekers. I think everybody knows the reason I am here and that's never been important to me until recently with all the problems with those people coming into the country, illegal immigrants and that, and not wanting them. (Jamaican female (3))

Conclusions

To summarise, the majority of the literature concerning ethnic relations in the UK has paid attention to the experiences of those BME people who live in England's largest conurbations and cities. This is understandable, given that 96.2 per cent of the UK's BME population resides in England, and that at least two-thirds of most of the largest minority ethnic groups live within its five largest cities (ONS 2003; Robinson 1993b). Nevertheless, census data and local studies have indicated that the black and minority ethnic population of rural areas is growing, propelled by the same trend to counter-urbanisation evident within the white population. For example, Magne (2003) has shown how the BME population of rural Devon has doubled between 1991 and 2001. However, our knowledge about the lived experience of these BME pioneers in rural areas is deficient in two ways. Firstly, the literature has for the most part only acknowledged their presence through accounts of how they have been victimised by white people and how they have been excluded from access to services and facilities, and secondly, many of the accounts we have pay insufficient attention to the diversity of the BME population in rural areas and the diversity of their lives. This chapter has therefore sought to unpick the dual stereotypes of BME people as victims and as an homogenous group about which it is easy to generalise, and to look at difference *within* rural areas.

Another major focus of this chapter has been to demonstrate how the BME rural experience is not only person-specific but also place-specific. In so doing, we have tried to unpick the conventional generalisations about BME rural experiences that fail to acknowledge the uniqueness of the local politics of inmigration, 'race' and identity, or the uniqueness of local cultural and community dynamics. We have therefore used our case study to make the point that rural racism in Wales is but one of a number of contemporary rural racisms that exist within the UK, and that differences *between* rural areas deserve more explicit attention than they have hitherto been given.

Notes

1   Due to the particularly low BME populations of some parts of Wales covered in the research, it was felt that the inclusion of interviewees' areas of residence would compromise the anonymity of respondents in certain cases.
2   In instances where there is more than one interviewee with the same ethnicity and gender, a difference has been indicated accordingly to distinguish the different respondents.

References

Ageyman, J. (1989) 'Black People, White Landscape', *Town and Country Planning*, 58 (12): 336–8.
Brown, C. (1984) *Black and White Britain*. London: Policy Studies Institute.
Chahal, K. (2003) *Racist Harassment Support Projects: Their Role, Impact and Potential*. York: Joseph Rowntree Foundation.
Chahal, K. and Julienne, L. (1999) *'We Can't All Be White!' Racist Victimisation in the UK*. York: Joseph Rowntree Foundation.
Clancy, A., Hough, M., Aust, R. and Kershaw, C. (2001) *Crime, Policing and Justice: The Experience of Ethnic Minorities. Findings from the 2000 British Crime Survey*, Home Office Research Study 223. London: Home Office.

Craig, G., Ahmed, B. and Amery, F. (1999) '"We Shoot Them in Newark!" The Work of the Lincolnshire Forum for Racial Justice', in P. Henderson and R. Kaur (eds), *Rural Racism in the UK: Examples of Community-Based Responses*. London: Community Development Foundation.

Daniel, W. (1966) *Racial Discrimination in England*. Harmondsworth: Penguin.

de Lima, P. (2001) *Needs Not Numbers: An Exploration of Minority Ethnic Communities in Scotland*. London: Commission for Racial Equality and Community Development Foundation.

Derbyshire, H. (1994) *Not in Norfolk: Tackling the Invisibility of Racism*. Norwich: Norwich and Norfolk Racial Equality Council.

Derounian, J. (1993) *Another Country: Real Life Beyond Rose Cottage*. London: National Council for Voluntary Organisations.

Dhalech, M. (1999) *Challenging Racism in the Rural Idyll: Final Report*. Exeter: National Association of Citizens' Advice Bureaux.

Evans, N. (1991) 'Immigrants and Minorities in Wales 1840–1990: A Comparative Perspective', *Llafur*, 4 (5): 5–26.

Evans, N. (2003) 'Immigrants and Minorities in Wales, 1840–1990: A Comparative Perspective', in N. Evans, P. O'Leary and C. Williams (eds), *A Tolerant Nation? Exploring Ethnic Diversity in Wales*. Cardiff: University of Wales Press.

Evans, N., O'Leary, P. and Williams, C. (2003) *A Tolerant Nation? Exploring Ethnic Diversity in Wales*. Cardiff: University of Wales Press.

Gardner, H. (2004) 'The Lived Experiences of Black and Minority Ethnic Groups in Rural Mid-Wales'. Unpublished PhD thesis, University of Wales Swansea.

Garland, J. and Chakraborti, N. (2002) *Tackling the Invisible Problem? An Examination of the Provision of Services to Victims of Racial Harassment*. Leicester: Scarman Centre, University of Leicester.

Giggs, J. and Pattie, C. (1992) 'Wales as a Plural Society', *Contemporary Wales*, 5, 24–63.

Henderson, P. and Kaur, R. (eds) (1999) *Rural Racism in the UK: Examples of Community-Based Responses*. London: Community Development Foundation.

Home Office (1981) *Racial Attacks*. London: Home Office.

Jay, E. (1992) *Keep Them in Birmingham: Challenging Racism in South West England*. London: Commission for Racial Equality.

Jones, O. (1997) 'Little Figures, Big Shadows: Country Childhood Stories', in P. Cloke and J. Little (eds), *Contested Countryside Cultures: Otherness, Marginalisation, and Rurality*. London: Routledge.

Magne, S. (2003) *Multi-Ethnic Devon: A Rural Handbook – The Report of the Devon and Exeter Racial Equality Council's Rural Outreach Project*. Devon: Devon and Exeter Racial Equality Council.

Malik, S. (1992) 'Colours of the Countryside: A Whiter Shade of Pale', *Ecos*, 13 (4): 33–40.

Modood, T., Berthoud, R., Lakey, J., Nazroo, J., Smith, P., Virdee, S. and Beishon, S. (1997) *Ethnic Minorities in Britain: Diversity and Disadvantage*. London: Policy Studies Institute.

Neal, S. (2002) 'Rural Landscapes, Representations and Racism: Examining Multicultural Citizenship and Policy-Making in the English Countryside', *Ethnic and Racial Studies*, 25 (3): 442–61.

Nizhar, P. (1995) *No Problem? Race Issues in Shropshire*. Telford: Race Equality Forum for Telford and Shropshire.

Office for National Statistics (ONS) (2003) *Census 2001: Key Statistics for Local Authorities in England and Wales*. London: Stationery Office.

Parker, M. (2001) 'Loaded Dice', *Planet: The Welsh Internationalist*, 148, 7–13.

Pollard, I. (1989) 'Pastoral Interludes', *Third Text*, 7, 41–6.

Robinson, V. (1993a) 'The Enduring Geography of Ethnic Settlement: First Results from the 1991 Census', *Town and Country Planning*, 62, 53–6.

Robinson, V. (1993b) 'Making Waves? The Contribution of Ethnic Minorities to Local Demography', in T. Champion (ed.), *Population Matters: The Local Dimension*. London: Paul Chapman Publishing.

Robinson, V. (1999) 'Neither Here Nor There: Refugees in Wales', *Contemporary Wales*, 12, 200–13.

Robinson, V. (2003) 'Exploring Myths about Rural Racism: a Welsh Case-Study', in N. Evans, P. O'Leary and C. Williams (eds), *A Tolerant Nation? Exploring Ethnic Diversity in Wales*. Cardiff: University of Wales Press.

Robinson, V. and Gardner, H. (2004) *Anybody out there? Minority ethnic people in Powys and their experiences*, Migration Unit Research Paper 18, University of Wales Swansea, Swansea.

Robinson, V. and Gardner, H. (forthcoming) 'Place matters: exploring the distinctiveness of racism in rural Wales', J. Agyeman and S. Neal (eds.) *The new countryside?: Ethnicity, nation and exclusion in contemporary rural Britain*, Policy Press, Bristol.

Robinson, V. and Valeny, R. (2004) 'Ethnic Minorities, Employment, Self-Employment and Social Mobility in Post-War Britain', in S. Teles and T. Modood (eds), *Race, Ethnicity and Public Policy in the US and UK*. Cambridge: Cambridge University Press.

Robinson, V., Andersson, R. and Musterd, S. (2003) *Spreading the Burden? European Policies to Disperse Asylum Seekers*. Bristol: Policy Press.

Scourfield, J., Beynon, H., Evans, J. and Shah, W. (2002) *Not a Black and White Issue: The Experiences of Black and Minority Ethnic Children Living in the South Wales Valleys*. Cardiff: Barnardos Cymru.

Smith, D. (1974) *Racial Disadvantage in Britain*. Harmondsworth: Penguin.

Virdee, S. (1997) 'Racial Harassment', in T. Modood, R. Berthoud, J. Lakey, J. Nazroo, P. Smith, S. Virdee and S. Beishon, *Ethnic Minorities in Britain: Diversity and Disadvantage*. London: Policy Studies Institute.

Williams, C. (1998) ' "Race" and Racism: Some Reflections on the Welsh Context', *Contemporary Wales*, 8, pp. 113–31.

Chapter 5

Cultures of Hate in the urban and the rural: assessing the impact of extremist organisations

Paul Iganski and Jack Levin

In applying a spatial analysis of hate crimes in both the United States and the United Kingdom, this chapter compares the locational dynamics of hate in the city and hate out of town. The little research that there is on the characteristics and motivations of hate crime offenders focuses on incidents in the city, suggesting perhaps that hate crime, and more specifically racist crime, is principally a feature of mobile and diverse metropolitan societies. Incidents in rural areas, and in small towns in such localities, rarely make the headlines in Britain, perhaps because there have been few cases that match the severity of some of the notorious hate incidents in London such as the murder of Stephen Lawrence who was stabbed to death on a street in south London in 1993, or Ricky Reel, who was found dead in the River Thames in West London in 1997 seven days after he and his friends were racially abused and attacked. In contrast, some notorious 'out-of-town' hate crimes in the United States achieved particular notoriety – perhaps due to the brutality involved.

The murder of James Byrd, an African-American, who was beaten unconscious, chained to the back of a pickup truck and dragged for miles along rural roads outside the town of Jasper, Texas in June 1998, attracted widespread media coverage. The brutality of the murder, and the fact that two of the perpetrators were members of a white supremacist organisation, evoked painful memories of lynching and historical racist violence in the United States. The callousness of the attack on the young gay man Matthew Shepard in Wyoming in October 1998, who was pistol-whipped and left lashed to a fence in freezing conditions to die later in hospital, generated considerable public and political debate about homophobic bigotry.

These incidents are some of the most extreme examples of crimes that have come to be labelled as 'hate crime': crimes in which the victim is selected by the offender because of some characteristic of their identity such as their 'race', ethnicity, sexuality, gender or religious belief. Following a brief analysis of the aetiology of racist hate crimes in urban areas, this chapter focuses upon the impact and popularity of white supremacist and far-right organisations in rural areas of the US and UK and how they fuel climates of hatred. We chart the history of extremist organisations in the US and assess how their ideas have found resonance among discontented rural communities. We also examine recent attempts by far-right parties in the UK to gain a political foothold in the countryside. The chapter concludes by suggesting that, while only a small percentage of racist hate crimes are carried out by members of extremist parties, individual acts of racism in rural areas may be symptomatic of cultures of bigotry evident in the wider community that extremist parties serve to inflame.

'Hate' in the city: defending neighbourhoods

Scholarship aimed at understanding the context, causes, motivations and consequences of so-called 'hate crime' is in its infancy, and it has been mainly limited in the UK and the US to crime in urban areas. Given the paucity of research there has been much speculation, and numerous explanations have been offered for the actions of 'hate crime' offenders, ranging from drunken pranks, social and economic crises, incitement by the media and many others. Given the range of victims of hate crimes, the variety of offenders involved and the different social situations in which they occur, there can obviously be no single explanation, and in any one incident there may be a range of explanations. It is instructive nevertheless to review some of the observations from the existing body of research as it illuminates processes that are likely to be at work out of town and in rural areas, as it shows that the geography of space and place clearly matters for understanding racist victimisation as experienced by offenders and victims.

In one of the few studies of the motivational dynamics of 'hate crime' offenders McDevitt *et al.* (2002) identified a 'defensive' logic at work (see also Levin and McDevitt 1993). They analysed 169 hate crimes in Boston covering the period July 1991 to December 1992 using police files on cases in which there was a known offender or suspect. One quarter of the crimes reportedly were committed, from the offender's prejudiced point of view, in order to protect his neighbourhood from those he considered to be 'outsiders or intruders'. The objective in some of these crimes 'was to convince the outsider to relocate elsewhere and also to send a message to other members of the victim's group that they too were not welcome in the neighbourhood' (McDevitt *et al.* 2002: 308).

Such crimes might be seen as an exclusionary process with a segregationist objective. These territorial dynamics of exclusion are, according to Hesse *et al.* (1992), a manifestation of 'white territorialism' whereby racist victimisation is an expression for the offenders of a sense of ownership, or propriety, of geographic space that they regard as 'white territory'. The presence and difference of the 'other', the 'outsider', is seen as a threat to the traditional spatial identity, or the 'ethnoscape', of the area.

It would seem to be logical that the greater the homogeneity of a community and the greater the community's identity is bound up with a locality, the greater the threat will be from those perceived to be 'outsiders' when they trespass on the territory of the 'insiders'. Research carried out by Donald Green and colleagues provides some statistical support to this logic (Green *et al.* 1998). Their analysis of hate crime data from the New York Police Department Bias Crime Unit for 1987–95 shows an association between racially motivated crime and demographic change. There is an evident rise in hate incidents when 'non-whites' move into traditionally white strongholds. The rate of increase of racially motivated incidents is positively correlated with the rate of 'non-white' migration into areas that are numerically traditionally white. Areas with larger and more established minority communities were observed to experience fewer incidents.

The analysis of hate crime data for New York City by Green, Glaser and Rich, and their additional analysis of time series data on lynchings in the United States (Green *et al.* 1998) has not found, in their words, 'a robust relationship' between hate crime and economic conditions. In a separate study, Green, Strolovitch and Wong (1998: 398) further concluded that 'racially motivated crime emanates not from macroeconomic conditions but rather from threats to turf guarded by a homogeneous group'.

Qualitative research in England and in the United States has, however, reported a combination of spatial and economic conditions in the aetiology of racially motivated crime. It also goes some way to bridge the link between the societal, or macrosociological, context of hate crime and microsociological explanations for the actions of individuals and groups of hate crime offenders. Larry Ray, David Smith and Liz Wastell (2003) (see also Ray and Smith 2002) draw on interviews with 64 offenders in contact with the probation service in Greater Manchester, England, to produce a variant of the frustration–aggression thesis (cf. Dollard *et. al.* 1938) to explain the motivations of offenders. Half of the offenders in their sample were unemployed, and those with jobs were generally in low-paid, low-skilled, casual or insecure work. Half had left school with no qualifications and half had convictions for other offences. In this context Ray and colleagues argue that much of the violence is related to the sense of shame and failure, resentment and hostility felt by young men who 'are disadvantaged and marginalised economically and culturally, and thus deprived of the material basis for enacting a traditional conception of working-class masculinity.' Such emotions, apparently, 'readily lead to violence only in the case of young men (and occasionally for young women) for whom resorting to violence is a common approach to settling arguments and conflicts' (Ray *et al.* 2003: 112). Ray and colleagues suggest that inclinations to such behaviour are widely shared among residents of disadvantaged neighbourhoods on the outskirts of Manchester.

They report that often the only contact offenders had with their victim's group was in commercial transactions – with shopkeepers and taxi-drivers, for instance. In these interactions offenders were faced with people who were more economically successful, but perceived to be undeservedly so because they were seen to be unfairly advantaged by stronger cultural bonds and kinship networks. Envy added to the emotional cocktail. Victims were scapegoated by offenders essentially looking for someone to blame for their situation. Ray and colleagues (2003: 125) suggest that:

> Against a background of the routine, taken-for-granted racism that characterised their neighbourhoods, and in the context of a shared sense of being invisible and ignored, young men and more rarely young women for whom violence is an accessible and habitual cultural resource will readily identify those who are visibly different and visibly (or apparently) more successful as the causes of their shame and humiliation.

The economic and structural context of racially motivated crime was also observed by Howard Pinderhughes (1993) from research with youths in New York City in 1990. Eleven focus groups were conducted with 88 youths attending a youth programme in southern Brooklyn working with white delinquents. The research revealed a combination of factors in the aetiology of racially motivated crime: structural, ethnic and racist attitudes, peer group dynamics and 'community sentiment'. Pinderhughes used a qualitative approach to tease out the interaction between structural, emotional and cultural forces behind offending. The youths in the study were economically marginalised and frustrated given limited job prospects in local and available labour markets. They perceived themselves to be victims of policy and practice that favoured minorities (an observation also made by Ray *et al.* 2003), reverse discrimination and growing black political power in the city. Living in economically disadvantaged neighbourhoods they saw themselves under siege and their attacks against blacks and other 'outsiders' instrumentally constituted a mission to maintain the ethnoscape of their neighbourhood. The hostile and potentially dangerous reputation of the neighbourhoods was well-known throughout the city and served as a deterrent against members of minority communities visiting and settling in the areas.

'Hate' out of town: defending turf

Taken as a whole, the small body of research on hate crime in urban settings suggests a number of logical propositions for developing an understanding of racially motivated crime in small town and rural environments. First, where there is a largely homogeneous local community on ethnic lines with a deep-seated traditional sense of identity attached to their locality, there will be a strong sense of who belongs and who does not: who is an 'insider' and who is an 'outsider'. Outsiders will be stigmatised by labels that express a sense of rivalry for those with only benign intent, and exclusionary sentiment for those with more malign feelings. The labels are likely to be incomprehensible to the outsiders, but for insiders they are laden with meaning. In Cornwall, in south-west England, for instance, outsiders are 'Emmets' and in nearby Devon they are 'Grockles': both derogatory terms have a long historical provenance. A second logical proposition is that when a sense of loss or grievance – perhaps a perceived erosion of cultural tradition, or on a material level the loss and decline of local industry and employment – is added to the cocktail, then bigotry against 'outsiders' is more likely to surface as they are scapegoated for the malaise. Third, when such areas also experience in-migration of outsiders then the environments provide fertile ground for the mobilisation of hatred. The history of organised racist groups in rural areas and small towns in the United States exemplifies these processes at work as shown by the case of the Ku Klux Klan and also the so-called Patriot movement and Militia groups.

The Ku Klux Klan began in 1865, in the aftermath of the civil war, at first as a social fraternity for ex-Confederate officers and later as a white supremacist organisation whose major purpose was to terrorise newly freed slaves. Although its influence was initially rather small, the Klan was soon notorious for its use of white robes and hoods and burning of large crosses at its meetings, all designed to intimidate black Americans into accepting their status as second-class citizens. During a short period of reconstruction following the civil war, when ex-slaves were granted genuine opportunities – under the law – to achieve a significant degree of equality, there was an escalation in the number of black people murdered by hooded Klansmen. In the South, slavery was soon replaced by violent methods of intimidation and segregation as means of racial domination (Lane 1997).

In the 1920s, the Klan was the main organisation in the United States dedicated to reactionary politics. Concentrating its activities in rural areas, the Klan was able to capitalise on the frustrations and anxieties of Americans who were eager to resist the growing importance of new technologies and the cultural dominance of the cities (Flint 2001). By the 1920s, membership in the Klan had peaked at about four million (Rice 1962), as more and more Americans, especially from rural areas and small towns, felt a growing sense of anxiety and loss in the face of massive cultural change.

For farmers, ranchers and small-town business proprietors, the cities represented a convergence of evil influences: the encroachment of unwanted technological innovations, immorality, separation of work from the home and foreign sources of change. In some circles, the traditional American way of life was regarded as disappearing under the impact of an unprecedented level of immigration from southern and eastern European countries, the advent of the automobile (known derisively as 'an apartment on wheels'), American involvement in the League of Nations, sex and violence portrayed in Hollywood movies, and the appeal to young people of working in large corporations away from the family farm or family business. In addition, income inequality left relatively few Americans between the rich and the poor. The Klan blamed blacks, Jews, Catholics, immigrants, and other minorities for a bad economy and what it regarded as widespread cultural depravity.

For several decades following the 'Roaring Twenties', the Klan gradually lost its popular support, as Americans increasingly became aware of, and appalled by, its role in intimidating the black community as well as the civil rights movement with murders, bombings and cross-burnings. But the problems for America's farmers continued to escalate. Beginning in the post-Second World War period, the number of farms fell dramatically across the country. In one county in upstate New York, for example, the number of farms dropped from 3,914 in 1945 to 1,427 in

1969. Some of this decline was a result of the concentration of farm ownership. During the same period, the average farm in this upstate county grew from 131 acres to 228 acres. The more general trend was simply for farmers to go out of business. In 1945, 79 per cent of the land in the county was devoted to farming; by 1969, only 50 per cent was occupied by farms. Exactly the same trend was profoundly changing the landscape of America (Thomas, 2003).

By the early 1980s, most white supremacists had switched their allegiance from the Klan to one of the newer hate groups – for example, The Order, White Aryan Resistance, Aryan Nations, Posse Comitatus, and Church of the Creator. From the 1920s to the 1980s, Klan membership had declined from millions down to about 5,000; the combined membership of all other white supremacist groups was estimated to be approximately 17,000. White supremacist organisations in rural areas were especially devastated by lawsuits. In the 1980s, the Southern Poverty Law Center (SPLC) successfully sued a local chapter of the Ku Klux Klan in Georgia for its role in the lynching of a black man. A few years later, a South Carolina Klan was similarly sued, this time for a church burning in rural Clarendon County. Also in the early 1990s, the SPLC sued Tom and John Metzger, leaders of California's White Aryan Resistance, for their part in the brutal murder of an Ethiopian man on the streets of Portland, Oregon. The Southern Poverty Law Center won a judgment for the victim's family to the amount of $12.5 million. More recently, they successfully sued the Aryan Nations for its assault on a visitor to its compound in Hayden, Idaho. As a result, this white supremacist group was forced to vacate its compound and relocate to rural Pennsylvania (SPLC 2002).

Yet the popular support for extremist politics can easily be underestimated. During the 1980s, there was rapid growth of civilian militia groups (a.k.a. the Patriot movement), whose members despised the federal government, communists, international bankers, the United Nations and proponents of a 'one-world order'. Militia members were convinced of the presence of a conspiracy in high places to destroy Americans' Constitutional rights. Many saw blacks, Jews, Latinos and Asians as part and parcel of that conspiracy.

Militia members argued that the sovereignty of the United States was under attack, that communists had already taken over the White House, and that revolution was just around the corner. As a result, many of them stockpiled weapons, built shelters in secluded areas and rehearsed collectively for what they saw as an inevitable war against the federal government. Typically, those Americans reputedly involved in right-wing terrorism are middle-aged, mostly white males who lack college degrees and are likely to be unemployed or impoverished. In the mid-1980s, a white supremacist militia group known as The Order sought to make good on its promise to foment revolution and to rid the nation of Jews, people of colour and liberals. In 1985, Andrew Macdonald's novel about the inevitability of a global race war came to the attention of the US Department of Justice, when members of The Order committed a number of robberies and murders in an effort to ignite the same kind of bloody war depicted in *The Turner Diaries* (MacDonald 1978). The group committed crimes ranging from robbing armoured cars and counterfeiting to gunning down a Jewish talk show host in the driveway of his Denver home (Dobratz and Shanks-Meile 1997). More recently, Eric Rudolph allegedly caused the deadly 1996 explosion that ripped through Centennial Olympic Park in Atlanta and in 1998 the fatal bombing of an abortion clinic in Birmingham, Alabama. Hiding in the hills of North Carolina, Rudolph was able to stay on the loose for five years until he was finally apprehended in 2003.

The ideological thinking of both white supremacists and militia members often had a basis in personal catastrophe. When economic recession hit the United States in the early 1980s, many farmers, ranchers, miners and timber workers in small towns and rural areas across the country lost their jobs or were put out of business (Flint 2001). Having suffered financial disaster, they believed that an inordinate amount of the attention of the nation had focused on the plight of minorities residing in large cities rather than on the troubles of the white residents of small-town and rural areas.

Toward the mid-point of the 1990s, the militia or Patriot movement had reached its pinnacle of success in terms of recruitment. Through the 1980s and into the early 1990s, more and more Americans – having seen their fortunes dwindle under the impact of economic recession and having witnessed major blunders of federal law enforcement at Ruby Ridge and Waco – were attracted to the cause. Many of the legal principles espoused by militia members continued to have a financial basis. They were brought into court over matters such as foreclosure on farm property, back taxes, unpaid debt and so on (Snow 1999). Many members of the Patriot movement are residents of rural and small-town America who experienced financial disaster beginning with the deep recession of the early 1980s, when ranchers, farmers, miners and representatives of the timber industry suffered profoundly. They were joined by blue-collar workers from major cities who lost their jobs when the automobile industry went into severe decline.

Then, in 1995, Timothy McVeigh blew up 168 men, women and children at a federal building in Oklahoma City, and even the most ardent of anti-government extremists simply felt that McVeigh had gone too far, that enough was enough. Recruitment to the militia cause became all but impossible. Finally, as the turn of the millennium came and went without revolution, many more militia members found themselves completely disillusioned. The militia movement was beginning to look frail and tired. Most Americans lost interest in it.

But rather than operate on their own, many former members of the Patriot movement transferred their allegiances to the white supremacist movement, causing the number of such groups to grow through the opening years of the new millennium. Over the same period, the structure of the white supremacist movement shifted away from large and highly organised groups to small 'cells' of a few close friends or acquaintances – so-called lone wolves who were only loosely connected to any larger movement. In addition to causing organised hatemongers to lose power and influence, this transition also served to increase the difficulty with which federal investigators were able to infiltrate and investigate groups of extremists.

The convergence of interests between the militia movement and white supremacist groups can be seen in the collective response to financial disaster of a group of American farmers who had borrowed heavily to enlarge and upgrade their farms, but ended up owing large sums of money they could not repay. During the farm crisis of the 1980s, a tax resistant movement known as the Posse Comitatus (power of the county) attracted a growing number of farmers who had been displaced from their land. By arguing that the only legitimate government was local government, they resisted the payment of federal taxes in a last ditch effort to maintain their agrarian lifestyles (Dobratz and Shanks-Meile 1997).

In the early 1990s, a group of financially strapped Posse members established a tract of land close to Jordan, Montana which they claimed was not part of the United States and outside of the jurisdiction of its laws (Snow 1999). Calling themselves the Freemen of Montana, they proclaimed themselves to be sovereign citizens who obeyed only the Constitution of the United States and its first ten amendments, and were no longer legally responsible for repaying their debt.

The Freemen also believed in the religious tenets of the racist Christian Identity church, tenets that provide a theological basis for believing that white Christians are intellectually and morally superior to people of colour and Jews. White supremacist organisations often cloak their hatred in the aura and dogma of religion. Followers of the Identity Church are only 'doing the work of God'. At Sunday services, they preach that white Anglo-Saxons are the true Israelites depicted in the

Old Testament, God's chosen people, while Jews are actually the children of Satan. They maintain that Jesus was not a Jew, but an ancestor of the white, northern European peoples. In their view, blacks are 'pre-Adamic', pre-Old Testament, a species lower than whites. In fact, they claim that blacks and other non-white groups are at the same spiritual level as animals and therefore have no souls (Levin and McDevitt 1993).

Membership in right-wing citizens' militias and survivalist groups together comprising the so-called Patriot movement has been estimated at between 15,000 and 100,000 (Karl 1995). Klanwatch suggests that these militia groups have declined every year since 1996, when the militia movement reached its peak with 858 groups. The widespread impression that Timothy McVeigh, just prior to his bombing of the federal building in Oklahoma City, had visited an Arizona chapter of the Patriot movement caused many Americans to turn away from right-wing extremist groups. By 2002, the number of groups in the Patriot movement had dropped to only 143. According to the Southern Poverty Law Center, many Patriot groups simply disappeared.

In Britain, far-right extremists and white supremacist groups have not achieved the same degree of activity and support as they have in the United States and also elsewhere in Europe. Historically, the far-right has been active in urban areas where Britain's minority ethnic communities have largely been concentrated as a consequence of the pattern of post-Second World War recruitment of a migrant labour workforce to address a chronic labour shortage. While elements of the far-right have embraced electoral politics, they exploit and fuel racial tensions where they are active. The House of Commons Home Affairs Committee concluded in the early 1990s (UK House of Commons 1994) that such organisations create an 'atmosphere of hatred'. Accordingly, in the Isle of Dogs in London, where the British National Party (BNP) won its first local council seat in 1993, there was an escalation of racist incidents recorded by the police. More recently, in local elections in 2002 and 2003 the party achieved the most significant electoral gains by the far-right in Britain since the earlier rise of the National Front in the 1970s. While their number remains small, their progress reflects popular opposition in Britain to asylum and immigration.

While the far-right in Britain has historically targeted urban areas it has also been turning its attention to small towns and villages in rural areas. In 1979 the National Front held its annual conference in Great Yarmouth, a seaside town in the rural county of Norfolk in the east of England. The far-right has also been active in and around Norfolk's major city Norwich, which in 1991 was dubbed by the National Front as 'the last white city in England' (Derbyshire 1994: 24). The BNP has also been active in the region, coming third in a local council by-election in the village of Yoxford in Suffolk in February 2004 (Rozenberg 2004). The BNP has had electoral success in rural areas elsewhere. In the May 2002 local council elections, voters elected BNP candidate David Edwards in the rural village of Worsthorne near the outskirts of urban Burnley, where they have been particularly active. The exploitation of countryside politics by the BNP (Purves 2004) has been clearly in evidence in the south-west of England in the rural county of Devon as they follow in the footsteps of the far-right National Front before them. The so-called 'Rural Affairs Circle' of the BNP distributes its newsletter *Land and People* in the area, and it even has a dedicated website where it proclaims that 'rural Britain needs nationalism'.[1] Its message is clear. It sees Britain's rural counties as the last line of defence against the threat to the British way of life (BNP 2004):

> You can't help but notice the presence of new housing development all over the British countryside, destroying the character and in most cases the sense of community in the areas affected. It's a tidal wave of concrete engulfing thousands of acres of prime farmland, ancient beauty spots and priceless wildlife habitats. But has anyone stopped to consider where all these people who are moving into these developments come from, who they are and why they are there? … they are mostly white, middle-class, city folk – ordinary people who, in the main, are sick to death of living in our in-creasingly alien, cosmopolitan, overcrowded, congested, polluted, crime-infested urban centres. People who see rural Britain as a refuge – a place to make a fresh start, away from the sordid, squalid towns and cities … The process is 'white flight' – ethnic cleansing by consent, if you will, and the people concerned are the 'white flighters'.

Conclusions: cultures of 'hate'

It is tempting to regard the wave of church burnings in rural areas of the United States in the mid-1990s as only some kind of wide-ranging conspiracy involving organised groups of white supremacist extremists. Indeed, the Ku Klux Klan was implicated in a sizable minority of the torched black churches in southern states. In June 1995, for example, the 125-year-old Macedonia Baptist Church located in rural Clarendon County was burned to the ground by four members of the Christian Knights of the Ku Klux Klan. Three years later, trial attorneys from the

Southern Poverty Law Center including Morris Dees filed a civil suit against the local chapter of the KKK on behalf of Macedonia Baptist Church, winning a $37 million judgement that effectively put the South Carolina Klan out of business.

Although the Klan was implicated in a number of church burnings, the evidence suggests that the majority of these racially-inspired arsons were the work of America's young people, most of whom had no connections with organised hate groups but were out to commit a thrill hate crime. In June 1996, for example, a 13-year-old girl was arrested and charged for an act of arson that destroyed the Matthews Murkland Presbyterian Church in Charlotte, North Carolina. Shortly afterwards, three men in their early twenties were prime suspects in the burning of the Lighthouse Prayer Church in Greenville, Texas. A year earlier, two boys, aged 9 and 10, were charged with destroying the Life Christian Assembly Church in North Charleston, South Carolina, and a 17-year-old was charged in the burning of Pleasant Hill Baptist Church in Roberson County, North Carolina.

The limited research that there has been on the characteristics of hate crime offenders – almost entirely within urban environments – suggests that organised hate groups and individuals with extremist views are responsible for a very small proportion of incidents, although those are the incidents that tend to make the news. The research instead exposes the everyday nature of hate crime. A snapshot analysis of racist incidents recorded by the Metropolitan Police Service in London in 2001 (Stanko *et al.* 2003: 133), for instance, reveals that neighbours and other local people such as local youths and school-age children are responsible for a substantial proportion of incidents. The limited research barely portrays premeditated extremism behind many incidents, and instead suggests that racist offending occurs as part and parcel of offenders' and victims' everyday lives. In such a context, as Rae Sibbitt (1997) suggests (also drawing from small-scale research in London), offenders are acting out the collective views of their local community: in essence, local cultures of bigotry. It is more instructive therefore, to use Sibbitt's words, to think of the individual perpetrator and their wider community as the 'perpetrator community'. Again, given that anecdotal evidence suggests that racist hostility and harassment are a common experience for minority residents in rural areas (cf. Derbyshire 1994), it seems logical to propose that racist offending in such areas does not occur in a vacuum, but in the wider context of local cultures of bigotry. While those cultures share the processes providing the context for racist hate crime in urban areas, given the stronger sense of attachment to locality, the greater the sense of social and economic marginalisation and the greater perceived threat by 'outsiders', racist offending is perhaps more likely to manifest a defensive exclusionary sentiment in rural areas than it does in many urban areas.

Although we have observed that the type of organised and extremist hate discussed in this chapter appears to play only a minor direct role in racist crime in total, it is not simply an aberration, and it too does not occur in a vacuum. Extremist groups tend to commit the most serious hate offences – the brutal assaults and murders. Their activities often inspire young perpetrators who do not hold group membership but who collect racist propaganda, visit hate websites and purchase hate CDs distributed by organised groups. Extremist groups exploit fertile ground, they mobilise local hatred and their activities serve as a barometer of the extent to which bigotry has become deep-seated in the areas in which they are active – whether it is in the city or out of town.

Note

1   See http:www.land-and-people.org/.

References

British National Party (BNP) (2004) *Land and People.* At http://www.land-and-people.org/countryside2.html.

Derbyshire, H. (1994) *Not in Norfolk: Tackling the Invisibility of Racism.* Norwich: Norwich and Norfolk Racial Equality Council.

Dobratz, B.A. and Shanks-Meile, S.L. (1997) *'White Power, White Pride!' The White Separatist Movement in the United States.* New York: Twayne.

Dollard, J., Doob, L.W., Miller, N.E., Mowrer, O.H. and Sears, R.R. (1938) *Frustration and Aggression.* New Haven, CT: Yale University Press.

Flint, C. (2001) 'Right-Wing Resistance to the Process of American Hegemony: The Changing Political Geography of Nativism in Pennsylvania, 1920–1998', *Political Geography,* 20 (6): 763–86.

Green, D.P., Glaser, J. and Rich, A. (1998) 'From Lynching to Gay Bashing: The Elusive Connection Between Economic Conditions and Hate Crime', *Journal of Personality and Social Psychology,* 75 (1): 82–92.

Green, D.P., Strolovitch, D.Z. and Wong, J.S. (1998) 'Defended Neighborhoods, Integration, and Racially Motivated Crime', *American Journal of Sociology,* 104 (2): 372–403.

Hesse, B., Rai, D.K., Bennett, C. and McGilchrist, P. (1992) *Beneath the Surface: Racial Harassment.* Aldershot: Avebury.

Karl, J. (1995) *The Right to Bear Arms: The Rise of America's New Militia.* New York: Harper.

Lane, R. (1997) *Murder in America: A History*. Columbus, OH: Ohio State University.

Levin, J. and McDevitt, J. (1993). *Hate Crimes: The Rising Tide of Bigotry and Bloodshed*. New York: Plenum Press.

McDevitt, J., Levin, J. and Bennett, S. (2002) 'Hate Crime Offenders: An Expanded Typology', *Journal of Social Issues*, 58 (2): pp. 303–18.

Macdonald, A. (a.k.a. William L. Pierce) (1978) *The Turner Diaries*. New York and Hillsboro, WV: National Vanguard Books.

Pinderhughes, H. (1993) 'The Anatomy of Racially Motivated Violence in New York City: A Case Study of Youth in Southern Brooklyn', *Social Problems*, 40 (4): 478–92.

Purves, L. (2004) 'A BNP Wolf Stalks Rural Britain, Scenting Victory', *Times*, 3 February.

Ray, L. and Smith, D. (2002) 'Hate Crime, Violence and Cultures of Racism', in P. Iganski (ed.), *The Hate Debate: Should Hate Be Punished as a Crime?* London: Profile.

Ray, L., Smith, D. and Wasell, L. (2003) 'Understanding Racist Violence', in E.A. Stanko (ed.), *The Meanings of Violence*. London: Routledge.

Rice, A.S. (1962) *The Ku Klux Klan in American Politics*. Washington, DC: Public Affairs Press.

Rozenberg, G. (2004) 'BNP Rural Ambitions Buoyed by Suffolk Poll', *Times*, 7 February, p. 13.

Sibbitt, R. (1997) *The Perpetrators of Racial Harassment and Racial Violence*, Home Office Research Study No. 176. London: Home Office.

Snow, R.L. (1999) *The Militia Threat: Terrorists Among Us*. New York: Plenum Press.

Southern Poverty Law Center (SPLC) (2002) 'The Roots of Hate', *Intelligence Report*, Spring: 58–60.

Stanko, E.A., Kielinger, V., Paterson, S., Richards, L., Crisp, D. and Marsland, L. (2003) *Grounded Crime Prevention: Responding to and Understanding Hate Crime*. Mainz: Weisser-Ring.

Thomas, A.R. (2003) *In Gotham's Shadow*. Albany, NY: State University of New York Press.

UK House of Commons (1994) *Racial Attacks and Harassment*, Home Affairs Committee, Third Report. London: HMSO.

Ward, D. (2002) 'Voice of BNP's New Stronghold: "No One in this Village is a Racist" ', *Guardian*, 4 May.

Chapter 6

Another Country? Community, belonging and exclusion in rural England

Jon Garland and Neil Chakraborti

> Now we often play cricket on our hunting ground
> The lads from the village they like to come down
> From their occupations they come just to play
> They'd rather play cricket than sleep in the hay

From *The Cricket Match* by 'The Singing Postman', 1965

Introduction

In the mid-1960s folk singer Allan Smethurst[1] enjoyed his own '15 minutes of fame' by popularising songs about rural Norfolk communities, typified by *The Cricket Match*, an excerpt from which is cited above. In this song, the images identified – 'hunting ground', cricket, traditional rural occupations and the 'sleepy, simple' nature of village life – symbolised, for Smethurst at least, the actualities of rural living in the latter half of the twentieth century. Yet, as his biographer noted, this life was 'fast disappearing even as he wrote and sang about it' (Skipper 2001: 8) and it may be the case that it was the (unwitting) nostalgia present in Smethurst's songs that held broad appeal to a public living through a turbulent decade of change and with the trauma of the Second World War still fresh in its memory.

In 1993, almost thirty years after Smethurst's idealisation of rural life, it was therefore somewhat surprising to discover his depiction finding resonance in the then Prime Minister John Major's portrayal of the essence of Englishness as 'County grounds, warm beer, invincible green suburbs ... and old maids cycling to Holy Communion through the morning mist' (Major 1993, quoted in Garland and Rowe 2001: 121). As is mentioned in the Introduction to this volume, Major's wistful idealisation of English life is not only old-fashioned and whimsical, its use of cricket, 'warm beer' and the church portrays a kind of rural and quaint, white Englishness that fails to take into account the complex, multicultural and multi-ethnic nature of contemporary English society.

Such notions also fail to acknowledge the presence of racism in rural locations that are characterised by overwhelmingly white populations, thereby leading some to conclude that, due to the lack of minority ethnic households present, racism is simply not a problem in these locations (de Lima 2001). However, in the summer of 2004 the experiences of a dual heritage man in Norfolk provided a graphic counterbalance to such 'common-sense' ideas. The man, of white English/Greek descent, found that his preconceived notions of Norfolk as being friendly and welcoming were shattered when, following the events of September 11 2001, he was continually victimised by white locals for having ostensibly darker skin and a beard, and thereby 'looking like a terrorist' (Ashworth 2004). Once this verbal abuse had degenerated into episodes of physical assault, the victim abandoned his ideas of living in the 'rural idyll' and left the county.

As will be outlined in this chapter, however, the linking of notions of Englishness solely with whiteness is still potent in the minds of many white rural communities in locations other than Norfolk. The inter-weaving of rural space, identity and belonging produces a process of exclusion of the 'other' in many village communities. It will be noted below that this process of 'othering' is often applied to any village 'outsider' who looks different or has a lifestyle deemed unconventional, or who simply comes from another town or village.

Using this 'othering' process as a framework, the chapter examines the nature of 'localism' and outlines the particular experiences of rural minority ethnic communities. These experiences, often typified by the endurance of racist harassment and a sense of isolation and exclusion from local communities, are illustrated here by drawing on the findings from a series of research studies undertaken by the authors in four rural and isolated areas of England – Suffolk, east Northamptonshire, and north and south Warwickshire. These studies examined the nature and levels of racism in these locales, the extent to which local agencies provided adequate support for victims, and also the values and views of white rural communities on 'race' issues.[2]

The chapter will utilise these findings in the light of a number of different explanations of 'community' in order to assess the nature of rural village life and the experiences of minority ethnic people within this context. It will note that while episodes of victimisation, such as those affecting the man in Norfolk described previously, are sadly not uncommon, developing an understanding of the nature of the risk of victimisation may actually assist in the reconstruction of the perception of rural minority ethnic communities as 'communities of shared risk' rather than as 'communities of place', as they are commonly understood. Such a conceptualisation may help to develop a fuller appreciation of the realities of rural living for those communities.

Deconstructing rural communities: localism, othering and belonging

The media's portrayal of the villages in England's countryside, typified by popular television dramas and comedies such as *Heartbeat*, *Last of the Summer Wine* and *The Darling Buds of May*, perpetuates the myth of the cosy village community, complete with its strong ties of kinship, shared values and sense of belonging (Neal 2002). Indeed, this sense of villages as 'warm' environs that are crime-free, where people look out for one another and where there is a certain shared sense of identity complemented by a strong feelings of belonging (Francis and Henderson 1992) are often reflected in traditional notions of community more generally. However, an oft-cited shared characteristic of such communities is their cautious, conservative and essentially 'circumspect' nature, whereby incomers from the city, and indeed even those from neighbouring towns and villages, are viewed with distrust and suspicion (see, for example, Burnett 1996). This point is vividly illustrated by the following two observations from a white district council policy officer from south Warwickshire and a white male in Mid-Suffolk, expressed to the authors during the course of their research:

> Generally populations, particularly in the rural part of the district, tend to be historically well established, everybody knows everybody else, and there is a lot of resentment to people coming in from outside the district of whatever kind. So irrespective of race, colour, creed, national origins, wealth, background, any of that, there is real resentment against people from outside coming in.

> Framlingham's a very close-knit community, isn't it? It's all inter-bred around here. It's the sort of place where people have lived for generations and everyone knows everyone, and when a stranger comes in you put your guard up – it's human nature.

This form of 'localism', involving an almost inevitable distrust of the 'other', was, according to the two interviewees above, reserved for all of those who are perceived to be different in some form. They argued that minority ethnic incomers to the village, whether residents or merely those visiting the village, are treated no differently from others whose faces are not familiar. Therefore, while acknowledging the common marginalisation of the 'other' in the rural, they suggested that any discrimination directed against those from different ethnic backgrounds was merely a symptom of this intense 'localism' and not racism *per se:* it was caused simply by the fact that 'outsiders' at least initially (and sometimes for extended periods of time) simply did not 'fit in' with the standard norms of the community.

Little (2002: 4) in his detailed study of the politics of community indicates that the problem may be deeper than one of mere difference by suggesting that communities 'still command certain behaviour from members and indeed this may take the form of expectations of obligation, reciprocity and so on'. Therefore anyone new to a tightly-knit and small social network may take time to understand the patterns of local behaviour and particularistic rural customs, and will experience pressure to learn and abide by them. As Giddens (1994: 126) notes, rather than being open and tolerant, such traditional communities can be limiting and oppressive towards individualism while exerting a 'compelling pressure towards conformism' upon anyone perceived to be somehow different.

In the course of the authors' studies of rural racism in various environments, this intolerance has been vocalised by a number of those interviewed, and has certainly been evident in the testimony of both white and minority ethnic participants. However, the fact that someone may look visibly different appears to act as a catalyst for forms of racism peculiar to environments where white communities are simply not familiar with, or used to, people with markedly different physical features, as the following research quotations demonstrate:

When I was working in a sales room ... there was one bloke in his late fifties who had never been abroad in his life, very rarely went out of Lowestoft. He would get so excited if he saw a coloured person. I remember one occasion where a black woman walked into the sales room and he shouted, 'Dave, Dave look at that, look at that, you don't see many as black as that!' (White male, East Suffolk)

I always think back to the very first, umm, ethnic girl that I had in a class, and no one knew how to refer to her. They were sort of saying 'Well, it's, er, you know the one I mean; the little girl in the red cardigan'. (White female schoolteacher, north Warwickshire)

The discomfort when talking about minority ethnic people illustrated in the last quotation was evident in a number of the testimonies from white rural dwellers, whether agency representatives or 'ordinary' members of the public, when interviewed by the authors for their studies. Whether intentional or not (a distinction rendered less important anyhow in the post-Macpherson climate) such behaviour reflects attitudes that have, in a broader context in England during the early part of the twenty-first century, manifested themselves most visibly in village campaigns against the Labour government's policy of dispersing asylum seekers into rural areas. As Hall (2004: 11) relates, fear of asylum seekers in rural south Nottinghamshire has caused local white residents to believe (without any factual foundation) that asylum seekers will 'attract trouble from young local men, frighten women, increase the risk of burglary, push down property prices and "tempt away" local teachers and doctors'. Tellingly, Hall noted that such attitudes were almost absent among white residents of inner-city Nottingham who were very familiar with multicultural environments and who were already living alongside asylum seekers.

A sense of exclusion for minority ethnic village dwellers from their local communities, brought on by negative reactions to their visible 'otherness', can be exacerbated in traditional rural environments when, as Saunders *et al.* (1978: 62) noted over 25 years ago:

> Both the size and density of settlement in most rural areas is of a kind which produces a highly particularistic social structure in which persistent face-to-face contact can be maintained. Where such particularism is accompanied by a rigidly hierarchical and ascriptive system of stratification then traditional forms of authority seem to ensue.

Such stratified social systems with their in-built hierarchies may have been in place for decades, if not centuries (Francis and Henderson 1992) and are almost impenetrable to newcomers. If minority ethnic families try to get involved in aspects of village life then they may find themselves victims of this rigid system and unable to become part of traditional village activities. As Magne (2003: 5.17) found when investigating rural racism in Devon in south-west England, only around a third of her minority ethnic research participants were involved in community-related activities and less than half participated in community life in any way at all. Reasons given for this lack of participation included: fear of cultural and linguistic problems, cultural connotations that caused concern about participation in organisations, and exclusion by virtue of the fact that village life is intertwined with church life (ibid., 5.20).

The inherently exclusive nature of basing so much rural community activity around the church (and most usually the Church of England) creates barriers that those from different religions find very difficult to surmount. However, the authors' own studies found that in some rural regions such as north and south Warwickshire where there are very few minority ethnic households, such households did not seek to form their own religious or cultural organisations in their own geographical area. This may be, as one interviewee suggested, because of fear of adverse reaction from the white population:

> If we did all get together the white population might think, 'We have got a problem here, brown people getting together', and it probably wouldn't work in our favour. It might be a negative thing, they might try and beat us up. (Indian female, north Warwickshire)

Instead, a white voluntary sector worker in north Warwickshire felt that minority ethnic households just looked back to the city or town they had originally left, or to the nearest significant urban settlement, and participated in activities there:

> People look to wherever they have moved from, so if they come from Coventry they look back to Coventry for their cultural, religious, family connections – or Tamworth or Birmingham or wherever. So I don't think there is any sense of ethnic minority community in north Warwickshire.

Other 'traditional' social activities are also exclusionary. The 'customary' visit to the village pub, especially on a Sunday, also causes problems for those whose faith dictates that they should not drink alcohol. It also causes pressures for those from other minority ethnic backgrounds who do drink alcohol but who feel that they are 'damned if they visit the pub and damned if they do not', as the following quotation from the authors' research shows:

> It's bad that you have to go to the pub and mingle with the locals, who often will ignore you. By the same token if you don't go they

are going to think you are strange and different, and won't talk to you anyway. (Indian female, north Warwickshire)

For some of those interviewed for the authors' studies the process of gaining acceptance into village life revolved around social status: they felt that having a 'respected' occupation, such as a general practitioner, helped ease the process of integration into the community. For others, the longer they lived in the countryside the easier it became, as local white people gradually became accustomed to their presence. In the case of one interviewee, having a good standard of spoken English was the key:

If you can communicate effectively that tends to go a long way. If you can't then that tends to hamper the whole thing, and then you are relying entirely on the good will of the other side, on the good nature of the other people. If you are able to communicate and are able to defend yourself that tends to speed up the process. (Indian male, north Warwickshire)

However, some of the language used by the interviewee above may tell a different story from the one he intended. By admitting that the integration into the community of those with poor linguistic skills rested 'entirely on the good will of the other side', he inadvertently showed that acceptance into village communities is often a one-way process, contingent on the inclinations of the white population (referred to in adversarial terms as the 'other side'). Equally striking is the interviewee's admission that effective communication skills enabled minority ethnic groups to 'defend themselves', thus illustrating the confrontational nature of much of the 'lived experience' of village life for people from those groups.

The quotation directly above also gives away another important aspect of the 'process of acceptance' into rural communities for minority ethnic people: it is a process of *assimilation*, rather than integration. Often, it appears that white rural communities expect minority ethnic households to adopt the pre-existing (and essentially white English) cultural, social and religious norms that characterise village life, whatever the implications of this may be. If they do so, minority ethnic individuals can attain the status of an 'honorary white person', as the following quotation demonstrates:

There's a chap who lives just down the road from me, he was saying 'It's all right love, we don't see you as one of them. You're one of us.' I don't want to be one of you, thank you very much. I'm me, thank you. (Female interviewee of dual heritage, Mid-Suffolk)

This 'honorary' status, whether accepted or not, is temporary and ephemeral in nature and can be just as easily withdrawn in the same way that it is conferred upon the recipient (Back *et al.* 2001). It is more often than not based upon an idealised notion of rural identity centred within an 'imagined', rather than actual, formulation of rural community life (Anderson 1991). As we shall see in the next section, this idealisation of the rural neglects to acknowledge, whether by accident or design, the realities of racist harassment and abuse in the countryside that undermine the traditional notions of rural village communities that appear so symbolically significant to many of their residents.

Deconstructing rural communities: cultures of racism in the countryside

The issue of racist harassment and violence in the rural is increasingly being seen as a serious problem and has been acknowledged as such by a relatively small but growing body of literature (see Chapter 2 in this volume for de Lima's concise summary of these developments). The authors of this chapter have themselves uncovered some shocking accounts of racist victimisation during their research, and as the first example below illustrates, some forms of this racism have their basis in the inherent 'fear of the other' and lack of familiarity with difference described above:

I was going out with a black guy and two local lads thought it would be really funny to knock on my back door with pillow cases on their heads and shout 'Ku Klux Klan!' It's since been passed on to me that I've been called a 'nigger shagger' behind my back. These people just can't comprehend that what they're saying and doing is not acceptable. (White female, north Warwickshire)

I've had fights in the public playing field when there's a football match going on, and all the dads turned round and watched five boys chanting names, throwing punches ... I'm sure if I had been a little girl with blonde hair, there's no way they would have stood and watched a little girl with blonde hair having all these boys throwing punches, calling names, pulling hair, and all this kind of business. (Female interviewee of dual heritage, Mid-Suffolk)

The last of these accounts shows how some white rural residents turn a 'blind eye' to incidents occurring in front of them, while the first quotation is especially instructive in revealing a fundamental lack of understanding of the hurtful nature of racist language and behaviour coupled with a barely hidden (and sometimes brutally open) resentment of dual heritage couples. While it is not being suggested here that such types of racism are solely confined to the rural and are absent from the urban, it may well be the case that the 'localism' (and its in-built 'fear of the "other" ') that strongly flavours the attitudes of white rural residents fuels the overt racism described above and in the quotation below:[3]

> We went to this supermarket and a lady was arguing with her husband, and her husband came and stood behind us in the queue and she said, 'I am not standing behind these monkeys'. I looked to see who was talking and I saw her and she actually moved away from me. (Iranian female, north Warwickshire)

It has been suggested by a number of commentators (see for example Derounian 1993; Robinson and Gardner in this volume) that the more hostile forms of rural racism may be located not in the sections of white communities who can trace their rural family lineage back centuries, but instead in the attitudes of new village residents – the so-called 'white flighters' – who have 'escaped' from the urban (with its perceived 'negatives' of crime and large minority ethnic populations) to what they view as the peaceful and ethnically homogenous countryside. These 'refugees from multiculturalism' (Jay 1992: 22) are therefore both surprised by, and resentful of, the presence of minority ethnic residents in their villages, and it is these feelings that have been manipulated by the far-right British National Party (BNP) in its specifically rural *Land and People* campaign, with its emphasis on the preservation of the essentially white nature of English rural communities.

However, the BNP's correlation of countryside with English national identity is in itself resonant of wider ideas of Englishness, whose formulation can be traced back to the nineteenth century and the development of a new nationalism based upon 'the characteristics of landscape, and in the forms of a (rapidly vanishing) rural life' (Kumar 2003: 209). In a society experiencing urbanisation and industrialisation at a bewildering pace, the rural was seen as the true heart of England, where the essence of national character had not been corrupted. The countryside's gently rolling hills, divided by meandering brooks and dotted with the spires of village churches, were often evoked, particularly at times of war, as the 'soul' of the English nation which must be preserved at all costs. As Colls (2002: 204) observes:

There always had to be a reason for [military] glory, and the English found it in the idea of a land and people living together softly and naturally ... it was in [the] mixing and comparing of hard political and soft geographical that modern Englishness was identified.

Therefore, key elements of this English identity were developed around not what it was, but rather what it was *not* (Cesarini 1996): it was not urban (with its connotations of poverty, squalor and the breakdown of community life); it was not Celtic or European; it was not Roman Catholic or any other religion; and it was not 'dark skinned'. As Neal (2002: 446) notes, there are those who trace the link between the soil and nationhood back further, and she cites an editorial from the Scilly Isles' *Tresco Times* (Spring 2001):

The beauty of our countryside is testament to millennia of careful husbandry, from which a community life developed. Not an urban, multicultural way of life, but the heritage of ethnic Britons – with roots going back 2,500 years.

English identity consequently became racialised, and it is its white character that the BNP is seeking to preserve in the rural, as indeed are others who are nostalgic for the nation they feel existed before postwar mass immigration. The implied 'whiteness' of the communities so beloved of the *Tresco Times* is, of course, inherently exclusive of those from a visible minority ethnic background, who feel disenfranchised and alienated from village life around them. Magne's (2003) study found that difficulties in forming cross-cultural friendships, experiences of racism and lack of contact with other co-ethnic people added to a sense of isolation for minority ethnic households in Devon. This sense of isolation is also evident in the quotations below, taken from the authors' own research:

I'm looked at like I'm a prostitute, I'm always getting funny looks ... I don't know of any other black people in this village. Actually I don't know one other black person round here whatsoever. (Female interviewee of dual heritage, East Northamptonshire)

This is such a close-knit community, everyone knows everyone. We are outcasts here ... We are outcasts cos we are Pakis. (Pakistani male, Waveney, Suffolk)

This sense of isolation, coupled with the harmful effects of the racist harassment described in this chapter, caused some of those interviewed by the authors to feel as if they existed 'apart' from the village life around them. It was almost as if the village had closed ranks against them by opposing their presence from the moment they moved into the village (see, for example, Chakraborti and Garland 2003). As Johnston (2000: 77) suggests, this may be part of the way that some communities define themselves, by finding 'suitable enemies' whom they can rally against. In the case of rural villages, often the most easily identifiable scapegoat is the 'outsider', and especially the person who looks so obviously different from everyone else. The villager who is seen to threaten the essentially (white) character of the community will be the one who is excluded by those who feel challenged by their presence.

However, it may not be the community 'closing ranks' against a perceived threat that leads to the isolation of minority ethnic households, as sometimes they will do it themselves. As the quotation below reveals, some victims of racism in rural areas are so psychologically damaged that they cut themselves off from the village around them for fear of experiencing further harassment:

> Sometimes the whole of winter passes and I will not go outside, all my life is in between these four walls, I don't go out the house ... you're conscious of it all the time, it's something that's in your head all the time, that you might get a bit of bother. (Indian male, East Northamptonshire)

Conclusions: minority ethnic communities as 'communities of shared risk'?

This chapter has attempted to deconstruct the nature of rural communities and assess the location of minority ethnic households within them. Research has indicated that many rural communities can be seen to be conservative and cautious in nature, and not the warm and welcoming places that they are commonly perceived to be. There is a strong sense of belonging and an identification with locality ('localism') which can result in the mistrust of the 'other' that habitually manifests itself in many rural environments. This mistrust can cause anyone who is perceived to be an outsider to be 'othered' and thereby marginalised from their local communities. This can happen to an incomer to the village or to someone who follows a lifestyle that is deemed to be alternative to the rural mainstream.

A key aspect of this chapter has been to investigate whether the discrimination and racism experienced by minority ethnic individuals and families in rural areas is in any way similar to this 'othering' process that can happen to 'outsider' white people. It has been shown that, while there are some similarities between the two (in that the 'fear of the unknown' may underpin them both) there are key differences too. The racist harassment experienced by minority ethnic communities takes specific forms, both verbal and physical, that separate it from the 'othering' of white newcomers to the village.

While the damaging effects of this marginalisation are not being disputed here, anecdotal evidence collected from the authors' own research indicates that, although it may even take some years, it is common for white newcomers to be accepted into village communities eventually. However, there are certain barriers – cultural, religious, linguistic, social – that are ever-present for minority ethnic people and are thus extremely difficult to overcome, even over a period of years. This can result in a sense of isolation and exclusion from local (white) communities which is exacerbated by the lack of presence of other minority ethnic people nearby and by the pernicious effects of racism.

This is not to say that the experience of minority ethnic rural dwellers is uniform across all rural areas or indeed between different ethnic groups. There are also factors, such as gender, age and sexuality, which can also profoundly affect the lives of rural minority ethnic people (see Kirkey and Forsyth 2001 for example), and it is acknowledged here that the situation for refugees also has its own complex sets of issues (Kelly 2003). As Robinson and Gardner eloquently argue in their chapter in this volume, there has also been a tendency among commentators to portray the lives of *all* minority ethnic people in the rural as being blighted by racism, when in fact their research shows that many of these experiences have, instead, been positive and largely unaffected by harassment: in some cases, for instance, minority ethnic households may claim to enjoy being so visibly different from most of the white population around them as it makes them feel special, exotic or unique. A concern that the authors of this chapter have with this argument is that these feelings seem to be complicit with the 'othering' process that the *vast majority* of minority ethnic people have to undergo in the rural. By 'playing along' with this process, there is a danger that such arguments are merely underlining the exoticisation of the 'other' and therefore confirming the 'outsider' status of minority ethnic households in the countryside.

Of course, the sense of geographical isolation felt by minority ethnic people is shared by many white residents in rural areas, and the lack of public transport and other services in the countryside are problems shared by all. Also significant, as Bevan *et al.* (2001) suggest, is the increasing frequency with which places where village residents can socialise, such as pubs or community centres, have been closing down, thereby further damaging people's sense of community. Although this chapter has shown that significant numbers of minority ethnic rural residents felt excluded from these places anyway, their disappearance cannot help but further compound the feeling of isolation felt amongst all sections of rural society.

A worrying aspect of rural village communities mentioned above is the tendency of some white residents to expect minority ethnic groups to assimilate into village life, complete with its traditional, specifically rural and therefore quintessentially white English customs and practices. Many of these customs and practices are outdated and relate to a notion of Englishness, exemplified by John Major's views cited at the beginning of this chapter, which has its roots in a countryside somehow seen as the true embodiment of English values and beliefs.

What those who subscribe to these narrow and nostalgic notions of national identity may fail to realise is that the equation of Englishness with the countryside in fact usually equates only with the countryside of certain southern English counties (Paxman 1999). As Kumar (2003) argues, the representation of the English rural used in the 'Your Britain, fight for it now' propaganda posters of the Second World War was Frank Newbould's painting of the South Downs. This painting had enormous impact and entered the national psyche as an icon of both England and the rural. However, this iconic picture cemented the notions of Englishness and the *southern* countryside together (ibid.: 210):

> The choice of [Newbould's painting] showed how strongly 'the south country' had imposed itself on the national consciousness, to the point where it was endlessly reproduced as an image of a 'timeless' England. England, in this image, *was* 'the south country'. It was cut off not just from Britain but from much of the rest of England, the England of the Midlands and the North.

In any case, as Young (2004) posits, Major's ideas may not be as ludicrous as they seem, at least not in the minds of some. In a survey of just over 1,000 British people in which they were asked to list the most distinctive symbols of Britishness, the most popular response was 'roast beef and Yorkshire pudding; fish and chips' at number one in the list; the Queen came next and Buckingham Palace fourth. Other symbols in the top 50 included 'drinking tea' (tenth), 'going down the pub' (twentieth), 'red telephone boxes' (thirty-fourth) and a 'stiff upper lip' (forty-ninth). There was no acknowledgement of multiculturalism, or of the achievements of minority ethnic communities, anywhere in the list.

Thus, while these depictions of both Englishness and Britishness appear to disregard the presence of minority ethnic groups in the rural and their contribution to wider society more generally, there are other, broader aspects of rural communities that are worth addressing. In their study of rural social housing, Bevan *et al.* (2001) found that many of the (presumably mainly white) participants in their research were not particularly interested in fitting in with village community life, but instead focused on their own social networks, such as family or friends, that may be geographically dispersed. This raises an important issue of whether the examination of the nature of rural communities needs to be based less around traditional, geographical notions and should be instead thought of in more abstract, non-spatial terms.

As Young (2001: 38) suggests, the characteristics of late modern communities are that they are pluralistic, fragmented, transient and constantly reinventing their history and boundaries. Although Young may have been talking about urban communities, rural ones will also be subject to the same stresses and strains of late modernity. While they may not be as pluralistic or as fragmented as their city counterparts, rural communities are nevertheless less stable and have more transient populations than may be commonly perceived. Equally, the populations of villages have multiple membership of a number of differing communities, whether they are based around leisure, employment or other areas of interest, as Smith (1988: 168) maintains:

> ... at any given time as well as over the course of anyone's life history, each of us is a member of many shifting communities, each of which establishes, for each of its members, multiple social identities, multiple principles of identification with other people, and, accordingly, a collage or grab-bag of allegiances, beliefs, and sets of motives.

Of course, village residents, and minority ethnic people among them, can subscribe to membership of a range of communities based around any of the factors listed above. However, although useful, the idea of community sketched by Smith is really one based around notions of 'shared interests' and is therefore too ephemeral to be applied to the situation that rural minority ethnic populations find themselves in. Moreover, it is important to recall at this point that research into service provision for victims of racist harassment in rural areas has shown that this provision suffers because many agencies simply do not regard tackling racism as being important or relevant; rather, they simplistically assume that if there are no substantial minority ethnic communities in rural localities then there can be no substantial problem of racism (Garland and Chakraborti 2004). These agencies are utilising a traditional concept of community, defined simply as large numbers of homogenous people living in close geographical proximity, and are thus missing, or inadvertently disregarding, minority ethnic groups that need assistance, but whose presence in the countryside is scattered and sporadic.

Clearly, then, it is important to move away from geographically-based and interest-based notions of community and towards those that examine the issue from other angles. A useful definition in this regard is that provided by Etzioni (2000: 9, quoted in Little 2002: 156), who suggests that:

> A community is a group of people who share criss-crossing affective bonds and a moral culture. By asserting this definition, I mean to indicate clearly that communities need not be local and are distinct from mere interest groups, in that they address a broad band of human needs. People who band together to gain privileged treatment for office equipment make an interest group; those who share a history, identity and fate, a community.

Etzioni therefore proposes that scattered populations can nevertheless form communities if they have certain cultural or historical ties that bond them together. While different minority ethnic groups do share these bonds (at least within each group), an added factor that may help in the formulation of this conceptualisation of community is that of risk. For instance, a factor that underscores the lives of all of the diverse minority ethnic populations in rural areas is that they are at risk 'on a daily basis' of experiencing racist harassment (Taylor 2003: 232). Johnston (2000) argues that populations should be thought of in terms of the risk that they face of becoming victims of crime, meaning that one could have 'high'- or 'low'-risk communities, or those of 'shared risk', who face a common problem collectively. In the case of rural minority ethnic groups at risk of racist victimisation, they could be conceived of as communities of 'shared risk', a concept which bypasses the need for such populations to live in the same shared space. Without this focus on 'numbers and geography', but with the added emphasis on risk, this alternative definition of rural minority ethnic communities may help to raise their profile in the countryside where previously they were often all but invisible. These communities may then receive the service delivery that their situation deserves.

Notes

1 Smethurst enjoyed a measure of success under the stage name of 'The Singing Postman', his biggest hit being *Hev You Gotta Loight, Boy?* which reached no. 20 in the EP charts in the summer of 1965. In the song *The Cricket Match*, the village cobbler, farmer, blacksmith, vicar and poacher all take turns to bat for the village cricket team, with everyone retiring to the local pub afterwards.

2 The research, conducted by the authors in all three counties and with the assistance of Parvinder Sandal in Suffolk and Katie Keetley in Northamptonshire, utilised a variety of qualitative and quantitative methods. In order to establish an understanding of minority ethnic communities' experiences of racist victimisation, questionnaire surveys, focus groups and interviews were conducted with a cross-section of members of these communities. Interviews and focus groups were also undertaken with a broad range of people from white rural communities, and interviews were conducted with representatives from a variety of statutory and voluntary agencies. For more specific and detailed findings from these studies, see Garland and Chakraborti (2002), Chakraborti, Garland and Keetley (2003) and Chakraborti and Garland (2004).

3 See Ray, Smith and Wastell (2004) for a fascinating (and in some ways contrasting) analysis of the motivations of violent racist offenders in outlying areas to the north and west of Manchester city centre.

References

Anderson, B. (1991) *Imagined Communities: Reflections on the Origin and Spread of Nationalism*. London: Verso.

Ashworth, H. (2004) 'Racism Drives Man Out of City', *Eastern Daily Press*, 22 April, p. 11.

Back, L., Crabbe, T. and Solomos, J. (2001) *The Changing Face of Football: Racism, Identity and Multiculture in the English Game*. Oxford: Berg.

Bevan, M., Cameron, S., Coombes, M., Merridew, T. and Raybould, S. (2001) *Social Housing in Rural Areas*. York: Joseph Rowntree Foundation/Chartered Institute of Housing.

Burnett, K.A. (1996) 'Once an Incomer, Always an Incomer?', in P. Chapman, K.A. Burnett, L. McKie, J. Nelson, M. Bain, F. Raitt and S. Lloyd (eds), *Women and Access in Rural Areas*. Aldershot: Avebury.

Cesarini, D. (1996) 'The Changing Character of Citizenship and Nationality in Britain', in D. Cesarini and M. Fulbrook (eds), *Citizenship, Nationality and Migration in Europe*. London: Routledge.

Chakraborti, N. and Garland, J. (2003) 'An 'Invisible' Problem? Uncovering the Nature of Racist Victimisation in Rural Suffolk', *International Review of Victimology*, 10 (1): 1–17.

Chakraborti, N. and Garland, J. (2004) *Racist Victimisation and Minority Ethnic Communities in North Warwickshire and Stratford-on-Avon: Issues and Responses*. Leicester: Department of Criminology, University of Leicester.

Chakraborti, N. Garland, J. and Keetley, K. (2003) *Responding to Racist Incidents in Wellingborough and East Northamptonshire: An Assessment of Agency Practice and Victim Satisfaction – Final Report*. Leicester: PRCI.

Colls, R. (2002) *Identity of England*. Oxford: Oxford University Press.

de Lima, P. (2001) *Needs Not Numbers: An Exploration of Minority Ethnic Communities in Scotland*. London: Commission for Racial Equality and Community Development Foundation.

Derounian, J. (1993) *Another Country: Real Life Beyond Rose Cottage*. London: National Council for Voluntary Organisations.

Francis, D. and Henderson, P. (1992) *Working With Rural Communities*. Basingstoke: Macmillan.

Garland, J. and Chakraborti, N. (2002) *Tackling the Invisible Problem? An Examination of the Provision of Services to Victims of Racial Harassment in Rural Suffolk*. Leicester: Scarman Centre, University of Leicester.

Garland, J. and Chakraborti, N. (2004) 'Racist Victmisation, Community Safety and the Rural: Issues and Challenges', in the *British Journal of Community Justice*, 2(3): 21–32.

Garland, J. and Rowe, M. (2001) *Racism and Anti-racism in Football*. Basingstoke: Palgrave Macmillan.

Giddens, A. (1994) *Beyond Left and Right: The Future of Radical Politics*. Cambridge: Polity Press.

Hall, S. (2004) 'May 1 Elections: Heart of England Divided on Asylum', *Guardian*, 23 April: 11.

Jay, E. (1992) *'Keep Them in Birmingham': Challenging Racism in South West England*. London: Commission for Racial Equality.

Johnston, L. (2000) *Policing Britain: Risk, Security and Governance*. Harlow: Longman.

Kelly, L. (2003) 'Bosnian Refugees in Britain: Questioning Community', *Sociology*, 37 (1): 35–49.

Kirkey, K. and Forsyth, A. (2001) 'Men in the Valley: Gay Male Life on the Suburban–Rural Fringe', *Journal of Rural Studies*, 17 (4): 421–41.

Kumar, K. (2003) *The Making of English National Identity*. Cambridge: Cambridge University Press.

Little, A. (2002) *The Politics of Community: Theory and Practice*. Edinburgh: Edinburgh University Press.

Magne, S. (2003) *Multi-Ethnic Devon: A Rural Handbook – The Report of the Devon and Exeter Racial Equality Council's Rural Outreach Project*. Devon: Devon and Exeter Racial Equality Council.

Neal, S. (2002) 'Rural Landscapes, Representations and Racism: Examining Multicultural Citizenship and Policy-making in the English Countryside', *Ethnic and Racial Studies*, 25 (3): 442–61.

Paxman, J. (1999) *The English: A Portrait of a People*. London: Penguin Books.

Ray, L., Smith, D. and Wastell, L. (2004) 'Shame, Rage and Racist Violence', *British Journal of Criminology*, 44 (3): 350–68.

Saunders, P., Newby, H., Bell, C. and Rose, D. (1978) 'Rural Community and Rural Community Power', in H. Newby (ed.), *International Perspectives in Rural Sociology*. Chichester: John Wiley and Sons.

Skipper, K. (2001) *Hev Yew Gotta Loight, Boy? The Life and Lyrics of Allan Smethurst, the 'Singing Postman'*. Newbury: Countryside Books.

Smith, B.H. (1988) *Contingencies of Value*. Cambridge, MA: Harvard University Press.

Taylor, K. (2003) 'Hatred Repackaged: The Rise of the British National Party and Antisemitism', in P. Iganski and B. Kosmin (eds), *A New Antisemitism? Debating Judeophobia in 21st-Century Britain*. London: Profile Books.

Young, J. (2001) 'Identity, Community and Social Exclusion', in R. Matthews and J. Pitts (eds), *Crime, Disorder and Community Safety: A New Agenda?* London: Routledge.

Young, R. (2004) 'Roast Beef and Fish 'n' Chips More British Than the Queen', *Times*, 28 April: 26.

Part 3
Tackling the Problem

Chapter 7

Supporting victims of rural racism: learning lessons from a dedicated racial harassment project

Shammi Jalota

This chapter considers the development and impact of a local authority-funded project, Suffolk County Council's Racial Harassment Initiative, in tackling the problems of racism in rural areas. The chapter focuses on how the Initiative supports those who suffer in both urban and rural locations, with emphasis on the differences and similarities between these approaches. The discussion provides examples of good practice, examines the requirements of effective multi-agency working and concludes by suggesting ways of improving upon the more traditional methods of combating racial harassment.

Background and demographics

The predominantly rural county of Suffolk in the east of England is commonly perceived as a beautiful place to live. It is also a place that has a comparatively small minority ethnic population. While the African Caribbean community has had a presence in the county since the 1950s, and the Bangladeshi community since the 1960s, other minority ethnic groups have arrived more recently, namely a large migrant population from Portugal, and those seeking asylum, primarily from the Balkan states and the African subcontinent (Refugee Council 2003). Nevertheless, the proportion of Suffolk's population from a black and minority ethnic background is still only around three per cent,[1] although over the last decade this population has grown by around 4,000, a substantial increase for such a relatively small section of the total population.

With regard to the rural/urban make-up of Suffolk, it has been documented that as many as 156 wards (out of a county total of 175) can be classified as rural (Hutchinson 2003). In terms of rural district areas, these are identified as the districts where the majority of the wards are rural (ibid.) and in Suffolk these are Babergh, Mid-Suffolk, St Edmundsbury, Suffolk Coastal and Waveney. Only the districts of Forest Heath and Ipswich are not classified as rural within the county. It should be pointed out that within some of the district areas larger towns do exist, such as Lowestoft (which is in the Waveney district), Bury St Edmunds (St Edmundsbury) and Ipswich (Ipswich district). Both Lowestoft and Bury St Edmunds in particular are not really deemed to be rural in nature, but they could be classified as 'isolated areas' – areas where the provision of access to a variety of culturally appropriate support services for black and minority ethnic people may be limited. This point is also echoed in the work of Johnson *et al.* (1998) who note that there has tended to be a problem nationally over the provision of suitable and culturally sensitive services in rural areas, partly due to the sheer geographical size of some areas and partly due to the financial costs of providing the interpreters, translators and other resources that some minority ethnic groups require.

Ipswich, on the other hand, could be classified as being 'urban' even though the town itself is surrounded, and heavily influenced both socially and economically, by farmland and agriculture. Ipswich is also home to the largest number of black and minority ethnic people in the county: the 2001 Census estimated that of its 117,000 residents, 7,700 were from black and minority ethnic backgrounds. Although demographically the number of visible and non-visible minority ethnic residents has increased since 1991, absolute numbers remain low and below the national average counts. The 2001 Census also indicates that the overall population in rural Suffolk is rising, with growth rates being above regional averages, while age breakdowns demonstrate that there are a significant number of elderly people in the county[2] (Hutchinson 2003). The overall increase in population over the 1990s has been reflected in the numbers of the county's black and minority ethnic people. At the same time, the structure and location of Suffolk's minority groups has started to change as more people begin to move into areas outside of Ipswich, with factors such as greater mobility, economic opportunities and the increased incomes of some minority ethnic groups having influenced traditional patterns of population movement (Lakey 1997).

This situation presents unique challenges when developing support services to address racial harassment in the county of Suffolk. It could be argued that the relatively small number of black and minority ethnic residents can lead to complacency among those responsible for public services, and even denial that such problems exist: for example, where some areas may invest in providing multilingual support for those who may be suffering racist abuse, others may unwittingly not give this adequate recognition. Historically, support for victims of racial harassment tended to be provided in the more urbanised parts of the country, such as Leicester, Birmingham and London. This 'common-sense' scepticism about the seriousness of racial harassment in rural communities was justified by immigration patterns to the UK over the last 50 years, with black and minority ethnic groups and communities most commonly settling in urban areas. Invariably, these groups and communities have also suffered from poor quality housing, having little prospect of employment and have generally been socially excluded (Henderson and Kaur 1999). Arguably, therefore, this tendency may to some extent have overshadowed the issue of racism in rural areas due to the 'invisibility' of minority ethnic people in such locations.

However, awareness and knowledge of the existence of rural racism either through research (Jay 1992; Derbyshire 1994) or through those actively engaged in dealing with its effects have led directly to policy interventions being implemented by agencies across the UK. The county of Suffolk is no different, with the formulation of policies, procedures and effective multi-agency responses to racial harassment occurring on a fairly broad scale during the 1980s and 1990s.

Indeed, Suffolk County Council's Racial Harassment Initiative (RHI), which sits within the Community Safety Unit,[3] is an example of a scheme where victims in a predominantly rural county are offered support and advice about racial harassment. Historically, the RHI has its origins in a Single Regeneration Budget (SRB) programme aimed at improving the social and economic prospects of Suffolk's black and minority ethnic groups. Representatives from local minority community groups and voluntary and statutory agencies were aware of the problems associated with racial harassment for many years, and also recognised the lack of any coordinated responses or dedicated resources to support victims across the county. To address the problem, the Multi-Agency Forum Against Racial Harassment (MAFARH) was formed in 1997 to assess the effectiveness of partners in combating racist hate crime through a series of consultation exercises based in Ipswich. Their prime aim was to analyse the nature and extent of racial harassment in Suffolk with a view to effecting change (MAFARH 1997). Initial findings and consultation with the community concluded that more action was required, in terms of supporting the small number of people who were actually reporting racial harassment. Consequently, this forum successfully secured SRB funding for the RHI for three years.

The Forum has developed significantly since it was first established in 1997 and has clear terms of reference, recently developing its own action plan aimed at supporting the work of the Racial Harassment Initiative. It concentrates mainly on the exchange and monitoring of information relating to racial harassment across Suffolk. The requirements of effective multi-agency working in tackling racial harassment across the county will be discussed in more detail shortly.

The extent of the problem

Between 1997 and 1998, the year preceding the development of the RHI, there were 74 racist incidents reported to the police in Suffolk.[4] Within its first year of operation there was a 56 per cent increase in the number of reported incidents,[5] and by 2001–2 this number had risen to 303. The RHI and partner agencies[6] believed that the rise in the number of reported incidents was at least partially due to an increase in victims' confidence in the availability of support and specialist advice. Community groups, aware of the specialist services provided and the high profile placed on tackling racial harassment across the county, gave partners the confidence to encourage those suffering to continue reporting racist incidents.

Partners of the RHI have embraced recommendation 12 of the Stephen Lawrence Report (Macpherson 1999) which redefined what constituted a racist incident. Outlined in the report, a racist incident is: 'any incident which is perceived to be racist by the victim or any other person' (ibid.: 328). Ground-breakingly, those who 'perceive' an incident as being racist now have the opportunity to identify it as such, and therefore this new definition has undoubtedly increased levels of reporting. It could also be argued that factors such as the adverse media coverage of Muslim and other minority ethnic communities following September 11 2001, the ongoing 'war on terror' and the debate surrounding asylum in the UK have led to an increase in the negative attitudes displayed towards minority ethnic groups. This has not only been directed towards those arriving in Suffolk, whether asylum seekers or migrant workers, but is also aimed at well-established minority ethnic populations scattered throughout the county. At this point, it must be stressed that this perception is solely based on the author's personal perspective and would require further investigation, though this view has been supported by discussions with various community members throughout the author's working experience in Suffolk since 1998.

Nationally, the emphasis given to acknowledging the presence of racism, and to the importance of *all* agencies being equipped to tackle the problem, has created a higher expectation among victims. The RHI has been instrumental in promoting this message across Suffolk, and increases in the reporting of racist incidents are therefore regarded as a positive outcome of the developments within Suffolk. The Initiative regularly produces detailed reports on the nature and level of racial harassment in Suffolk, which help to inform agencies, to raise awareness of key issues and to secure support for new initiatives within local areas.[7] Such detailed reports not only help agencies identify what interventions they would like to see in their areas, but also allow them to monitor the actual number of reported incidents within their particular localities.[8]

Supporting victims in urban and rural areas: differences and similarities

The RHI is based in Ipswich, due in part to partner agencies being based there also.[9] This has allowed the rapid exchange of information pertaining to racial harassment cases and for these to be discussed and assessed readily, in order for action to be taken. More importantly, this is where historically the majority of incidents have been reported and where the bulk of the county's black and minority ethnic people live. While there has been much focus on the increasing number of incidents reported in Ipswich since 1998, this should not by any means suggest that the care and support provided to victims in Ipswich is different to that offered in other parts of the county. In fact, it is quite the contrary, as over recent years the RHI has been aware of the increasing number of incidents reported outside Ipswich in rural and isolated areas. It could be argued that those who suffer racial harassment in such areas require a particular *type* of service, one which differs from that received by victims and their families in more urban areas, such as Ipswich. The operational role of the RHI has primarily focused on providing support and care to victims who have either 'self-referred' themselves to the project or who have been referred to the RHI, for example by the police, housing or any other partner agency.

Approximately 90 per cent of all the RHI's referrals from across Suffolk are forwarded to the Initiative by the police and arrive within 24 hours of an incident having been recorded by the constabulary. Procedurally, the RHI's internal service standards state that once an incident has been received, a letter outlining the support role that the Initiative can offer will be sent to those suffering within 24 hours of receiving the initial notification. This is in addition to a telephone call which is made within 48 hours, offering a personal visit to further ascertain what the needs of the victims and the family might be.[10] The RHI also makes use of Language Line, an interpreting and translation service which can be accessed 24 hours a day by RHI staff. This facility is often utilised, particularly where letters have to be translated and sent to victims in their own language outlining that the Initiative will make contact with them via a Language Line interpreter. This latter service allows for a three-way conversation to take place in order to ascertain the facts of a particular incident, regardless of where the victims live within the county. This initial contact allows victims, particularly in rural areas and/or where their English is limited, to feel empowered, supported and listened to and to have a sense of security in the knowledge that help is on its way. An interesting point to make here is that the timescales for initially contacting victims via letter and offering a personal visit remain the same, regardless of whether the victim lives in a rural or urban area.

The range of services that the RHI offers victims is not determined by where victims live. An important feature of service delivery in this regard is that the entire range of interventions is available to victims and their families across a 50-mile radius. Such interventions may include coordinating a response through initial client casework, offering home visits and liaising with a raft of agencies that may have a vested interest in the case. The immediate impact of racist harassment may also lead the RHI to work with its partners in order for community alarms or CCTV cameras to be installed.[11]

The casework role undertaken by the RHI is largely aimed at raising awareness of the victim's rights, while offering realistic expectation of what the outcomes of an incident might be. A wide range of solutions can be offered. One of these is the possible use of mediation, particularly if the racial harassment is between two neighbours. Another option is the RHI's specialist counselling service, specifically designed and developed for victims who have particular trauma, anxiety and depression issues which need attention. Here, trained counsellors are at hand to offer expert care and guidance to those who require it. The counsellors used by the RHI are located across different parts of the county, so their accessibility to victims in rural or isolated parts of Suffolk is made much easier as victims do not need to travel to Ipswich to access these specialist services.

In addition, the police Administration of Justice (AJU) unit notifies the RHI when the preliminary court hearing is set against defendants.

Although the victim and their family may already know this date, they are reminded by the RHI in case they have forgotten about it or may not have received any correspondence from the police. Once trial dates are set, the Initiative will usually act upon requests arising from victims and their families in court, regardless of whether incidents occur in urban or rural areas. Alternatively, if charges have been reduced or altered by the Crown Prosecution Service (CPS) prior to a court hearing, the RHI has an agreement with the CPS that CPS staff will meet victims, explaining their decisions for changing the charges.

Furthermore, the RHI has also developed a free-phone helpline. This service provides information to those simply wanting to know what constitutes racial harassment, while also catering for those who wish to inform the Initiative that they have been verbally or physically attacked. The facility allows victims to leave a message in one of nine community languages in order for the RHI to coordinate a response to a reported incident. Again, this not only enables victims across the county to access the same advice and support regardless of whether they live in an urban or rural environment, but allows them to do so from the comfort of their own homes. The RHI has been able to develop these facilities by marketing and advertising these particular services across the entire county.

These examples, therefore, help to illustrate how the RHI supports victims in both urban and rural areas. It was argued earlier that the range of services available for victims does not depend on where they live, and this has been demonstrated and given credence via the examples discussed. However, although there are clear similarities in terms of the types of support services provided by the RHI in rural or urban Suffolk, there are also practical differences in delivering those services. The chapter now turns to examine these differences.

As previously mentioned, the RHI is located in Ipswich, from where it can support all the districts and borough councils in respect of policy issues. More problematic, however, is the level of physical contact that can be offered to victims of racist crime who are based away from more urbanised areas. As the RHI is based in Ipswich, the response time, in terms of visiting victims and coordinating appropriate action, can be more immediate in that particular town than in other areas. This is simply due to the geographical location of those reporting racial harassment. Travelling within Ipswich itself is obviously easier and quicker for caseworkers, who can reach clients based there in less time than it takes them to reach those living 30 or so miles away in an isolated village. This speed of access not only assists the RHI in developing a holistic response to the needs of victims, but also allows the RHI caseworkers to have direct access to the family and other agencies within the local vicinity.

In contrast, victims needing the same level of service in rural areas may not receive the same rapid response, purely because of the logistic difficulties of reaching them. Therefore, due to the sheer size of the county, the response time depends on *where* the incident has occurred, rather than *what services* the RHI can offer the victim. Furthermore, the RHI has only one casework officer whose remit is to cover the entire county, which is a sizeable responsibility.[12] This invariably means that from time to time the caseworker may be travelling all day across rural Suffolk attempting to accommodate a number of home visits. However, with time being restricted, the caseworker will only be able to spend a limited amount of time offering help and trying to resolve the complaint.[13]

Arguably, the coordination of responses to victims in rural Suffolk could be less time-consuming if more preparatory work was undertaken prior to victims being visited. While correspondence with key stakeholders is routine prior to any home visits taking place both in Ipswich and rural Suffolk, often the RHI will not have met individual officers from the various agencies in rural Suffolk who would be jointly involved in resolving a victim's plight. However, in Ipswich and the surrounding area, the RHI is well informed and more joined-up to a range of officers and key agencies who may be 'championing' racial harassment issues. This is somewhat different in areas outside Ipswich where key contacts with specific officers from a range of agencies may at times be limited.

Once an incident has been referred into the RHI from villages or other rural areas, it can become fraught with difficulties, caused by problems with coordinating a response, as previously mentioned, or more importantly by the victim's own concerns. Often, victims who request an RHI visit may ask for discretion when the visit takes place: for example, those who are experiencing racial harassment may request that the RHI officer (or any other agency worker) park their car away from where the harassment is taking place. This is so as not to draw the visit to the attention of the alleged perpetrators, which could potentially make the situation worse. Although this type of response is occasionally requested in Ipswich, it is much more evident in areas where the number of minority ethnic households is small. In other words, a considerable amount of practical thought goes into the logistics of visiting clients in rural, as opposed to urban, areas.

Additionally, the take-up of target-hardening measures, such as the community alarms (linked to the police) in rural or isolated areas is less extensive than, for example, in larger towns such as Ipswich. Again, the reason given for this by victims when questioned by the RHI is that they would not feel comfortable or safe if a police car was to respond to an incident, as this would be an indicator to other villagers that the police had been informed,[14] as one dual heritage victim explained to the author:

It would probably make the situation worse for me. I can just see it now, a police car responding to dog mess being posted through my letterbox. I've been there with that stuff – drawing more attention to it with alarms would be catastrophic for me and the family.

In 2001 research was undertaken by Garland and Chakraborti into the nature and extent of racism in Suffolk, with particular emphasis given to assessing the effectiveness of agency responses to victims. The study highlighted the difficulties facing minority ethnic households in rural Suffolk and the fact that their vulnerability was compounded by a sense of isolation, a lack of support networks and also a lack of understanding of the issues facing victims among local agencies (Garland and Chakraborti 2002). The research gave further credence to what the RHI has been trying to do since its inception in 1998, namely seeking to lobby, influence and change the manner in which key agencies and organisations in rural and isolated areas respond to the needs of victims. It could be argued that negotiating and influencing such changes in the policies and practices that support victims is far less exhausting in urban areas, and on occasions more productive, than it is in more rural environments. This may be due to the extent to which agencies in rural or isolated locations *fail* to understand the impact that racial harassment has on its victims, coupled with, at times, the assumption that low numbers of minority ethnic residents in such areas mean that racism does not exist (de Lima 1999). Moreover, supporting victims by way of developing appropriate policies and procedures to benefit them in the long term becomes more problematic in rural areas when racist incidents are seen as isolated, one-off events rather than forming part of a continual stream of harassment (Bowling 1998).

Finally, the complexities of being victimised on the basis of one's colour, culture, religious belief or ethnic origin in areas outside of Ipswich may mean that recipients of racist abuse continue to feel isolated and disempowered, regardless of whether the victimisation has stopped and a resolution found. Although the RHI is able to provide victims and their families with immediate attention and care through casework, the feeling of being 'left alone' in order to take back control of their lives is often daunting for many. Victims in these areas may experience a form of isolation which, to a large extent, cuts them off from a majority of activities within their community. As a consequence, RHI staff are required to work more rigorously in rural areas in a 'befriending' role to ensure that culturally sensitive and appropriate local support is identified. The situation described differs considerably from how the RHI may help victims based in urban areas. For instance, there are a number of initiatives and projects already in place in Ipswich which aim both to empower victims and to provide general informal support.[15]

Thus, although it can be seen that clear similarities exist in terms of the range of responses that the RHI can offer victims, regardless of whether they live in an urban or rural area, practical differences are also evident. Difficulties of delivery of services to victims in rural Suffolk may occur due to location, while victims themselves may continue to feel a sense of isolation once the harassment has ceased and agencies such as the RHI have stopped supporting them. Thus the level of service, as opposed to the types of services, may differ according to the urban/rural divide.

Structure and requirements of effective multi-agency working

The range of support measures the RHI is able to offer victims, both in urban and rural Suffolk, has benefited from agencies working together effectively. These have been developed through the work of the county-wide Crime and Disorder Reduction Partnerships (CDRPs) which derived from the inception of the Crime and Disorder Act 1998. In addition to this, the local MAFARH quickly realised at the time that the first wave of crime audits and strategies were being written in 1999 that there was a need for the development of anti-racist strategies to become an integral part of the CDRPs' crime reduction agenda. The introduction of CDRPs across the county has given the RHI a much wider platform upon which to influence, develop and assist in amending the agenda within the confines of the multi-agency banner. As a result, all district and borough councils across Suffolk are now actively engaged in the debate around racial harassment.

Challenging racism through multi-agency cooperation is dependent upon a firm commitment among partners to the prioritisation of the prevention and reduction of racism, which demands from partners a plan of action. As such, key stakeholders should mainstream the issues within their own organisations, rather than expect elements of the voluntary sector, as it has done so for many years, to lobby for changes to be made in terms of how racial harassment is dealt with. This task has been left to multi-agency forums and committees for too long when, in essence, what is needed is a 'top down' approach within organisations whereby senior figures take a lead on such issues. This requires recognition of the issues and a shared vision by leaders and decision-makers to deal with racial harassment in order for good practice to filter down through individual organisations.

An important feature of the Suffolk experience has been the clear demarcation of roles and responsibilities as a prerequisite for effective multi-agency working. For example, the RHI, Victim Support and the Constabulary have a service level agreement outlining which agency is responsible for fulfilling certain tasks when victims need to be cared for. This policy not only ensures that staff within the respective organisations are aware of their duties, in the short, medium and long term, but also that agencies within the partnership can respond effectively to the needs of those suffering. Without defined responsibilities, confusion would invariably arise in the event of a breakdown in communication, hence decreasing the value of any effective working arrangements.

Clear roles and responsibilities go hand in hand with issues of ownership. It should be noted that only a handful of areas in the UK exist where local authorities have mainstreamed racial harassment support projects. Instead, many projects are resourced in an ad hoc manner, by charities such as Comic Relief, lottery funding or charitable trusts, and therefore struggle to continue due to these uncertainties (Chahal 2003). This has led to a lack of clarity over, and ownership of, who should be championing support for victims. With regard to Suffolk, the RHI has been a mainstream service to residents throughout the county since 2001. This has meant that the unit has been regarded as a co-ordinating body, encouraging many partner organisations to claim ownership of the issue, rather than adopt an 'it's not a concern of ours' mentality.

The requirements of effective multi-agency operating also include working with partners internally; indeed there is a considerable amount of coordination between directorates and departments within Suffolk's own county council. The RHI has developed close relationships with directorates such as education, where work is jointly designed and delivered around liaising with schools across Suffolk, while the Youth Offending Service has received detailed training around dealing effectively with racist and racially motivated offending. These few examples illustrate that a high level of 'intra-' as well as 'inter-agency' work is beginning to take shape, resulting directly from detailed planning, communication and flexibility, and from clear roles and responsibilities being agreed.

Having briefly examined some of the ingredients required to develop effective multi-agency working, it has been shown that although partners in Suffolk have divided and defined roles, they can also work effectively as a group under the crime and disorder banner, usually led by the RHI. The discussion now turns to illustrate examples of good practice, resulting from the requirements of effective multi-agency work.

In order to continue encouraging victims to report racist incidents, the RHI has, from the very outset, embraced recommendation 15 of the Stephen Lawrence Report as a prerequisite of good practice.[16] The Lawrence Report drew attention to the importance of developing systems of reporting and recording racist incidents and, as a result of this, a county-wide common reporting form was developed in Suffolk. This has enabled the RHI to capture accurate and timely information about racist incidents, with a view to assisting victims and sharing information with appropriate agencies. In addition to this, the recommendation stressed the importance of steps that should be taken by key partners towards enabling victims of racism to report incidents at places other than police stations, and possibly throughout the entire day and night. The RHI has worked with over a dozen Citizens' Advice Bureaux spread across Suffolk, enabling the Bureaux to take third-party racist incident details from those who may be suffering in both urban and rural areas. Due to the small but significant increase in the number of attacks on refugees and people seeking asylum in Suffolk, this network has been expanded to include the Refugee Council, where staff are trained to record and refer cases to the RHI.

These examples of good practice have recently been furthered to encompass a 24-hour pre-recorded helpline for victims to utilise. This method of reporting enables those who are suffering to find out about the availability of support and where it can be accessed. It could be argued that the greater the flexibility and options for reporting incidents, the more likely that an accurate picture of the situation will be given. Schemes which allow victims to report racist incidents more easily also then require provisions to be made which ensure that staff who are supporting victims provide a sensitive and appropriate response to their needs. Research by Chahal (2003) into the role, impact and potential of racial harassment support projects in a number of case study areas across the country highlighted the perception among caseworkers who were interviewed that specific counselling skills needed to be developed within racial harassment projects. Interviews with staff across the country also revealed that the lack of formal counselling qualifications, together with time and resource restrictions, often meant that it was not always possible to offer such a service. However, and as previously stated, the RHI has developed a unique support service offering specialist trauma, stress and anxiety counselling to those who have suffered racist harassment throughout the county. This work can either take place on an individual or family basis, and is led by trained counsellors.

Finally, in order to ensure that agencies are working to full capacity to find a resolution to the plight of victims, the RHI has developed case conferencing and case review panels. The case conference panel aims to ensure that cases are mapped and tracked both to assess risk and also to ensure that agencies share information about any ongoing cases. The aim of case review panels on the other hand is to ensure that agencies can learn from incidents of racist harassment that have been dealt with. Key agencies such as the police, housing, education and the CPS take part in these panels.

In summary, the effective multi-agency approach adopted in challenging racial harassment in Suffolk has enabled the RHI to co-ordinate traditional but effective responses through its casework approach, and has also allowed the unit to develop innovative methods which build on the more conventional ways of dealing with the issue. The final section concludes by illustrating the significance of developing interventions which value the notion of education and prevention in combating racial harassment, the importance of training as a means of learning, and finally by considering whether the RHI model could be replicated in other rural environments.

Conclusions: developing a model response to victims?

The Racial Harassment Initiative's role in such a predominantly rural county as Suffolk has developed over the seven years of its existence. The chapter has sought to highlight the range of services which can be made available to victims across Suffolk. However, this does not necessarily suggest that the way in which services are delivered is the same in urban and rural areas. This chapter has illustrated that although many similarities are present in terms of the types of support services available for those experiencing racial harassment, regardless of the urban/rural divide, some clearly defined differences do nevertheless exist. These differences are mainly based around the problems associated with the geography of Suffolk, in terms of the time taken to physically visit victims, as well as, at times, a less informed understanding of the immediate need of victims by agencies and the lack of support networks for individuals and families.

As already mentioned, in the short term the main aim of racial harassment projects is to coordinate responses to incidents. These traditional approaches could arguably be deemed as reactive as they respond to the immediate needs of victims, and this process, termed the 'bread and butter' method, is the one which many agencies understand and adhere to. Although casework will continue to be an essential facet and requirement of any support project, the need for a proactive stance in combating race hate crime through educative and preventative methods should also be given equal weight as, undoubtedly in this context, prevention is better than cure.

It is envisaged that over time the level of negativity towards minority ethnic groups will shift as a result of the work undertaken by the RHI and partner agencies. In order to work towards this change agenda, the RHI has developed a comprehensive range of educational programmes with young people and communities, such as annual young people's conferences which have been taking place in Suffolk since 1999. The focus of these events has been upon young people being able to share their experiences of prejudice and discrimination, either as victims or perpetrators, with others. Such events are 'needs-led', based on the local education authority's statistical returns on the number of reported incidents which highlight trends among victims and perpetrators according to year groups. Such an approach ensures that the problem of racism can be discussed and debated through cognitive-based modules which aim to dispel myths and stereotypes about black and minority ethnic people.

In addition to this, further methods of improving upon the more traditional ways of combating racial harassment have involved developing educational photographic portrait exhibitions which explore and celebrate the diversity of Suffolk. By using photography as a tool, exhibitions such as these aim to precipitate a long-term change in attitudes. The general idea with pieces of work such as these has been to challenge stereotypes, encourage inclusiveness and tackle racist beliefs among the young and old across Suffolk. Agencies such as the Youth Offending Service and schools have visited and debated the content of the exhibition. This indirect method assists in combating racial harassment through dialogue, with a view to making it unacceptable, thereby helping to break down commonly held myths about 'difference'.

Moreover, a thorough training programme has been developed by the RHI which benefits partner agencies. The Initiative routinely researches good practice methods around developing effective strategies, and holds regular training events aimed at raising general awareness of the impact of racial harassment. The overall intention is therefore to enable agency staff to respond effectively to the needs of those experiencing racist harassment in any area across Suffolk. Equally important have been the programmes developed around working effectively with perpetrators of racial harassment. Certainly, it would appear crucial for any training programme aimed at meeting victims' requirements also to consider the need to work with specialist agencies such as Youth Offending and Probation Services, with a view to training staff to deal with those charged with racially aggravated offences. In Suffolk, where absolute numbers of offenders charged with racially aggravated offences are small, staff from these agencies have received detailed training, co-facilitated by the RHI, to enable them to be vigilant and aware of how to respond to those actually perpetrating these offences, with the ultimate aim of reducing repeat victimisation rates. It could be argued that the development of such educative and preventative interventions based on cognitive reasoning allows people think through the reasons for their having particular values which may be prejudicial and discriminatory towards minority ethnic groups. In essence, the non-traditional methods described may not necessarily combat racial harassment per se simply by reducing the number of reported incidents. However, what this work is intended to do is to act as a catalyst for people to reflect upon the reasons why they racially abuse, and the possible impact and consequences of such actions.

The Suffolk Racial Harassment Initiative could supply the basis for a model which can be replicated across the UK, provided that leaders within respective organisations make resources available to deal with the issue. Furthermore, the lack of reported incidents should not be regarded as an indicator of the rural being a 'racial harassment-free zone'. Just as significant is the requirement of effective partnership working, where clear roles and responsibilities among partners are defined. A lack of an agreed and overarching purpose for responding to racial harassment will inevitably mean few or no services will be made available to those who are suffering. It should be noted that those projects that do exist, but which do not have mainstream funding sources and which may be time-limited, should align themselves with their local CDRPs with a view to persuading them that combating racial harassment should become a key priority within their areas. This in turn may bring about the desired outcomes required by agencies in the UK who currently work with victims of racial harassment.

However, providing an effective response may prove difficult where there is an absence of a central body specifically funded to support victims, develop intervention programmes and offer strategic support to partner agencies. In essence, funding racial harassment work on a short-term basis will not bring about the desired changes necessary, for both victims and the community at large. This chapter has illustrated that every effort should be made to highlight racial harassment as an issue, both in urban and rural areas through the appropriate channels, but while sufficient recognition may be paid to the problem in an urban context, many counties will not have a specific unit, such as Suffolk's RHI, to provide services to victims in the rural. Nonetheless, the day-to-day plight of those suffering in silence continues to be a reality in rural locales. It is up to us all to redraw the landscape for the better.

Notes

1 Suffolk's population in 1991 stood at just under 622,000, and black and minority ethnic residents made up fewer than 14,000 (2.25 per cent) of this total. Figures from the 2001 Census indicate that the county's population has increased to 668,000, with minority ethnic residents now standing at just over 18,000 (2.69 per cent), signifying an increase in the minority ethnic population of nearly 29 per cent in ten years.
2 There are over 210,000 people in wards of rural Suffolk aged over 50 based on the 2001 census. Twenty-one per cent of the population of rural Suffolk is over retirement age.
3 Information about the RHI is available online at: www.suffolkcc.gov.uk/srhi.
4 Community groups and agencies in the county were aware that there were many incidents not being reported. This was backed up by national research indicating that as little as 1 in 17 incidents of racial harassment were actually being reported (ACPO 1998).
5 In October 1999, the RHI was one of ten regional winners of the British Crime Prevention and Community Safety Awards for its innovative work around racial harassment in Suffolk. In presenting the award, the Princess Royal praised the efforts of those organisations in Suffolk, led by the RHI, that were helping to encourage the reporting of racist incidents.
6 These agencies include Mid-Suffolk District Council, Suffolk Coastal District Council, Waveney District Council, Suffolk Police, East of England Development Agency (EEDA), Learning Skills Council, Youth Offending Service, Education, Suffolk Health, Social Care and Connexions.
7 This two-page fact sheet is available upon request from the Racial Harassment Initiative.
8 One hundred and thirty-three incidents were reported to Suffolk constabulary in 1998/99, 236 in 1999/00, 280 in 2000/01, 303 in 2001/02, 286 in 2002/03 and 350 for the first ten months of 2003/04.
9 The RHI was initially based at the Ipswich and Suffolk Council for Racial Equality (ISCRE) between 1998 and 2001, with the view of raising the profile of the project. As the RHI was mainstreamed in 2001, it co-located with the Community Safety Unit to Suffolk County Council.
10 The RHI, police and Victim Support have a service level agreement which

was produced in 2003. It outlines how each agency should care for and support victims of racial harassment, thereby avoiding duplication of work. The RHI is the only agency in the county that offers *all* victims of racial harassment a personal visit regardless of where they live.

11 The RHI, in conjunction with the police, is able to offer victims and their families a community alarm dependent on the severity of the incident. These alarms are linked to a central control room and once activated by the victim, a police response will follow. These target-hardening devices tend to reduce both the fear associated with racial harassment, and also reassure the victim that support is available to them. The 20 alarms are distributed across policing areas according to the number of reported incidents in any given area and are installed by crime reduction officers employed by Suffolk Constabulary.

12 The increase in reported racist incidents and the expectations of victims has meant that the casework officer who covers a large geographical area ensures that clients are seen on an appointment basis.

13 It is not being suggested that due to limited time the casework officer will spend with victims and their families that additional support will not be provided once the officer departs from the victim's home. The RHI may be able to resolve the harassment from its base in Ipswich by liaising with partner agencies such as the police and housing in those respective areas.

14 Six victims in rural Suffolk were questioned between October 2003 and January 2004 about target-hardening measures such as the use of community alarms. All responded by stating that they would not have them installed if offered.

15 Community education in Ipswich, local community activists (with a vested interest in race equality issues) and Ipswich and Suffolk Council for Racial Equality (ISCRE) are all potential sources of additional support for victims, if for example, they do not want to discuss their case with the RHI, police or any other 'formal' agency.

16 Recommendation 15 calls for the creation of a 'comprehensive system of reporting and recording of all racist incidents and crimes' (Macpherson 1999: 329).

References

Association of Chief Police Officers (ACPO) (1998) *The Good Practice Guide for Police Response to Racist Incidents.* London: Home Office.

Aust, R. and Simmons, J. (2002) *Rural Crime: England and Wales,* Home Office Research Development and Statistics Directorate, Statistical Bulletin 1/02. London: Home Office.

Bowling, B. (1998) *Violent Racism: Victimisation, Policing and Social Context.* Oxford: Clarendon Press.

Chahal, K. (2003) *Racist Harassment Support Projects: Their Role, Impact and Potential.* York: Joseph Rowntree Foundation.

de Lima, P. (2001) *Needs Not Numbers: An Exploration of Minority Ethnic Communities in Scotland.* London: Commission for Racial Equality and Community Development Foundation.

Derbyshire, H. (1994) *Not in Norfolk: Tackling the Invisibility of Racism.* Norwich: Norwich and Norfolk Racial Equality Council.

Garland, J. and Chakraborti, N. (2002) *Tackling the Invisible Problem? An Examination of the Provision of Services to Victims of Racial Harassment in Rural Suffolk.* Leicester: Scarman Centre, University of Leicester.

Henderson, P. and Kaur, R. (1999) *Rural Racism in the UK: Examples of Community-Based Responses.* London: Community Development Foundation.

Hutchinson, J.C. (2003) *A Profile of the Rural Suffolk Economy.* Cambridge: SQW Limited.

Jay, E. (1992) *Keep Them in Birmingham: Challenging Racism in South West England.* London: Commission for Racial Equality.

Johnson, M.R.D. with Powell, D., Owen, D. and Tomlins, R. (1998) *Housing and Social Care Needs of Ethnic Minorities in Warwickshire.* Coventry: University of Warwick/Friendship Group.

Lakey, J. (1997) 'Neighbourhood and Housing', in T. Modood, R. Berthoud, J. Lakey, J. Nazroo, P. Smith, S. Virdee, and S. Beishon, *Ethnic Minorities in Britain: Diversity and Disadvantage – Fourth National Survey of Ethnic Minorities.* London: Policy Studies Institute.

Macpherson, Sir W. (1999) *The Stephen Lawrence Inquiry: Report of an Inquiry by Sir William Macpherson of Cluny.* London: HMSO.

Multi-Agency Forum Against Racial Harassment (MAFARH) (1997) *Annual Report.* Ipswich: MAFARH.

Office for National Statistics (2004) *Census 2001.* At http://www.statistics.gov.uk/census2001/

Refugee Council (2003) *Information for Advisers: Eastern Region.* At http://www.refugeecouncil.org.uk/downloads/publications/ipswich_ap.pdf

Chapter 8

Challenging rural racism through education

Kate Broadhurst and Andi Wright

Introduction: setting the debate in context

The suspension in April 2004 of a maths teacher from a secondary school in Solihull in the West Midlands, following his declaration of candidacy for the far-right British National Party in the 2004 June European elections, again raised concerns, both nationally and locally, about the problem of racism within education (Crace 2004). Central to this discussion was the question of whether Britain's education system could be branded 'institutionally racist' in the same vein that the Metropolitan Police Service was criticised in the 1999 Lawrence Report (Macpherson 1999). With this in mind, this chapter seeks to examine concerns relating to the education sector's response to racism and highlights ways in which the problem can be challenged.

The authors would like to acknowledge that the majority of the research reviewed in this chapter focuses primarily upon those issues pertaining to racism within education more broadly, as opposed to concentrating specifically, and exclusively, upon rural contexts. This has been intentional for two reasons. First, the dearth of investigations into racism in education in the rural has necessitated the use in this chapter of findings from urban environments, where research has been much more plentiful and insightful. Second, a number of parallels may still be drawn from reviewing current literature that examines the situation in those urban schools classified as predominantly white (see, for example, Cline *et al.* (2002) who view this as when between 4 and 6 per cent of pupils are from minority ethnic backgrounds), and consequently extrapolation of such research findings in this context is highly useful when giving consideration to the potential ways in which to address racism within rural educational settings. Therefore, rather than abandoning the findings of research conducted within more urbanised settings, the authors have sought to examine those findings and consider their applicability to rural educational contexts. It would be mistaken to suggest that such research bears little relevance for schools in the rural, as it can help to shed light upon ways in which urban schools have developed anti-racist strategies that mainly white, rural schools can learn from.

Defining education

In order to understand the complexity of the problem there is a need to deconstruct the education system into its various components, and in so doing to acknowledge the many forms that education can take. This is instructive in facilitating a fuller appreciation of the numerous tiers of the system that are open to racial intolerance, as well as the enormity of the potential role that education can play in challenging racism at every level.

It is suggested here that educational establishments vary greatly both *between* sectors (i.e. primary, middle, secondary, special educational needs, further education, higher education) and *within* sectors, even though government legislation calls for all statutory education service providers to implement key policies, such as the Race Relations Amendment Act 2000, among others. As a result, any difference between urban and rural educational contexts may be exacerbated or reduced by policy awareness, implementation and practice. Furthermore, this issue is compounded when considering the case of private educational establishments that are not underpinned by certain aspects of government legislation and are therefore not obliged to address racism in any specific way. It is also widely, and perhaps naively, assumed that statutory educational establishments are closely monitored and regulated by agencies such as the local education authority (LEA), the Office for Standards in Education (OFSTED), the Department for Educational and Skills (DfES), the Home Office and national teachers' unions, and that therefore legislation is implemented to the same level of integrity both within, and indeed across, all statutory educational sectors within the UK. While most commonly within the education system there are schools maintained by the state through the LEA, there are also a wealth of private, independent and special schools that fall outside of the powers of the LEA, and as such responsibility lies with the proprietor of these establishments.

There are important issues to address surrounding the promotion and regulation of anti-racist practices which are located 'outside' the realms of statutory educational contexts. When defining education more broadly than the confines of the school environment, there are a number of key stakeholders that have a similar educative role supporting young people, such as local authority youth services, home tutors, adult education, community education, youth offending teams, and private sector educational establishments (including nursery provision). Thus with all these factors in mind, it becomes clear that in terms of tackling racism within the education system, the situation is far more complicated than simply thinking in terms of central government policy being translated through the LEA into procedures and ethos within state schools.

Understanding the problem

Underachievement of minority ethnic students

By far the most researched area in the context of 'race' and education is that of the underachievement of minority ethnic pupils. There is a significant body of research exploring the achievement gap between white pupils and their minority ethnic classmates. A number of key studies were undertaken between 2000 and 2004, all of which provide insights into the ways in which racial inequalities and/or racism (in all its forms, including verbal harassment, name-calling and physical assault) have been identified and addressed within the education sector. One example includes a review of both statistical data returns and key documentation from a variety of agencies including the Department for Education and Employment (DfEE), the Ethnic Minority Achievement Grant (EMAG) statistical returns,[1] and information produced to date from the Youth Cohort Study of England and Wales (Gillborn and Safia Mirza 2000). This research sought to establish the level to which racial and ethnic inequalities impact upon educational attainment in comparison to other factors, such as gender and social class. As a result of undertaking detailed analyses of all relevant data and documentation, it was found that despite variances in geographical locations, minority ethnic pupils in general experienced lower levels of educational attainment when compared to pupils from non-minority ethnic backgrounds. Furthermore, it was concluded that although the variables of gender and social class do impact upon educational attainment, these factors are far less instrumental in affecting educational attainment than 'race' and ethnicity.

Reasons that have been put forward to explain the gap have ranged from the influence of racist teachers to the existence of a racist curriculum and racist education systems. Others, such as Amin *et al.* (1997) argue that 'race' cannot be separated from class and other linked socio-economic factors. When comparing the inequalities by 'race', class and gender between 1988 and 1997, Amin *et al.* (1997) discovered that the largest disparity was found between children from managerial/ professional families and those from unskilled and manual families.

Raising the achievement of minority ethnic pupils is a complex issue with no simple answers, although the problem is being addressed through initiatives such as *Excellence in Cities* and the *National Literacy and Numeracy Strategies*.[2] A wealth of guidance now exists (see, for example, DfES 2002; Runnymede Trust 2003) for LEAs, teaching staff and governors, which suggests that, if it is implemented effectively across the education system, then the complex causes of underachievement can begin to be tackled. Previous research conducted in the field by OFSTED, the DfEE and the Commission for Racial Equality (CRE) is consistent with this view, and supports the conclusions produced as a result of the review undertaken by Gillborn and Safia Mirza. All of these agencies advocate the case for moving towards the development of inclusion strategies both within schools and their respective LEAs, including a number of key considerations that should underpin the development of any effective strategy to tackle racism. These involve adopting a strong approach to leadership with respect to equal opportunities and social justice; using pupil and parent consultation as a means of obtaining qualitative information; offering a transparent process for reporting and recording racist incidents; and reviewing curricular and pastoral approaches to ensure sensitivity and appropriateness of response from school staff. Therefore the fundamental philosophy underpinning the effectiveness of all these strategic approaches relates to developing and maintaining an ethos that is open and vigilant, and utilising ethnic monitoring as a routine and rigorous part of school management and performance (Gillborn and Safia Mirza 2000).

Stunted progression for minority ethnic staff

In a similar vein to the underachievement of minority ethnic pupils, research conducted with teaching staff funded by the Commission for Black Staff in Further Education found that despite being better educated than their white colleagues, many black staff failed to progress to senior positions, with only one per cent of college principals in England being black (Commission for Black Staff in Further Education 2002). Significant under-representation in senior management posts was also noted, while a high proportion of black staff were found to be in transient, part-time teaching posts in subjects such as community education and English as a second language. The report found that black staff were under-represented compared with the number of minority ethnic students, and suggested that schools adopted a holistic approach to equality, including race equality training. Recommendations made in the Race Relations (Amendment) Act 2000 require all public bodies to monitor ethnic representation in their workforce and, within the education sector, to monitor students as well.[3] Even with these checks and regulations in place, the under-representation of minority ethnic teaching staff, particularly in senior positions where they can affect policy and practice, undoubtedly influences the ways that schools tackle racism. In rural contexts this situation is likely to be even more acute where numbers of minority ethnic staff are considered to be at their lowest.

Racist victimisation in schools: the experiences of pupils and teachers

Research that has examined the ways that racism affects pupils and teachers presents a worrying picture of a failure to stem a growing problem within schools. A number of studies conducted in the last decade have found racist prejudice to be endemic (see, for example, Whitney and Smith 1993; Hatcher 1995; Stuart et al. 2003). A recent illustration of this concern was provided at the Spring 2004 conference of the teaching union the National Association of Schoolmasters Union of Women Teachers (NASUWT), where a paper presented by a religious education teacher from Wakefield, West Yorkshire suggested that the growing influence of far-right groups on children and parents has led to an increasing problem of racial intolerance among pupils (Ward 2004).

Research by Cline et al. (2002), conducted in mainly white schools across LEA areas throughout the UK, is useful to consider in the context of this discussion, as the low numbers of minority ethnic pupils in those schools examined allow comparisons to be made with schools in rural contexts (which also have a similar student demographic profile). The primary aims of this research were to elicit information regarding pupils' experiences of racism in schools and the extent to which teaching staff were prepared to address and challenge racist behaviour, while also exploring strategies deployed by mainly white schools to promote diversity through the curriculum, and examining the training received by teaching staff with respect to diversity, ethnicity and 'race'. In summary, Cline et al. found high levels of name-calling and racist verbal abuse directed towards pupils from minority ethnic backgrounds by their peers, both within the context of the school setting and indeed, when travelling to and from the educational establishment. This harassment had, more often than not, been taking place over a lengthy period of time. Furthermore, the study revealed that parents and pupils often did not report incidents of race-related bullying due to their lack of faith in the ways in which schools undertook investigations into racist incidents, and indeed due to the lack of transparency of processes undertaken by schools to successfully resolve the situation. Those pupils whose needs teaching staff found most difficult to address were those from dual heritage backgrounds. Not only did teachers have limited, if any, awareness of the problems faced by dual heritage pupils, such as the difficulties these pupils can have with relating to either minority or majority communities, but also they had no real understanding or awareness of those concerns held by the pupils' parents.

Each of these factors was compounded by the fact that of all the schools participating in the project, none had successfully designed and implemented curricula that explored cultural diversity. Disappointingly, very few schools valued cultural diversity as an integral and mainstream element to the pupils' learning environment, and this was largely attributable to the majority of teachers involved in the study failing to truly understand the concept of a multicultural approach to education. The research also found that there was little or no support, or internal training, provided by school management to improve knowledge, awareness and skills.

An integral element of Cline et al.'s work was, however, to identify promising practices that can be implemented in an attempt to raise the current standard of addressing racism in mainly white schools. These included encouraging head teachers to provide a lead for other staff in combating the problem; informing victims and their parents of the outcomes of any follow-up to a report of racist behaviour; installing 'bullying boxes' in schools to allow pupils to post messages that would receive staff attention within 24 hours; using a racist incident log book for school management to complete following the reporting of a racist incident; and using 'circle time' and thinking sheets for pupils to reflect upon what they had done wrong and why, which were also required to be signed by parents (Cline et al. 2002). Therefore, as shall be discussed more fully shortly, while problems of racism may potentially be many and varied in the context of schooling, recognition should be afforded to the mechanisms that can be developed to counter such problems.

Policy and legal frameworks

Research undertaken by the University of Brighton (Cole and Hill 2001; Cole 2002) has called for the implementation of recommendations contained in the Macpherson Report and the empowerment of LEAs to create and enforce anti-racist policies through codes of practice, coupled with the amendment of the National Curriculum to raise awareness of existing prejudice.

There are already a number of legislative and guidance frameworks that seek to safeguard the education system from racism to protect both pupils and teachers alike. One such framework is provided by the Race Relations Act 1976, and subsequent Amendment Act 2000, whose provisions make it unlawful to discriminate against a person, directly or indirectly, in the field of education. Guidance offered by the CRE (2003) outlines the ways that such discrimination can manifest itself, from crude racist remarks to subtle differences in assessment, expectation, provision and treatment. Such behaviour may be unconscious or even well-intentioned, but is nonetheless unlawful.

Within educational establishments it is illegal for an establishment to discriminate in the terms with which it offers admission or refuses to accept an application; in the way it affords, or refuses to afford, its pupils or students access to any benefits, facilities or services; or by excluding them from the establishment or subjecting them to any other detriment. This applies to all educational institutions and includes LEA-maintained schools and colleges, grant-maintained schools, independent schools and colleges, universities, polytechnics and colleges of higher education. Similarly, it is unlawful for LEAs to discriminate in carrying out any of their functions, including, for example, the provision of school meals, school transport, educational welfare, liaison and psychological services or English as a second language. Indeed, LEAs have a general duty to provide all their services without unlawful racial discrimination, enforceable by the Secretary of State for Education. Local authorities have a general statutory duty to ensure that their various functions are carried out with due regard to the need to eliminate unlawful racial discrimination and to promote equality of opportunity and good relations between persons of different ethnic groups.

As a result of the Education Reform Act 1988, school and college governors have increased responsibilities for educational provision in their institutions. These will include employment, admissions, exclusions, resource allocation and the implementation of the National Curriculum. Many sections of this code are of particular relevance to governing bodies in ensuring that they too discharge their respon-sibilities without racial discrimination.

The 1996 Schools Inspection Act sets out a broad framework for school inspections focusing on quality, standards, the management of financial resources and the spiritual, moral, social and cultural development of pupils. In March 1999 the government, in its response to the Stephen Lawrence Inquiry, gave OFSTED a lead role in monitoring the imple-mentation of strategies designed to prevent and address racism in schools. The CRE, however, appeared critical of OFSTED's failure to openly recognise the existence and causes of racism, concluding that '… it is difficult to see how OFSTED and its leadership can contribute to the prevention of racism through the inspection of schools while they continue to avoid any direct discussion of racism in its standard policy documents and public statements' (Osler and Morrison 2000: xviii). The CRE recognised that while OFSTED has published research focused on 'race' issues (Gillborn and Gipps 1996) and conducted thematic inspections on the achievement of minority ethnic pupils, these were yet to inform their work overall.

Promising practice

The bulk of research conducted to date in the field of tackling racism through education has been focused predominantly at the 'school' level, in an attempt to identify inconsistencies and commonalities with regard to the ways in which schools across the UK address and challenge racism. The overarching non-departmental public body known as the Qualifications and Curriculum Authority (QCA), sponsored by the DfES, has a remit to help maintain and develop the National Curriculum and associated assessments, tests and examinations, and to accredit and monitor qualifications in colleges and at work. The QCA is also concerned with working closely in partnership with other agencies such as, for example, the Office for Standards in Education and the Teacher Training Agency, in order to help inform and achieve its aims. Therefore, although the majority of studies focus upon what schools are not doing with regard to addressing racism, the QCA exists to offer curriculum guidance to teachers nationally so that mainstream activities such as Personal Health and Social Education, Religious Education and the National Curriculum more generally are used in a manner that values diversity and challenges racism in the classroom.

As with many agencies, the key to improving the ways in which racism is tackled within the education establishment is the use of schools as the starting point from which to develop better working practices. Thus the National Curriculum (delivered to all pupils within statutory educational sectors) is only one way in which rural racism can be tackled through education: education extends beyond the realms of the school grounds and reaches out to parents and the community more broadly. Correspondingly, consideration should also be given to the level of commitment from nominated members of school management to act in a manner that consults with pupils, parents and community members in the locality in order to adopt a truly inclusive approach to educating individuals in anti-racist practices.

National agencies and organisations have been instrumental over a number of years in undertaking ongoing programmes of research into the educational attainment of young people within statutory education. In particular, research conducted by OFSTED adopts a proactive approach to addressing the experiences of pupils from minority ethnic backgrounds. Two significant studies undertaken in 2002 (OFSTED 2002a, 2002b) focus upon educational attainment in both primary and secondary schools within the UK and highlight promising practice surrounding the ways in which schools identify, monitor and challenge underachievement and racism within schools. This research involved an in-depth examination of school data, structures, processes and systems for documenting incidents of racism, as well as observational activity both within classroom lessons and within the school grounds. A further qualitative perspective was deployed using discussions with both school pupils and parents, and staff working within the school.

The findings from this research provide clear examples of 'what works' in addressing and challenging racism, and are thus worthy of consideration as they provide a baseline from which schools (both statutory and private) within rural settings can work. These examples include providing complete clarity surrounding the school's stance on racism, adopting streamlined procedures to effectively address racist language or behaviour and ensuring that the type of offence committed and the age of the pupils involved (both offender and victim) are taken into consideration. Strong leadership from senior management to communicate the policy of the school with regard to racist practices, as well as the establishment of key objectives and targets ensuring that all staff are working towards the same objectives and adopting the same standpoint with respect to challenging racism, is fundamental in further developing a school's ethos, as is the forging of strong links with pupils' parents and the community in which the school is located.

OFSTED's research studies also identify a number of recommendations that should be adopted by all schools[4] regardless of whether they are located in urban or rural areas. These recommendations relate, for example, to the use of data analysed by ethnicity to check participation and achievement of minority ethnic groups; to gathering and debating the views of staff, pupils, parents and the wider community about barriers to achievement; to focusing on the school response to the Race Relations Amendment Act on what can be done to remove any such barriers and to reflect ethnic and cultural diversity; to setting clear targets to improve participation and achievement; and to providing staff with access to high-quality training to tackle needs with confidence (OFSTED 2002a, 2002b).

Two areas where little research surrounding tackling racism has been undertaken are those of both further and higher education. In line with the underlying philosophy surrounding the study of racism in education (in the light of available projects undertaken in the UK), the unwritten assumption seems to be that by identifying issues as they arise within primary and secondary educational establishments, it is hoped that the problems that currently exist may be targeted and ultimately eradicated. However, a fundamental flaw with this philosophy lies in the fact that the bulk of this research relates to young people between the ages of 4 and 16 years, and hence has a tendency to overshadow the significance of developing and maintaining anti-racist practice in non-statutory education (i.e. post-16 and higher education). As highlighted by Turney *et al.* (2002: 1):

> The lack of attention to 'race' and racism issues in higher education is worrying and indicates a need for the development of conceptual and methodological tools and resources to assess, review and reconstruct educational policy and practice.

Nonetheless, a small degree of literature does exist which aims to help tackle the problem of racism through higher education, such as, for example, the CRE's *The Duty to Promote Race Equality: A Guide for Further and Higher Education* (CRE 2002), which aims to give information and guidance on racial discrimination to those working within the field of further and higher education, and a toolkit produced by the Open University (*Open Teaching Toolkit: Equal Opportunities* 1996). A further extremely useful piece of research conducted by the University of Leeds has resulted in the production of an 'online' toolkit entitled *Institutional Racism in Higher Education* (Turney *et al.* 2002) containing key sections on conceptual, legal and organisational tools, anti-racist strategies and a review of institutions.[5] This toolkit was produced as a direct result of the Race Relations Amendment Act (2000) with the primary aim of ensuring that higher education establishments are aware of, and indeed are instrumental in the development of, policies and procedures to effectively tackle racism, as it would seem that:

> ... institutions across the UK need to consider and rethink attitudes to black and minority ethnic staff and students and actively address 'racism' by moving beyond the current climate of complacency that suggests these issues matter less in Higher Education Institutions (HEIs) than in other organisations. (Turney *et al.* 2002: 1)

Conclusions: applying interventions to the rural context

In summary, in spite of the existence of legal frameworks governing race relations and education, recent research portrays a worrying picture of a failure to stem a growing problem of racism in the education system. The lack of attention paid to the needs of minority ethnic groups in the classroom is well documented, and within a rural context the nature of the broader aspects of the problem becomes even more apparent. A number of key factors fuse to further exacerbate the situation. In rural locations, demographic studies indicate that the percentage of minority ethnic households within the overall community is often minimal, something reflected in the make-up of the pupil composition and teaching staff. The needs of these scattered populations are frequently overlooked, and the service provision they receive is consequently often poor (Garland and Chakraborti 2003). The same situation exists within the education sector, meaning that lessons are habitually taught from a white perspective, leaving minority ethnic pupils feeling disillusioned and isolated (Patel 1994; Benyon *et al.* 1996; Gaine 1995). The concerted efforts of the British National Party to campaign in rural areas in recent years, coupled with a lack of the support networks that exist in equivalent communities in cities and towns, have made the situation even more acute.

In addition, the greater prevalence of independent and private schools in rural locations, and the fact that they fall outside of the responsibilities of LEAs, adds another troubling dimension to the rural perspective. While it is not being suggested here that such schools are inherently or necessarily institutionally racist, the fact that they are not accountable in the same way as state schools may mean that racist policy and practice, whether intentional or not, may be allowed to continue untouched. The rural 'idyll' may therefore be anything but idyllic for minority ethnic pupils resident in private schools in the countryside, and this situation highlights a clear need for initiatives and policies that tackle racism in schools to transcend the mainstream state system and enter the private sector.

More broadly, the CRE remains critical of the current attempts to address the problem of racial prejudice within the education sector and there is a clear case for ensuring that existing policy, guidance and examples of good practice are implemented across the whole education system, from central government down, in a consistent and coherent manner. In the rural context, where the problems may well be intensified for reasons offered above, the case is all the more important to acknowledge and address.

Headway is being made, however, with respect to gaining a greater level of understanding of the precise nature of the problem of racism within schools, and to an extent this is reflected by some of the interventions that are proving helpful in making schools more proactive in tackling racial intolerance. A series of regional conferences held across the UK hosted by the DfES that began in late 2003 has, in part, examined issues relating to eradicating racism through education. This has resulted in the production of a number of key recommendations to assist schools with raising their current standards of policy and practice to help reduce, and ultimately eradicate, the prevalence of racist behaviour and language.

Some of the recommendations produced as a result of collating information obtained via regional conferences include having a shared understanding among *all* staff (including support and administrative officers as well as teachers) of why and how bullying based on background, colour, religion or heritage is even more serious than most other kinds of bullying; developing a more informed understanding, including acceptance and use of the definition of racist incidents proposed by the Stephen Lawrence Report; and utilising a code of practice which clearly outlines specific procedures to be followed for recording and dealing with racist incidents on the school premises and on journeys to and from school.

From a strategic standpoint, those recommendations also urge governors to take seriously their responsibility to report regularly to the LEA the number and nature of racist incidents at their school, and indicate in their reports how the incidents were dealt with, as well as the development of a user-friendly leaflet that details for pupils and their parents what they should do if they experience racism. Similarly, with respect to empowering young people to address racism in schools, pupils themselves should be encouraged to make clear that racist remarks and behaviour are unacceptable by supporting each other in being assertive as opposed to being aggressive or submissive when incidents occur, and should be given the chance to report incidents of racism anonymously as they occur. Moreover, schools should become involved from time to time in national anti-racist projects, giving thorough coverage within the curriculum to interpersonal behaviour among pupils, including racist and sexist name-calling and bullying, with this being linked with wider issues of learning for citizenship and participation in society (DfES 2004).

Crucially, each of these points arising from the DfES regional conferences could be extrapolated to rural contexts to help shape the development of a more informed strategy for tackling racial intolerance. Indeed, if racism in all its forms is to be effectively challenged through education, consideration must be given to ways in which mechanisms and interventions can be successfully utilised in the rural, and this requires recognition of the particular dynamics of rural environments, their schools and the needs of their pupils. In such environments, where unfamiliarity with 'difference' may be a common and enduring feature, the need for sustainable educational responses to racism is arguably all the more pressing. However, if some of the positive ideas outlined within this chapter are acknowledged and consistently implemented, then real progress can be made in this regard.

Notes

1   With regard to these Ethnic Minority Achievement Grant (EMAG) statistical returns, 118 local education authorities out of a total of 120 contributed their data for analysis for the purposes of the study.
2   For further information, see http://www.standards.dfes.gov.uk/sie/ and http://www.standards.dfes.gov.uk/literacy/.
3   For further information on provisions of the Act, see http://www.legislation.hmso.gov.uk/acts/acts2000/20000034.htm.
4   This refers to all schools in the statutory sector at least; private sector establishments, though autonomous, should nevertheless consider the extent to which these recommendations could impact upon their own circumstances.
5   For further information, see http://www.leeds.ac.uk/cers/toolkit/toolkit.htm.

References

Amin, K., Drew, D., Fosam, B. and Gillborn, D. with Demack, S. (1997) *Black and Ethnic Minority Young People and Educational Disadvantage*. London: Runnymede Trust.

Benyon, J., Garland, J., Lyle, S. and McClure, A. (1996) *Education Matters: African Caribbean People and Schools in Leicestershire.* Leicester: Scarman Centre, University of Leicester.

Cline, T., de Abreu, G., Fihosy, C., Gray, H., Lambert, H. and Neale, J. (2002) *Minority Ethnic Pupils in Mainly White Schools.* London: DfES Research Report RR365.

Cole, M. (2002) *Education, Equality and Human Rights.* London: Routledge/Falmer.

Cole, M. and Hill, D. (2001) *Schooling and Equality.* London: Kogan Page.

Commission for Black Staff in Further Education (2002) *Challenging Racism: Further Education Leading the Way.* London: Commission for Black Staff in Further Education.

Commission for Racial Equality (CRE) (2002) *The Duty to Promote Race Equality: A Guide for Further and Higher Education.* London: CRE.

Commission for Racial Equality (CRE) (2003) *The Race Relations Act 1976 (Amendment) Regulations 2003: A Briefing by the Commission for Racial Equality.* London: CRE.

Crace, J. (2004) 'Booted and Suited', *Guardian*, 4 May.

Department for Education and Skills (DfES) (2002) *Removing the Barriers: Raising Achievement Levels for Minority Ethnic Pupils: Exploring Good Practice.* London: DfES.

Department for Education and Skills (DfES) (2004) *Make the Difference: Anti-Bullying Conference.* Brighton, 19 January.

Gaine, C. (1995) *Still No Problem Here.* Stoke-on-Trent: Trentham Books.

Garland, J. and Chakraborti, N. (2003) 'Countryside Alliance? An Assessment of Multi-Agency Responses to Racism in Rural Suffolk', *Crime Prevention and Community Safety: An International Journal*, 5: 61–73.

Gillborn, D. and Gipps, C. (1996) *Recent Research on the Achievements of Ethnic Minority Pupils. Report for the Office for Standards in Education.* London: HMSO.

Gillborn, D. and Safia Mirza, H. (2000), *Educational Inequality: Mapping Race, Class and Gender. A Synthesis of Research Evidence.* London: OFSTED.

Hatcher, R. (1995) 'Racism and Children's Cultures', in M. Griffiths and B. Troyna (eds), *Antiracism, Culture and Social Justice in Education.* Stoke-on-Trent: Trentham Books.

Macpherson, Sir W. (1999) *The Stephen Lawrence Inquiry: Report of an Inquiry by Sir William Macpherson of Cluny.* London: HMSO.

OFSTED (2002a) *Achievement of Black Caribbean Pupils: Three Successful Primary Schools.* London: OFSTED.

OFSTED (2002b) *Achievement of Black Caribbean Pupils: Good Practice in Secondary Schools.* London: OFSTED.

Open University (1996) *Open Teaching Toolkit: Equal Opportunities.* Buckingham: Open University.

Osler, A. and Morrison, M. (2000) *Inspecting Schools for Racial Equality: OFSTED's Strengths and Weaknesses: A Report for the CRE.* Stoke-on-Trent: Trentham Books.

Patel, K. (1994) *Multicultural Education in All-White Areas*, Aldershot: Avebury.

Runnymede Trust (2003) *Complementing Teachers: A Practical Guide to Promote Race Equality in Schools*. London: Runnymede Trust.

Stuart, J. and Cole, M. with Birrell, G., Snow, D. and Wilson, V. (2003) *Minority Ethnic and Overseas Student Teachers in South-East England: An Exploratory Study*. London: Teacher Training Agency.

Turney, L., Law, I. and Phillips, D (2002) *Institutional Racism in Higher Education Toolkit Project: Building the Anti-racist HEI*. Leeds: University of Leeds.

Ward, L. (2004) 'Fears of a Rise in Classroom Racism', *Guardian*, 14 April.

Whitney, I. and Smith, P.K. (1993) 'A Survey of the Nature and Extent of Bully/Victim Problems in Junior/Middle and Secondary Schools', *Educational Research*, 35: 3–25.

Chapter 9

Responding to rural racism: delivering local services

Richard Pugh

Introduction

While there is a growing body of research into rural racism and increasing attention is now being given to the delivery of public services to ethnic minorities, there has been relatively little research into how local services respond to racism in rural areas. Within the UK the results of the few studies that have been undertaken rarely surface beyond their immediate context, as the dissemination of findings is often confined to the publication of a local research report. As a result, examples of good (and bad) practice barely receive wider attention and there is little accumulation of knowledge (Craig and Manthorpe 2000). Consequently, while some parts of this chapter are reasonably well-supported by research, much of the discussion is based upon extrapolation from more general sources about racism and rural services, or is informed by potentially less reliable sources, such as news reports, personal observations and anecdotal experience. This is unfortunate but unavoidable at this time. We have to start somewhere, and it is hoped that this chapter will help to stimulate interest and further research into these issues.

The chapter looks at how local services respond to the needs and problems of black and ethnic minority service workers and service users who have experienced racism. It is written from the perspective of public sector health and social service organisations, but much of the discussion is relevant to other services such as housing, criminal justice and the voluntary sector.

It should be evident from the preceding chapters that in many respects racism in rural areas is similar to that in urban areas. However, the rural context is likely to have some significant features which do make a difference, such as the increased social visibility of black and ethnic minorities in small communities, and the greater potential for social isolation given the absence of other similar individuals and groups who might provide advice and support. As well as the particular problems of racism, members of black and ethnic minorities also face the same sorts of problems that beset many other individuals and groups in rural areas, namely those arising from poor general infrastructure, poor transport networks, higher living costs, patchy or non-existent public services, and stereotypical perceptions by politicians and service planners of rurality.

Furthermore, as I have explained in some detail elsewhere (Pugh 2000, 2003) there is no simple picture of rural life, for rural communities differ considerably in terms of their histories, wealth, perceptions of community, expectations of daily life and reactions to difference and diversity. Racism, like other forms of discrimination, is a potent force which can be mobilised by bigoted individuals or re-energised un-scrupulous politicians, and is sadly a common and well-established feature of many communities. Nonetheless, we should be wary of assuming that it is an inevitable feature of rural life or of the life of every black or ethnic minority person living there (see Chapter 4 by Robinson and Gardner in this volume). While it may well be the case that rural communities tend to a conservatism, they are by no means universally illiberal places or places that are resistant to newcomers. To assume otherwise is to ignore the reported experience of some individuals (Myers 1995) and, more significantly, tends to lead to a deterministic and pessimistic view of the prospects for change. After all, the crucial point that follows from the acceptance of a social constructionist view of racism is that what is 'man-made' always has the potential to be unmade or reconstructed.

There are two fundamental premises upon which the response of public services to racism should be based. The first is an explicit acknowledgement of the statutory duty to promote race equality placed upon most public bodies by the Race Relations (Amendment) Act 2000. The second is the recognition that for many public sector workers their professional codes of ethics and professional standards require them to challenge racism. For example, all registered social workers and their employers in England are required by the General Social Care Council to promote equal opportunities, to respond to diversity and different cultures, and to report, challenge and respond to discrimination.[1] Similarly, the National Health Service Plan, and related documents such as the Mental Health National Service Framework[2] and the report *Inside Outside* (Sashidharan 2003) on improving mental health services for black and ethnic minority communities, make general and specific commitments regarding reducing and eliminating inequalities in services. These two statements might seem to be somewhat redundant in a book such as this, but it is important to rebut any presumption that social care and health workers might make about personal choice. Challenging and responding to racism is not a matter of professional or personal discretion, it is a statutory duty and a professional obligation. There may well be room for the exercise of judgement and discretion in deciding how best to respond, but respond they must.

Effective challenges and responses to racism must be built upon a sound understanding of the different forms of racism and their consequences. Important distinctions need to be made between overt and covert racism, personal and structural/institutional racism, and intended and unwitting racism. Moreover, we need to recognise that while racism in the UK is often predicated upon presumed differences signalled by skin colour, it is a far more complex phenomenon, and the term should be understood as embracing discrimination based upon a variety of assumptions made about real or imagined cultural and ethnic difference. To do otherwise would be to ignore the historical potency and threat of anti-Semitism, to ignore the experience of Irish people, to exempt from consideration the experience of Gypsies and Romany people, and to ignore the racist discrimination against other minorities such as asylum seekers and refugees. Similarly, in avoiding over-simplification we should also avoid any predilection for establishing hierarchies of discrimination either between different forms of racism or different groups, or between different forms of discrimination, such as sexism and ageism.

All individuals occupy multiple dimensions of social location, that is in terms of their age, class, ethnicity, gender, sexuality and so on. If we wish to understand how best to meet their particular needs, we need to acknowledge that individuals and groups may differ widely in their experiences and their perceptions of the difficulties they face. For example, while crude and violent racists may see little difference between them, the everyday experience of a middle-class Indian doctor living in a rural community may be significantly different from that of poorly paid Bangladeshi workers in a village restaurant, or the experience of temporarily resettled asylum seekers. However, the aim of this chapter is not to provide an exegesis of racism but to highlight three important points, that:

- without a clear understanding of the myriad ways in which racism may be manifested social services agencies are unlikely to recognise its existence in the first place, and even when having made some recognition, are unlikely to devise effective responses;

- individual social locations and community contexts vary greatly. Thus personal social status, community perceptions of utility, together with an individual's wealth, their geographical location, the availability of private transport; and their social networks not only influence their susceptibility to overt racism but may well shape their personal reactions to it as well;

- the presence or absence of any supportive response from the wider community, including those who provide public services, can be a salient factor in terms of personal experience and the likelihood of any continuing risk of discrimination, insult or injury.

The following section in this chapter focuses upon the broader context of service provision and begins by outlining how idyllicised misconceptions of rural life contribute to the invisibility of social problems. It then explains how urbanist assumptions have contributed to the political neglect of rural needs and notes some of the important policy changes that are taking place. There is then a review of the most salient points regarding the experience of service users and service workers followed by an analysis of the particular problems of initiating change in rural services.

Understanding the context

Idealisation and invisibility

The British countryside is home to substantial numbers of people, but rural life is often subject to idealisation and oversimplification (Pugh 2000). A recurring feature of social problems in rural areas is that they are often unnoticed by policy-makers and service providers. In part, the 'invisibility' of rural problems stems from the uncritical acceptance of rather idealised conceptions of what rural life is like. Thus it is assumed that poverty is non-existent, that there are no drug problems, and that loneliness and isolation cannot be a problem in rural communities. This is often underpinned by the assumption that rural communities are self-sufficient, homogenous entities which lack both the diversity of urban areas and the sorts of problems associated with urban life. Thus racism or homophobia are not perceived as problematic issues because these forms of difference upon which discrimination is subsequently based are presumed not to exist in the countryside. Furthermore, the overlooking of minorities and the assumption of homogeneity are not always happenstance but may be quite deliberately manipulated for political ends. Far from being a haven of bucolic bliss, the countryside is the subject of some fiercely contested ideas about who should be in it. Sibley (1997), in a perceptive essay on how public order legislation has been used to confer the status of 'non-belonging' upon Gypsies, New Age Travellers, ravers and hunt saboteurs, notes how these groups are perceived as alien and damaging to the countryside. The countryside often has a significant role in constructing ideas of identity and otherness and in representing particular ideas about nationalism, boundaries and belonging. Sibley makes the point that in England, the countryside has long been invested with a 'sacred' quality, arising from the notion that it represents the essence of Englishness. Thus the idealisation of a sup-posedly unchanging landscape populated by peaceful homogenous communities may at times be seen to be threatened and 'endangered by the transgressions of discrepant minorities' (Sibley 1997: 219).

The point is that service planners and providers need to look beyond stereotypical notions and gather accurate information about the com-munities they are supposed to serve. Although the diversity of rural areas may seem insignificant in comparison to the obvious diversity of many urban areas, every rural community will contain some social minorities. Within these communities, as several studies have shown, relatively isolated individuals who are perceived as 'different' or not 'belonging' may not only lack the support of a wider community, but may be exposed to significant risks arising from intolerance and hostility (Chakraborti and Garland 2003; Dhalech 1999; Henderson and Kaur 1999; Jay 1992). Consequently, one of the most fundamental problems facing rural dwellers is getting public services to recognise their particular needs and problems in the first place. In the absence of service, many potential service users struggle because they lack other financial or social resources which they could mobilise to meet their needs. Thus, racism, along with other types of discrimination, can lead to dis-advantages which are not unique to the countryside but are reinforced by the rural context.

Urbanist models and assumptions

Until quite recently much government policy has largely been blind to the particular circumstances of rural communities. Although, as we shall see in the following section, there are significant changes taking place, the current situation in regard to funding and models of service delivery adopted in rural areas is very much the product of a history of neglect and oversight. For example, while the costs of service delivery in rural communities are often 20 to 30 per cent dearer than in urban areas, there has been no comparable uplift in funding for most public services. Thus higher costs which derive from additional time and transport costs in delivering services to small and scattered populations, combined with fewer opportunities for economies of scale, result in reduced levels of provision for many rural dwellers (Pugh 2003; Social Services Inspectorate 1999; Spilsbury and Lloyd 1998).

Throughout much official and guidance policy there has been a 'one size fits all' mentality, which is evident in the de facto assumption that what works in urban areas will also work in rural areas. Thus, the models for service delivery which are promoted in urban areas are unthinkingly applied to rural contexts with little or no consideration of their viability in somewhat different contexts. For example, the centralisation of domiciliary services which makes sense in a geographically compact urban district may become an expensive and unresponsive option in a large rural area where locally distributed management and provision is likely to prove more effective. Even in instances where it has been recognised that not only do rural dwellers get fewer and poorer services, but that ethnic minorities who live in rural areas are possibly even worse served, the solutions advanced in urban areas are unlikely to work in rural areas. Moreover, the absence of other organisations with good knowledge and which might have credibility with minority groups and individuals means that there simply are no existing alternatives to draw upon.

Urbanist assumptions are not solely the province of government agencies; they can also arise in the voluntary sector too. For example, Dhalech (1999: 29), in reporting the development of anti-racist initiatives in south-west England, noted that:

[Some] Black agencies come into the area wanting to undertake development work but they typically lack an understanding of rural issues ... An officer from a national agency offered support for developing a telephone help line modelled on a London borough. The several meetings between the officer and representatives of local Black agencies proved to be remarkably un-constructive because there was no recognition of rural issues. As soon as the local agencies started discussing the idea between themselves an immediate consensus was reached and the ideas were developed.

Perhaps the most pervasive urbanist assumption, and one which is arguably inaccurate even for some urban areas, is the notion that service innovation and development is a neutral process and that good ideas will self-evidently be recognised and accepted as such by the local community. This is often accompanied by the premise that the workers who will provide these services somehow 'float free' from their communities, which completely ignores the fact that since personal connection is the basis of much of rural life anyway, service provision in small communities is typically highly personalised. Who you are and where you come from are often key elements in the interaction between workers and clients. In relatively stable and small communities it is often the case that even when workers and clients do not personally know each other, they will often know *of* each other and probably have other connections, and be able to easily obtain information about each other. Sometimes these connections and this information may be helpful, in that they help to establish the worker's credibility and engender the expectation that the worker is likely to understand 'how things are' for the client. But sometimes, the fact that the worker is local can be counterproductive, especially when clients are fearful of confidentiality and possible stigmatisation if their difficulties were to become more widely known. For example, black workers who are long settled in a district, who have perhaps gone to school and grown up locally, may be relatively well-known and well accepted by prospective service users. Their personal history and professional credibility will almost certainly precede their first direct interaction with prospective service users. This personal history is likely to include information about the worker's family and her/his local social networks. In contrast, a black or ethnic minority worker who moves into a district with their job may find it much more difficult to establish the initial rapport with the service user, as they may be wary of her/his reliability and confidentiality.

The changing policy context

National government is becoming more attuned to rural needs and problems, and since the *Care in the Country* report (Social Services Inspectorate 1999), there have been a number of significant developments. In 2000 the rural White Paper, *Our Countryside, The Future*, established a Rural Services Standard which aims to 'give people in the countryside a better understanding of access to services they could expect' (Countryside Agency 2003: 2). At the same time, the government is trying to ensure that its policies are not developed solely from an urban perspective and that they are 'rural proofed'. The intention is to get policy-makers and planners to:

- think about whether there will be any significant differential impacts in rural areas;

- if there are such impacts, consider what they these might be;

- consider what adjustments/compensations might be made to fit rural circumstances (DEFRA 2003a).

Although much of the Standard relates to schools, the police, employment services and access to benefits, there are a number of elements that bear upon health and social services. These include: collecting evidence to be used to develop rural standards and targets; efforts to improve access to information about available services, especially through the use of information technology; efforts to improve access to services themselves; and establishing clear lines of responsibility for rural issues across government departments.

Social inclusion is presented as an integral part of the framework for rural development and while this is predominantly directed towards poverty reduction, there is an explicit recognition of the particular problems of racist incidents and crimes directed towards ethnic minorities in rural areas. It is too early to come to any conclusive assessment of the effectiveness of these initiatives. However, as progress in relation to health and social care generally has been limited, with even the government noting that there was 'scope for improvement' (Countryside Agency 2003: 12), it is unlikely that measures aimed at improving the situation of ethnic minorities have had much impact so far. For example, only 7 out of 75 projects approved for funding under the Connecting Community initiative included any focus upon rural racism (DEFRA 2003b).

The newly established Commission for Healthcare Audit and Inspection and the Commission for Social Care Inspection are also expected to consider the extent to which health and social care services meet the needs of rural populations, and they will be developing further performance indicators to measure progress (Department of Health 2003c). The Department of the Environment, Food and Rural Affairs has a checklist of policy issues and information and guidance for the development of public services in rural areas (DEFRA 2002) which makes no specific reference to racism. In contrast, since the publication of *They Look After Their Own, Don't They?* (Social Services Inspectorate 1998b) the Department of Health has produced some valuable reports (Alexander 2000) and helpful guidance on service development and delivery to Britain's ethnic minorities generally (Department of Health 2002, 2003a, 2003b), and in which there is some reference to the rural context (Department of Health 2001a; see also *From Lip Service to Real Service* 2001b).

The increasing awareness of government agencies is also evident in the work of the Local Government Association. In a report on social inclusion Moor and Whitworth (2001: 7) make the point that:

> There are a number of other less obvious issues which local authorities and other local agents should address in their rural proofing work. An example is supporting the needs of ethnic minority individuals and families. For ethnic minority citizens, families and communities living in rural areas, particular issues include: comparative lack of sensitivity to their needs from public service providers; relative isolation from support services and from self-help and community groups; relative lack of information on services (including translation services); and additional costs in accessing services.

This report also emphasised the need for accurate local information upon which to develop policy and practice, including such things as surveys of experiences of racial harassment, a point which is repeated in many Department of Health reports.

The Local Government Association has also had some success in persuading central government of the case for devolved and decentralised systems of service delivery, as the Haskins Review (Haskins 2003) has explicitly accepted the need for further decentralisation. This recommendation would ameliorate the predominance of urban models and permit service delivery systems to better match local circumstances and meet local needs. It is too soon to tell how effective the plethora of recent initiatives has been. Indeed, apart from the specific efforts directed at reducing racist crime and improving the response to such crimes, much of what is proposed would appear to have little direct bearing upon other local responses to racism. Nevertheless, many of these measures do have potential for improving the provision of services to ethnic minorities in rural areas in that they require service providers to gather much more comprehensive information about who accesses and uses their services, and require public services to develop and publish plans aimed at meeting the needs of all sections of the community.

Understanding the issues

This section looks at the experience of black and ethnic minorities who are, or might be, potential users and providers of public services. Although the general experience of racism in rural communities has been reviewed in the preceding chapters, it is nonetheless important to recognise that the general experience of daily life in a small community sets the context for both the personal and professional lives and interactions of black and ethnic minority workers and clients. Both may be very 'visible' in their small communities, both may feel isolated, and both may be subject to harassment and discrimination as they go about their daily life. Clearly, the experiences of black and ethnic minority workers and service users overlap to some degree, but there are important differences too. Prospective service users often need help at times of stress and vulnerability, they may lack sufficient financial resources, and they may lack information about how to access services and about what services they can expect. In contrast, public service workers are less likely to be in a similar position. They are much more likely to be in good health, in steady employment and living relatively stable lives. Most important is the fact that they are not seeking help or needing information. Thus the most fundamental difference between ethnic minority clients and ethnic minority providers arises from their differential positions in the provider/user relationship. Nonetheless, public service workers too may be at risk from racism within their employment, either from colleagues or from other agencies that they come into contact with in their formal capacity. Furthermore, even their relatively favourable position in the helper/helped interaction will not always protect them from racism from service users.

The experience of black and ethnic minority service users

While the possibility of overt and direct personal racism aimed at individuals is always present in any formal interaction with public service providers, because of the increasing sensitivity of public bodies to legal and professional sanction, the changing social context and the impact of professional training, it is likely that such crude forms of discrimination are less frequent than perhaps they were some years ago. However, it depends very much upon which type of service a person has contact with. In general, the 'helping' services such as health, social work and social care are more likely to be viewed with positive expectations by Britain's ethnic minorities, while the 'coercive' services such as the police and the criminal justice system are viewed with more trepidation and much lower expectations of fair treatment. The report *Race Equality in Public Services* (Home Office 2002) described the results of research into white, black and Asian respondents' perceptions of how they thought they were (or would be) treated by different public sector organisations. While there were small increases in negative expectations in most categories of public services between white, black and Asian respondents, the differences were most marked in the responses regarding the police, the prison service, the probation service, the courts and the Crown Prosecution Service. Interestingly, there were some marked differences between black male and female respondents' perceptions, with black women being much more likely to report negative experiences with council housing departments and housing associations. This probably reflects the fact that they are the family members most likely to have dealings with these bodies.

It was noted in the introduction to this chapter that relatively little research has been conducted on issues of health and social service provision and take-up for ethnic minorities in rural areas, but what has been done shows patchy or non-existent provision allied to very low expectations of service from minorities (Social Services Inspectorate 1998a). Given that the situation in terms of the provision of public services to rural residents generally is erratic, the experience of members of ethnic minorities in rural areas is likely to mirror that of their counterparts in urban areas (Bhui 2002; Bracken and O'Sullivan 2001; Home Office 2002; Smaje 1995), namely worse than that of the majority communities. Indeed, with regard to mental health, Sashidharan (2003: 10) has concluded that:

> There does not appear to be a single area of mental health care in this country in which black and minority ethnic groups fare as well as, or better than, the majority white community.

Similarly, the reports of the Social Service Inspectorate into services for ethnic minorities with physical disabilities and sensory impairments led the Department of Health to conclude that these were 'less well developed than most other services' (Department of Health 2001a: 7).

In 1995 Shropshire County Council, which covers a predominantly rural area centred around the county town of Shrewsbury, undertook a study into community care provision to ethnic minorities and found evidence of continuing discrimination, lack of cultural awareness among staff, ignorance of the needs and preferences of ethnic minorities, a lack of culturally appropriate services and a lack of good public information about what was available (Nizhar 1995). Subsequent Social Service Inspectorate reports throughout the country (Department of Health 2001a) noted similar findings and stressed the importance of under-standing the feelings of ethnic minorities, and in particular recognising how previous negative interactions and experience of racism inhibited service take-up.

A large survey of 87,000 people over the age of 65 who had received home care in England in 2002/23 showed that on each question regarding users' satisfaction with the service, black and ethnic minority respondents were less satisfied than white respondents. Overall, 58 per cent of white respondents were satisfied with their services compared to 44 per cent of black and ethnic minority respondents (Department of Health 2003b). Unfortunately the report does not allow a comparison of different ethnic groups' satisfaction by type of authority to be made, although a crude comparison of the satisfaction rates of all respondents from unitary authorities and metropolitan districts with the more rural shire counties does not show any clear pattern of greater satisfaction in urban areas in comparison to rural districts. There is considerable variation within each type of local authority, together with considerable overlapping of the range of variation between types of authority. Indeed, many of the lowest overall satisfaction rates are to be found among the inner London authorities.

A small study by de Lima in four areas of Scotland – Angus, the Highlands, North Ayrshire and the Western Isles – found that it was commonly assumed that minority ethnic groups did not have any needs because they were small in number, 'invisible' and 'silent' (de Lima 2001). This invisibility, as noted earlier, is a common feature contributing to the neglect of social problems in rural areas. Furthermore, it is not simply a matter of raising the profile of particular issues as the fear of increased 'visibility' leading to accusations of 'scrounging' or dis-crimination may also deter ethnic minorities from seeking service or lobbying more assertively for improvements in existing provision. The Department of Health has been unequivocal in stating that 'Councils that play the numbers game (that is, "there are too few black older people in our areas to bother about service developments specially for them") are falling down in their duties' (Department of Health 2001b: 5).

The situation with regard to voluntary sector services is similarly depressing. Following a survey in four rural counties in 1992 which showed that both public and voluntary sector agencies consistently underestimated the size of their ethnic minority populations, the National Council for Voluntary Organisations launched a nationwide initiative aimed at developing race equality practices among rural voluntary groups. This included the development of more specific local services for ethnic minorities, training materials for staff and ways of supporting isolated rural workers. Nevertheless, as a more recent study of community care services for North Warwickshire Council for Voluntary Services indicated, progress has not been uniform. This study found a lack of specific services for ethnic minorities, that information was available only in English, that there was little cultural awareness training provided and that many of those from an ethnic minority had to travel out of the area to access appropriate services (Marsh 1996).

When it comes to seeking advice and support in challenging racism, the situation for ethnic minorities in rural areas is also poorer than in urban areas. Not only is there not the support of a wider community, but there will be fewer formal bodies able to help. Indeed, the Commission for Racial Equality (CRE) has acknowledged the patchy provision of such services throughout the UK and especially in rural areas. Through its *Getting Results* programme, the CRE is now providing additional funding for a number of rural districts including Ayrshire, Devon, Dorset, East Fife, the Grampian region and North Wales, to ensure that local race equality work is delivered consistently across the UK (Blink 2003).

The changing policy context outlined earlier requires local public services to provide more detailed and specific information about their work. For example, one of the requirements of 'Best Value' (HMSO 1999) is for local authorities to monitor the ethnicity of people who are assessed for services and those who receive them, but the immediate prospects of improvement are not promising. While the national data from the first year of returns on the new performance indicators showed that the proportion of black and ethnic minority adults and older people receiving an assessment for community care services in 2000–1 almost matched their proportions in the general population at 0.97 per cent, with the proportion going on to actually receive a service compared to all others only a little lower at 0.96 per cent (Home Office 2002; Department of Health 2003a), these figures should not be accepted uncritically. Their reliability is compromised by the incomplete data return, i.e. with around 20 per cent of cases missing, and because the baseline data for the proportion of black and ethnic minority people in the population probably under-recorded the actual numbers since these comparisons were based upon the 1991 Census data. The data analysis for the following year which utilised the 2001 Census showed that there were some significant variations between different shire counties in the likelihood of members of ethnic minorities receiving services after an assessment (Department of Health 2003a). Again these figures should be treated with some caution, since there is considerable variation between and within different ethnic minority groups and the returns from different authorities vary considerably with some authorities recording and returning the ethnicity for every case, while others only do so in 58 per cent of cases. In the future, it is anticipated that not only will more comprehensive information become available, but that there will be greater sophistication in the indices and in their interpretation.

The relatively small numbers of ethnic minorities in rural areas means that there is less pressure for culturally appropriate services in the first place, and fewer knowledgeable people and organisations who are available to advise or directly provide them once needs have been recognised (Patel 1999). Consequently, it is probable that in rural areas, as in urban areas, members of black and ethnic minority communities are more likely to experience the following – a basic lack of recognition of their existence and of their problems, both personal and social (hence, the deleterious effects of racism upon prospective service users may not even be considered by service providers); problems in accessing services in the first place; cultural and language barriers in assessments (especially in terms of understanding of language preferences and linguistic sensitivity); lower rates of provision of supportive services and higher rates of involvement with coercive ones in child care and mental health; lower involvement of service providers with service users, family and carers leading to a lack of understanding of circumstances and needs; lower rates of satisfaction with services and lower expectations of service (leading to a consequent aversion to seeking help from statutory bodies); and finally, feelings of isolation and vulnerability.

The experience of workers

There are two main dimensions to rural workers' experience of racism within their employment – racism from other workers and from other agencies, and racism from service users. Unfortunately, little research appears to have been done into either aspect within rural contexts. However, the social context of personal service provision in rural areas has some distinctive features (Pugh 2000) which are likely to affect the experience of workers. In small communities all professionals are likely to have a higher social visibility than they might in many urban areas. They will tend to find it harder to maintain a separation between their professional and personal lives and this visibility brings both benefits and disadvantages. For many workers this is a positive experience, in that they value the sense of belonging, recognition and achievement, and for workers from ethnic minorities there may be greater opportunities for them to be accepted as individuals, perhaps exempted from the stereotypical expectations that might otherwise be held about minority groups (Pugh 2004). But for others it can be a more isolating experience as they struggle to establish themselves and their service without the support of a larger team of colleagues, and often without other professional support networks. In small communities service users may often attempt to 'place' the worker, that is to discover something about the worker's background, family and personal networks and their professional capability, before committing themselves. Consequently, when the personal credibility of workers is based upon a wider consideration of their behaviour and social comportment within the local community, then workers from black and other ethnic minorities may face additional difficulties in establishing themselves.

A common problem reported by black and ethnic minority workers in urban areas and also noted by those in rural services, is the 'ghettoisation' of problems of racism as all efforts and responses become identified with them. What often begins as a well-meaning attempt by managers to gain knowledge and enlist the support of existing black and ethnic minority staff rapidly becomes sidelined as managers lack confidence in dealing with issues of racial equality and react to other priorities. This often leaves workers in an invidious position. They may find themselves expected to take on additional tasks without sufficient recognition in terms of time and remuneration. Dhalech (1999) in his report found that one agency had exploited the knowledge and experience of minority ethnic professionals and race equality agencies by consulting with them to develop their guidelines, but then failed to acknowledge their contribution publicly and did not include them in further development. Black and ethnic minority workers who are personally and professionally committed to challenging racism and improving services may find themselves perceived as the 'expert' on all matters concerning ethnic minorities and receive little support from managers or colleagues. As they attempt to respond to local problems, more damaging consequences may follow. They may begin to be perceived as a nuisance by their colleagues and other agencies, and so become even more isolated, and are likely to become increasingly frustrated and disillusioned at the lack of support and response to their work.

The failure to 'mainstream' racial equality measures, that is to ensure that policies and practices are understood, 'owned' and permeate through all aspects of the service, extends beyond the misuse and exploitation of workers noted above. For example, the response of many services to workers' reports of racism directed at them from service users is often confused and unhelpful. Some services have instituted procedures to investigate such incidents but fail to provide adequate support for the staff member concerned and often fail to recognise the additional stresses and perceived risks that may accompany a reference to the procedure. Even when the outcome of the investigation finds clear evidence of racism from the client, instead of the service responding as if this were an institutional problem, the matter is still treated as if it were an individual incident between a single user and a single worker, a problem compounded by the absence of any clear policy and practice on the conditions under which service will be provided, modified or withdrawn from the user. In the face of such ambiguity black and ethnic minority staff may feel unsupported, let down or betrayed.

Responding to racism: initiating change

This section is premised upon the assumption that rural agencies like urban ones must have effective training strategies on equality issues, including anti-racist work, if they are to meet the various duties and responsibilities which arise from equal opportunities legislation and government policy. While the main focus of this section is upon the additional strategies that will help to develop a more responsive local service, training is the bedrock upon which all service development rests so it is vital that it encompasses what the Department of Health has called the 'three Rs', that is:

- the *recognition* of black and ethnic minorities and their diverse range of needs, aspirations and experiences;
- of *respect* for their right to appropriate and effective services;
- the aim of *relevant* services, to meet specific needs in culturally appropriate and accessible ways (Department of Health 2001b: 32).

This training should be broad based and should encompass information and exercise on a wide range of minority groups. Otherwise, as Cemlyn (2000) found in a study of social services' response to Travellers, semi-settled and nomadic lifestyles may be wittingly and unwittingly pathologised by the assumptions and expectations that agencies and workers may have about them. Many people whose notion of what constitutes a 'normal' and acceptable lifestyle encompasses the desirability of home ownership and a stable and settled existence have great difficulty in appreciating the extent to which Travellers' preferred ways of living are exactly that – a preference and a conscious choice – which they make. Instead, they often make stereotypical assumptions that poverty, or a reluctance to work, is the primary determinant of their situation. Without good knowledge of how different groups operate, public service workers will often impose their own meanings upon unfamiliar situations, and these almost invariably simplify the complexity of what is happening.

Understanding the community and getting accurate information

Without accurate information about demographic and cultural diversity, service providers are likely to continue to omit from consideration even the presence of ethnic minorities in their districts, let alone begin to develop access to effective services for them. While the national census provides some basic information, this is often insufficient for the purposes of service planning and development. Fortunately some local authorities carry out their own local surveys which may provide useful information or can be adapted to do so. Thus information is needed about the range of minorities, their ages, their situations and, most crucially, their perceptions of their needs and their preferences for service. Some of this can be obtained by formal methods of research but for the purposes of service provision information about needs and preferences should ultimately always be gathered from personal contact with individuals and groups. Otherwise there is a risk of assuming an homogeneity of needs and preferences which may not exist. Useful advice on constructing survey categories in terms of what terminology and nomenclature to use, and advice on how to handle self-ascription of ethnic identity, can be obtained from the Commission for Racial Equality (CRE), the Office of National Statistics and also from the Scottish Social Care Data Standards Project (SSCDSP). In addition to the usual ethical considerations involved in setting up any research, agencies should bear in mind the advice given by the National Institute for Social Work and reiterated by the SSCDSP, that agencies seeking to conduct research involving ethnic minority data should be clear about what information is sought and to what purposes it will be put.

It should be remembered that 'research and consultation are not ends in themselves' (Department of Health 2001b: 5) but are the means to the ends of providing fair, responsive and culturally sensitive services to all sections of the community. In rural areas, because there may be no well established local organisations or other formal connections between different ethnic minorities, it is not only important to try to contact every group, not just the largest or most visible, but also to work through existing networks of friendship and association. Aside of any scepticism or even fear that ethnic minorities may have about why information is being sought and to what purposes it will be put, the credibility of service providers with potential users will be diminished if action is not eventually forthcoming. Thus agencies should avoid long delays in responding to the results of the research, or if this is unavoidable, then at the outset they should signal clearly to respondents and participants that this is likely to be the case.

Nevertheless, rural agencies seeking to consult with ethnic minorities are unlikely to face the same scale of problems that the Department of Health noted in their report upon developing services for older people:

> Where a new initiative is being proposed for a black community or where there has been little focus on the needs of that community, there will be a tendency for the consultation to be overwhelmed by requests for improvements. This may make it difficult to keep, or refine, a focus upon the priority issues that need to be tackled. (Department of Health 2001b: 28)

However, rural agencies do need to be aware that consultation will itself raise expectations and increase demands for service. If it is perceived that there is no effective response, or that the response is biased towards some groups rather than others, then the willingness of black and ethnic minorities to cooperate in service development will ebb away. From the start agencies need to communicate clearly what their primary purpose is in seeking consultation so that expectations are not unrealistically raised.

It was noted earlier that rural communities vary considerably, so workers will need to develop a good understanding of how particular communities work. This is a complex subject which can only be noted in a chapter such as this. But we should recognise that experienced workers who usually gain this sort of knowledge slowly through direct experience buttressed by their personal knowledge of an area, often take it to be 'common sense'. Workers who lack or ignore it will find great difficulty in working effectively. For example, Boushel in a study of child welfare identified some of the strengths and weaknesses of Irish Traveller communities, in which 'Traveller children are in some ways well-protected by their community's shared values of family life and close social interconnectedness ... [they] will go to great lengths to tolerate and ameliorate socially unacceptable behaviour by members of the group' (Boushel 1994: 185). However, within these closely linked communities, the fact that there are 'religious and cultural traditions [that] place a high value on marriage, [and] there are fewer single parents than in the settled communities in which they live, and Traveller women are less likely than other Irish women to have paid employment outside the home' (ibid.: 186), means that when things to wrong 'the options facing vulnerable women and children within the Traveller community are very limited' (ibid.: 186). Consequently, Traveller women who have experienced the general hostility and discrimination aimed at their communities are much less likely to seek help from social services and other public services.

Auditing and evaluating existing provision

There are two forms of service audit which may be used to develop local services. The first is a self-audit of what an agency already provides or undertakes. For example, the Local Authorities Race Relations Information Exchange has developed a web-based tool kit to assist local authorities in developing their race equality policies (see www.ig-employers.gov.uk/equal-pol-small.html). Similarly the CRE provides much useful general information which employers and service providers can use to review their own work.

The Department of Health has also produced audit tools for the purposes of service development. A good example, and one which can easily be adapted to other services, is *Developing Services for Minority Ethnic Older People: The Audit Tool* (2002). The second form of service audit focuses outside of the agency to ascertain the level and appropriateness of existing voluntary and independent sector provision. This should be a broad-ranging review and should include existing organisations who may not see themselves as having any primary focus upon ethnic minorities, but who may be responsive to locally identified needs and gaps in provision, or may be able to lend support to lobbying and innovation, such as Age Concern, the parish council and local Women's Institutes.

In many rural areas, especially where there is little or no existing provision to ethnic minorities, it is crucial that some understanding is gained of informal care arrangements. These arrangements may provide exemplars for the development of formal services because they will illustrate gaps in provision, and may also establish contact with individuals who may then be formally employed to help others. Finally, where some service provision to ethnic minorities already exists it is good practice to evaluate its effectiveness and users' views of its appropriateness (see the earlier reference to the home carers' survey (Department of Health 2003b) for an example).

Information and improving access to services

One of the clearest messages from research is that rural dwellers generally, and black and ethnic minorities in particular, often lack information about what services are available and about how to access them (see Garland and Chakraborti 2003). Unsurprisingly the goal of improving the information available to service users is a constant theme in Department of Health policy and strategy and this can be seen in all the national service frameworks for health and social care and in the recommendations and guidance in many of the reports cited earlier in this chapter.

The Social Service Inspectorate's report into rural services noted that 'Innovations such as databases in libraries and advice centres tended to be located in towns' (Social Service Inspectorate 1999: 9) and the distribution of other sources of information such as might be found in free local papers was often very limited in rural areas. Even shops and post offices did not display much information, though one Citizens' Advice Bureau had held sessions in a local GP's surgery, while others used advice workers who could visit people at home. Mobile offices, information displays and the use of school IT facilities all provide useful ways of spreading knowledge about services. However, efforts at improving information dissemination need to be sensitive to the perceptions of local minorities. For example, while the low take-up of childcare among parents and carers from ethnic minorities is partly due to financial constraints and lack of information, it is also due to their perception that existing provision is 'a white service to a white clientele' (Stephens 2001: 9). The Rural Race Equality Project in Cornwall, Devon and Somerset (Dhalech 1999) undertook an audit of relevant resources in the area and compiled these into a directory of useful contacts. They also disseminated information through the web, newsletters, posters, leaflets, sympathetic local media and one-off events such as a conference, by contributing to training and awareness raising in schools, colleges, youth clubs and by working with other agencies including the police, prison and social services.

Women from ethnic minority groups face additional problems in getting appropriate help. One response suggested by de Lima (1999) is to seek other links with ethnic minority groups by looking at what contacts they may already have with other organisations not normally associated with social services or community development. For example, a Chinese language course for the Chinese children in the Highlands helped the children maintain confidence in their bilingualism and brought parents together as they transported their children to and from the classes. MacKay has noted how 'the assumption is often made that because domestic abuse crosses all racial, ethnic and class boundaries, every woman's experience of it must be the same' (2000: 16), whereas help-seeking patterns vary culturally and are also modified by the woman's particular context. Thus women from Traveller families may be extremely reluctant to seek help from formal agencies which they regard as alien to their community, while Indian and Chinese women are less likely to seek informal help within small tightly-knit ethnic communities.

In minority groups where women's status is strongly linked to that of their partner, there may be intense pressure not to 'go outside' to seek help as this may bring the group into disrepute, or cause shame. For women who do not speak English the risks of help-seeking may seem insurmountable, for gaining access may be beset with problems. As MacKay notes, even attempting to seek help might 'expose women to culturally alien agencies and refuges, if not institutional racism ... [and] the interpreting service may pose risks as well as a lack of understanding' (2000: 16). For example, untrained voluntary interpreters may be reluctant to convey information which they feel discredits their community and may even exert pressure directly upon women to conform to their cultural expectations (Pugh 1996).

Collaborative working and building networks

Cheers (1998), writing about rural services in Australia, makes the point that understanding the local context is paramount to developing and providing effective services. While there is a considerable literature on community development in the UK, very little attention has been paid to the question of how local contexts impact upon the development of new initiatives in social services. The rural context may not necessarily be a more conservative context than its urban counterpart, but is often perceived by those who live there as a less diverse one. Consequently, an appreciation of particular problems and difficulties may be much harder to promote and establish, and it is clear from many rural projects that it does take much longer to create and develop new services (Edwards *et al.* 1999; Mason and Taylor 1990). Indeed, the explicit or even tacit support of the wider community seems to be a much more significant factor in establishing and promoting services than might be expected (Eaton 1995; Francis and Henderson 1992; Lindow 1999; Midgely *et al.* 1997).

Initiatives that are well-grounded in local communities rather than being perceived as imposed from without are much more likely to mobilise the support of significant people in the community, and thus ensure the longer-term viability of new services. But before this can happen, there is often a fundamental challenge facing those who seek to develop new services, which is to persuade others of the need for particular initiatives at the outset. For example, Dhalech, in his report on an anti-racist project in south-west England, notes that the project began with rather ambitious aims, given the realities of existing circumstances and the prevailing attitudes within major local agencies, but the team quickly realised that they would have to develop a more holistic approach than they had originally envisaged. This was largely because of the widespread ignorance and denial of the existence of racism in the region. Subsequently they established a reporting system to record racist incidents, which became the 'most compelling answer to those who say we have "no problem here"' (Dhalech 1999: 4). The reports that were received demonstrated that discrimination was occurring in virtually every aspect of everyday life – in local shopping, in leisure and social activities, and in public services like housing, education and social services.

The problem-centred approach adopted by most personal social service agencies tends to underplay the role of the broader community; thus community development and education are not included as significant elements in service plans, but it is precisely these aspects which might be most fruitfully developed if services are to be improved. A useful source of information on community-based responses is published by the Community Development Foundation (Henderson and Kaur 1999), which reports on projects undertaken in Cornwall, Devon, Somerset, Lincolnshire, Northern Ireland and Scotland.

In rural areas where resources are limited and local knowledge and expertise in working with ethnic minorities is scarce, cooperation and partnership with other agencies and with organisations from other areas is often a necessity. It can provide opportunities for some economies of scale and allow a more effective use of the available resources: for example, in developing a joint register of interpreters and advisors, establishing joint commissioning arrangements for services, or in developing multi-use facilities. Nevertheless, agencies need to develop a more sophisticated appreciation of the problems that independent service providers face. Many voluntary sector and minority group organisations have considerable difficulty in managing short-term planning and funding cycles (Alcock *et al.* 1999; Hague 1999). Agencies should also avoid any tendency to outsource all initiatives developed in response to racism because this leaves them vulnerable to marginalisation.

Finally, there is much to be gained by developing networks for supporting black and ethnic minority workers and service users. Efforts to reduce isolation can take the form of mentoring schemes, joint training, professional networks, support groups and joint use premises. The point is that initiatives which are not feasible for one agency alone may become viable with cooperation. For example, in Bath and north-east Somerset the local Youth Justice Board established a mentoring scheme as part of a series of projects aimed at young people from depressed rural areas. This scheme sought to tackle the vulnerability of black and ethnic minority young people to rural racism in the community and within the projects. Like many other rural initiatives, they experienced difficulty in recruiting sufficient 'ethnic minority or dual heritage staff ... [to] adequately represent and reflect the needs of these young people' (Youth Justice Board 2004), but were able to progress through the support of a black police officer working in the area.

Conclusions

A fundamental difficulty in many organisations is the lack of an effective corporate approach to racism. Consequently, it is often left to individuals to decide whether or not to participate in or contribute to initiatives. While this may have some benefits, particularly at a grass-roots level in allowing particular individuals the leeway to get involved, it leaves new developments highly vulnerable to shifts in personnel and fails to secure the support of those senior managers and local politicians who decide priorities and allocate resources. In such circumstances, even where partnership of some kind is established, it can still be undermined by an institutionalised racism that makes no commitment to the basic principles of partnership, and by the thoughtlessness, ignorance and personal racism of individual workers.

Clearly changing attitudes is always likely to be slow work, but ethnic minority communities will not have confidence in agencies that fail to acknowledge the problems that they may have within their organisations. We know that many of those who suffer racism, or would benefit from services in rural areas are reluctant to seek help or 'make a fuss' because they fear that in drawing attention to their problems and needs they may be blamed for their own situation, or even worse become the subject of further discrimination. As de Lima observes: 'There is often a reluctance to become involved in any initiative which they feel would focus attention upon them as individuals, and they are often not keen to discuss their experiences' (de Lima, 1999: 37). Workers seeking to develop responsive policies and services should be careful to recognise how significant this reluctance is. For although it may be a reasonably successful strategy for 'not being noticed', it may also indicate a considerable anxiety and fear on the part of ethnic minorities about exposing themselves. It should also remind us just how fragile and contingent the appearance of tolerance may be in a small community.

Hitherto, the numbers of black and ethnic minority people living in rural areas have been much smaller proportionately than those living in urban areas, but there are indications that this is changing. For example, increasing success and affluence for some members of the Asian communities in Leicester has resulted in some residential migration to the outer suburbs and rural areas surrounding the city. A study into the needs of Asian elders and carers (Jewson *et al.* 2000) found that while family members were heavily involved in providing informal care, they often lacked culturally appropriate public services and were relatively isolated. The point is that the rural context is changing. Many of the immigrants who first came to Britain in the 1950s and 1960s are beginning to enter retirement and as they age, their need for health and social care will increase. We may also see further migration into rural areas as the succeeding generations develop similar aspirations in terms of housing and quality of life to those evident within the white majority. If this happens then the demand for services will not simply change as numbers increase, but the needs of ethnic minorities living in rural areas will change too. For example, the elevated levels of learning disability among some Asian communities will probably diminish as social conditions, maternal nutrition and access to pre-natal care improve. Thus it is likely that what are common issues now, such as the need for interpreters and for particular types of culturally appropriate service, will also change. Furthermore, the newer generations of ethnic minorities moving into the countryside may not only have different needs, but may also be more confident about asserting their preferences. It is already evident that many local providers of public services struggle to meet existing needs, yet the determination of the Department of Health to respond to the health and social care needs of Britain's ethnic minorities will create even more pressure for the provision of effective and appropriate services.

Currently, there is insufficient research and knowledge about how best to organise and provide rural services generally, and very little specific information about what works best for minority communities in rural areas. The Government's Social Exclusion Unit has concluded that the provision of effective mainstream services rather than the provision of more specialised local initiatives is usually the best way of addressing social exclusion. For as other equal opportunity initiatives have shown, a failure to mainstream the desired policies and practices often marginalises the intended developments in service. Sashidharan (2003: 8) made a similar point when he contended that the solution to the problems around 'race' and ethnicity in mental health services should be met 'within the mainstream of service development rather than in segregated or otherwise specialised services or initiatives'. His view is that the problems are not a 'product of the specific cultural or ethnic requirements of people seeking mental health care' (ibid.: 8). While we should indeed be wary of pathologising cultural difference, the whole point of personal social services is that they should be 'personal'. Therefore a responsive service for ethnic minorities should, if necessary, have differentiated provision within it, but because its fundamental policies and practices should be based upon common principles and processes of assessment which permeate the entire service, it will remain responsive to the legitimate and diverse needs of all sections of society.

Notes

1   See the General Social Care Council's website at www.gscc.org.uk for further information.
2   See www.nelh.nhs.uk/nsf/mentalhealth/default.htm.

References

Alcock, P., Harrow, J., Macmillan, R., Vincent, J. and Pearson, S. (1999) *Making Funding Work: Funding Regimes and Local Voluntary Organisations*. York: Rowntree Foundation.

Alexander, Z. (2000) *Study of Black, Asian and Ethnic Minority Issues*. London: Department of Health.

Bhui, K. (2002) *Racism and Mental Health*. London: Jessica Kingsley.

Blink (2003) *Equalities Support for Rural Communities*. At www.blink.org.uk/pdescription.asp?key=2167&mid+&grp=69&cat=262.

Boushel, M. (1994) 'The Protective Environment of Children: Towards a Framework for Anti-oppressive, Cross-cultural and Cross-national Understanding', *British Journal of Social Work*, 24: 173–90.

Bracken, P.J. and O'Sullivan, P. (2001) 'The Invisibility of Irish Migrants in British Health Research', *Irish Studies Review*, 9 (1): 41–51.

Cemlyn, S. (2000) 'Assimilation, Control, Mediation or Advocacy? Social Work Dilemmas in Providing Anti-oppressive Services for Traveller Children and Families', *Child and Family Social Work*, 5 (4): 327–41.

Chakraborti, N. and Garland, J. (2003) 'An Invisible Problem? Uncovering the Nature of Racist Victimisation in Rural Suffolk', *International Review of Victimology*, 10 (1): 1–17.

Cheers, B. (1998) *Welfare Bushed: Social Care in Rural Australia*. Aldershot: Ashgate.

Countryside Agency (2003) *The Rural Services Standard: Second Progress Report 2002/03*. Wetherby: Countryside Agency; also available at www.countryside.gov.uk

Craig, G. and Manthorpe, J. (2000) *Social Care in Rural Areas: Developing an Agenda for Research, Policy and Practice*, Rowntree Research Findings 5110. At www.jrf.org.uk.

de Lima, P. (1999) 'Research and Action in the Scottish Highlands', in P. Henderson and R. Kaur (eds), *Rural Racism in the UK: Examples of Community-Based Responses*. London: Community Development Foundation.

de Lima, P. (2001) *Needs Not Numbers: An Exploration of Minority Ethnic Communities in Scotland*. London: Commission for Racial Equality and Community Development Foundation.

Department for Environment, Food and Rural Affairs (DEFRA) (2002) *The Way Ahead for Rural Services: A Guide to Good Practice in Locating Rural Services*. London: Department for Environment, Food and Rural Affairs.

Department for Environment, Food and Rural Affairs (DEFRA) (2003a) *Our Countryside: The Future – A Fair Deal for Rural England: Rural White Paper*. London: Department for Environment, Food and Rural Affairs, at www.defra.gov.uk/rural/ruralwp/whitepaper/chapter13.htm

Department for Environment, Food and Rural Affairs (DEFRA) (2003b) *Rural White Paper: Implementation Plan*. London: Department for Environment, Food and Rural Affairs at www.defra.gov.uk/rural/ruralwp/timetable.htm.

Department of Health (2001a) *Responding to Diversity: A Study of the Commissioning of Services for People of Black and Minority Ethnic Origin with Physical Disabilities and/or Sensory Impairment, Aged 18–64 Years*. At http://www.dh.gov.uk/Publications/fs/en.

Department of Health (2001b) *From Lip Service to Real Service: Responding to Diversity*. At http://www.dh.gov.uk/PublicationsAndStatistics/fs/en.

Department of Health (2002) *Developing Services for Minority Ethnic Older People: The Audit Tool*. At http://www.dh.gov.uk/PublicationsAndStatistics/fs/en.

Department of Health (2003a) *Community Care Statistics 2001–2002: Referrals, Assessments and Packages of Care for Adults*. At www.doh.gov.uk.

Department of Health (2003b) *Personal Social Services Survey of Home Care Users in England Aged 65 or Over: 2000–2003*. At http://www.dh.gov.uk/PublicationsAndStatistics/fs/en.

Department of Health (2003c) *Social Services Performance Assessment Framework Indicators 2000–2003*. At www.doh.gov.uk.

Dhalech, M. (1999) *Challenging Racism in the Rural Idyll: Final Report.* Exeter: National Association of Citizens' Advice Bureaux.

Eaton, S. (1995) *Multi-Agency Work with Young People in Difficulty*, Rowntree Research Findings 68. At www.jrf.org.uk.

Edwards, B., Goodwin, M., Pemberton, S. and Woods, M. (1999) *Partnership Working in Rural Regeneration*, Rowntree Research Findings 039. At www.jrf.org.uk.

Francis, D. and Henderson, P. (1992) *Working with Rural Communities.* London: Macmillan.

Garland, J. and Chakraborti, N. (2003) 'Countryside Alliance? An Assessment of Multi-Agency Responses to Racism in Rural Suffolk', *Crime Prevention and Community Safety: An International Journal*, 5 (2): 61–73.

Hague, G. (1999) 'Smoke Screen or Leap Forward: Interagency Initiatives as a Response to Domestic Violence', *Critical Social Policy*, 53: 93–109.

Haskins, C. (2003) *Rural Delivery Review – A Report on the Delivery of Government Policies in Rural England.* At www.defra.gov.uk/rural/ruraldelivery/default.htm.

Henderson, P. and Kaur, R. (eds) (1999) *Rural Racism in the UK: Examples of Community-based Responses.* London: Community Development Foundation.

HMSO (1999) *Explanatory Notes to the Local Government Act.* At www.hmso.gov.uk.

Home Office (2002) *Race Equality in Public Services.* London: Home Office.

Jay, E. (1992) *'Keep Them in Birmingham': Challenging Racism in South West England.* London: Commission for Racial Equality.

Jewson, N., Jeffers, S. and Kalra, V. (2000) *Success at a Price.* At www.le.ac.uk/press/press/asianelders.html

Lindow, V. (1999) *Evaluation of the National User Involvement Project*, Rowntree Research Findings 129. At www.jrf.org.uk.

MacKay, A. (2000) *Reaching Out: Women's Aid in a Rural Area.* St Andrews: East Fife Women's Aid.

Marsh, B. (1996) *Community Care Needs of People from Minority Ethnic Groups in North Warwickshire.* Warwickshire: North Warwickshire Council for Voluntary Service.

Mason, S. and Taylor, R. (1990) *Tackling Deprivation in Rural Areas: Effective Use of Charity Funding.* Cirencester, Glos.: ACRE.

Midgley, G., Munro, I. and Brown, M. (1997) *Integrating User Involvement and Multi-Agency Working to Improve Housing for Older People*, Rowntree Research Findings, Housing Research 205. At www.jrf.org.uk.

Moor, C. and Whitworth, J. (2001) *All Together Now? – Social Inclusion in Rural Communities.* Local Government Association. At www.lga.gov.uk.

Myers, P. (1995) 'Country Matters', *Guardian*, 21 March, pp. 4–5.

Nizhar, P. (1995) *No Problem? Race Issues in Shropshire.* London: Commission for Racial Equality.

Patel, N. (1999) *Community Care Services For Black and Ethnic Minority Elders.* Unpublished paper presented at CCETSW/University of Wales seminar at the North East Wales Institute, Wrexham, 19 February.

Pugh, R. (1996) *Effective Language in Health and Social Work*. London: Chapman and Hall.

Pugh, R. (2000) *Rural Social Work*. Lyme Regis: Russell House.

Pugh, R. (2001) 'Globalisation and Social Change; the Fragmentation Thesis and the Analysis of Difference in Rural Social Work', *Rural Social Work*, 6 (3): 41–53.

Pugh, R. (2003) 'Considering the Countryside: Is There a Case for Rural Social Work?', *British Journal of Social Work*, 33: 67–85.

Sashidharan, S.P. (2003) *Inside Outside: Improving Mental Health Services for Black and Ethnic Minority Communities in England*. Leeds: National Institute for Mental Health.

Sibley, D. (1997) 'Endangering the Sacred: Nomads, Youth Cultures and the Countryside', in P. Cloke and J. Little (eds), *Contested Countryside Cultures: Otherness, Marginalisation and Rurality*. London: Routledge.

Smaje, C. (1995) *Health, Race and Ethnicity*. London: King's Fund.

Social Services Inspectorate (1998a) *Inspection of Community Care Services for Black and Ethnic Minority Older People*. Bristol: Department of Health.

Social Services Inspectorate (1998b) *They Look After Their Own, Don't They?* London: Department of Health.

Social Services Inspectorate (1999) *Care in the Country – Inspection of Community Care Services in Rural Areas*. London: Department of Health.

Spilsbury, M. and Lloyd, N. (1998) *1997 Survey of Rural Services – A Report to the Rural Development Commission*. London: Rural Development Commission.

Stephens, S. (2001) *Challenging Inclusion – Childcare: The Way Forward*. Ipswich: Suffolk ACRE.

Youth Justice Board (2004) *Practitioners' Portal*. At www.youth-justice-board.gov.uk/PractitionersPortal

Index